A Limited Bounty

The United States Since World War II

A Limited Bounty

THE UNITED STATES SINCE WORLD WAR II

Otis L. Graham, Jr.
University of North Carolina, Wilmington
University of California, Santa Barbara

THE McGRAW-HILL COMPANIES, INC.

New York   St. Louis   San Francisco   Auckland   Bogotá   Caracas
Lisbon   London   Madrid   Mexico City   Milan   Montreal
New Delhi   San Juan   Singapore   Sydney   Tokyo   Toronto

McGraw-Hill

A Division of The **McGraw·Hill** Companies

A LIMITED BOUNTY
The United States since World War II

This book is printed on acid-free paper.

1 2 3 4 5 6 7 8 9 0 DOC DOC 9 0 9 8 7 6 5

ISBN 0-07-023979-7

This book was set in Palatino by ComCom, Inc.
The editor was Lyn Uhl;
the production supervisor was Louise Karam.
The cover was designed by Joan E. O'Connor.
Cover photo: Reuters/Bettmann
Project supervision was done by Spectrum Publisher Services.
R. R. Donnelley & Sons Company was printer and binder.

Library of Congress Cataloging-in-Publication Data
Graham, Otis L.
    A limited bounty : the United States since World War II / Otis L.
Graham, Jr.
        p.   cm.
    Includes bibliographical references and index.
    ISBN 0-07-023979-7
    1. United States—Politics and government—1945-1989.   2. United
States—Politics and government—1989-   3. Environmental policy—
United States—History—20th century.   I. Title.
E743.G725   1996
973.92—dc20   95-43709

About the Author

OTIS L. GRAHAM, JR., teaches in the History Department and the Cameron School of Business at the University of North Carolina, Wilmington. His previous books include *An Encore for Reform* (1966), *The Great Campaigns: Reform and War in America* (1973), *FDR, His Life and Times* (with Meghan Wander, 1985), and *Losing Time: The Industrial Policy Debate* (1992). A Guggenheim fellowship recipient, he has served on the Council of the American Historical Association and as editor of *The Public Historian.* Dr. Graham has taught history at the University of California, Santa Barbara (1966–1980, 1989–1995) and at the University of North Carolina, Chapel Hill (1980–1989).

For Eric Van Horne,
Elizabeth Koed,
and Lady Dee.
They kept the faith.

A nation that offered its people—a century ago—uncharted forests, broad sparkling rivers, and prairies ripe for planting, may have expected that bounty to endure forever.

But we do not live alone with wishful expectations.

We live with history. It tells us of a hundred proud civilizations that have decayed through careless neglect of the nature that fed them.

We live with the certain future of multiplying populations, whose demands on the resources of nature will equal their numbers.

We are not immune. We are not endowed—any more than were those perished nations of the past—with a limitless natural bounty.

Lyndon Baines Johnson
Message to Congress
February 8, 1965

Contents

PART FIVE

1978–1988   211

9.   The Political Resurgence of American Conservatism   213

10.   It Was Not Morning in America: Reagan and Reality, 1984–1988   236

PART SIX

INTO THE 1990s   259

11.   End of the Cold War, Beginning of What?   261

Introduction:
A Usable Past?

One would expect the United States in the 1990s to be a triumphant country in a positive mood about the future. America's prosperity and democratic political institutions are enviable among nations and the Western coalition led by the United States during the long Cold War has been declared the victor in that titanic struggle.

But America is deeply troubled, with "its charter fading, its goals diverging," in the words of *Time* magazine in 1994. The nation's commentators, scholars, and civic leaders talk increasingly of a crisis, of a menacing future of internal division and directionless drift. The American economy faces mounting international competition with more anxiety than optimism. The gap is steadily widening between the educated, successful classes on top and a vast bottom tier of people who sense themselves slipping down declining wage scales toward, if they have not already arrived there, poverty. National, state, and local political institutions and leadership have steadily lost the confidence of a public that is increasingly disinclined to vote and expresses little faith in the government's competence or credibility. Another one-term, "failed presidency" is possible in 1996, at the end of Bill Clinton's four years, but the Republican Party faces the same skeptical public. There is much talk of third parties and of political instability unknown since the other end-of-century crisis in the 1890s. Similar to that crisis of 100 years ago, cities in the 1990s are declared crime-ridden and unsafe, the urban and natural environments are besieged with pollution, and massive immigration appears to swamp the nation's capacity to absorb the incoming millions.

Can we look to history to shed light on our national situation, even to somewhat illuminate the way ahead? Historians are of two minds—no and yes. Both are correct.

Historians almost universally believe that the first purpose of historical study is not to solve contemporary problems, but to understand and reconstruct the past in its own terms. Historians agree that "presentism" is *the* cardinal sin in dealing with the past by forcing today's views and perspectives on another period of time, which had its own horizons, problems, truths, and errors.

Conversely, most historians also believe that the study of history often has some contemporary usefulness—after we have reconstructed it as faithfully as possible. History offers "perspective" on the present and may aid contemporaries to make better decisions by avoiding the mistakes of the past. However, historians usually become quite vague about the benefits that historical study may bring to the present.[1] They know that our agenda and problems today are so different from any but the most recent past that historic "lessons" may not apply, and that history must be used cautiously because the future is full of surprises.

The *recent* past. Here, perhaps, we have a special case. Does recent history provide more useful insights as compared to those found in the maneuvers of Roman legions or the community and civic life of colonial New England? Historians have not been polled on this, but the proposition has logic on its side. A few historians have proposed that, if we write history *backward*, starting with our contemporary situation (as well as we understand it) and ask the past, especially the recent past, to illuminate the arrival and current form of our circumstances and dilemmas, then we can find insights into the present.

This book is conceived in that spirit of looking backward. We move forward in time from World War II through the Cold War, to struggles over the role of government in a capitalist economy, and to the social movements of the 1960s and after. Throughout this account, the core themes and questions are derived from today's public life and agenda. In that sense this is history written backward, from a contemporary vantage point. A half-century of history is asked to illuminate what seem to be the underlying elements of our predicament.

1. The long combat and gradual enfeeblement of the political traditions of liberalism and conservatism that dominated the second half of the century, and the parallel weakening of electoral and governing political institutions;

2. The emergence of a global economy in which American capitalism faces uncertain prospects, with the possibility that the nation may divide even more sharply into economic winners and losers;

3. The widespread acknowledgment of an intensifying "cultural war" between traditional values and a new cultural ethos variously called "post-modernist" or "multiculturalist"; and

4. The most important element and central focus of this book—that America and the entire human race move deeper into an unprecedented era of ominous, accelerating buildup of population pressures on the American and planetary environments, resource bases, and national borders. The French term "problematique," or "problem cluster," directs attention to this triad of concerns—population, resources, and environment.

---

[1]For a discussion of the uses and misuses of history, see Otis L. Graham, Jr., *Losing Time: The Industrial Policy Debate* (Cambridge: Harvard University Press, 1992), chapter 11.

These concerns have been familiar to the human race since its origins but are reaching awesome dimensions as the twenty-first century brings the prospect of an unprecedented doubling (or tripling) of the global (and possibly also the U.S.) population.

The history of the public life of the American people since World War II is much more than the seedbed of our contemporary challenges. I attempt a sufficient account of the chief events of earlier decades, whatever their relevance to today. But this book makes no claim to comprehensiveness. Aiming to understand the public life and dilemmas of contemporary America, it hews closer to political than social history, although some of the book's themes have to do with cultural transformation. The narrative is built around American society's experience as a nation, not as individuals engaged in the important preoccupations of marrying, working, consuming, making music, and other daily fare of private life. Above all, this book represents an effort to watch the contemporary world emerge from a half century of national experience.

I would like to acknowledge the following text reviewers for their helpful suggestions: William Graebner, State University of New York, Fredonia; David Hamilton, University of Kentucky; Barbara Havira, Western Michigan University; Judy Johnson, Wichita State University; Steven Lawson, University of North Carolina, Greensboro; Mark Lytle, Bard College; Norman Markowitz, Rutgers University; Richard Pells, University of Texas; and Daniel Pope, University of Oregon.

I have incurred many obligations in working on this book over a period of years longer than anyone intended. A close collaborator at the outset was Eric Van Horne, who brought essential research skills and helped me clarify the project concept. Dr. John Tanton has been supportive in many ways, not least in the funding of a conference in which I received indispensable commentaries from Stuart Burns, Barbara Lindeman, Paul Relis, Mark McGinnis, and Barton J. Bernstein. My brother Hugh D. Graham read the manuscript more than once and with his usual astute sense of history and prose style.

More than anyone else, Elizabeth Koed became a collaborator whose matchless research and computer skills, editorial judgment, and unflagging energies meant all the difference.

Delores Graham brought a scientist's skepticism, a deep knowledge of environmental and public health issues, and an endless patience. She was the wind beneath my wings.

Otis L. Graham, Jr.
University of North Carolina, Wilmington
University of California, Santa Barbara

PART ONE

1945–1950

So God created man in his own image . . . and said unto them, "Be fruitful, and multiply, and replenish the earth, and subdue it; and have dominion over the fish of the sea, and over the fowl of the air, and over every living thing that moveth upon the earth."

—GENESIS 1: 27–28

CHAPTER 1

Victory and Postwar Issues

AMERICAN PROSPECTS: 1945

Few Americans could have anticipated the dramatic changes that the year 1945 would bring. As it began, life ran in familiar channels: the ordeal of World War II, now in its thirty-eighth month for Americans; and the presidency of Franklin D. Roosevelt (FDR), entering its thirteenth year. The grip of winter was firm and the celebration of Christmastime holidays was altered only by the red stars in the windows of those proud, anxious families with members in the armed services.

But change was in the air. In February, Allied armies contained the last-ditch German counterattack in Belgium and Luxembourg, and resumed the push toward Berlin. Spring would bring decisive events: the sudden death of FDR on April 12, Adolf Hitler's suicide in his bunker on April 30, and the German surrender on May 8. Bitter Japanese resistance on Iwo Jima in February and on Okinawa in March and April did not blunt the momentum of the American drive toward Tokyo, as U.S. air and naval forces bombarded Japanese targets almost at will and plans went forward for a massive invasion of the home islands in the fall. The war would not extend beyond 1945. The age of atomic energy had arrived at Alamagordo, New Mexico, where a test bomb was detonated on July 16. Later, at Hiroshima on August 6 and Nagasaki on August 9, Japanese urban populations were attacked by U.S. atomic weapons. It was a year of significant endings—the era of FDR, World War II, and the expansion of Western colonialism. There were also many beginnings—peace, a new American presidency, a pioneering effort at world government through the United Nations, and the new anxieties of living with atomic weapons.

These were changes on a vast scale, but even these war-brought transformations did not alter the fundamental underpinnings of American life. The U.S.

Winston Churchill, Franklin D. Roosevelt, and Joseph Stalin meet at Yalta, February 1945. FDR would die 1 month later, and Harry S Truman would complete The Big Three at future conferences.
(Courtesy of Franklin D. Roosevelt Library, Hyde Park, New York.)

economy remained the world's dominant engine of production, whether measured by size or technological superiority. American democratic political institutions came out of an era of global depression and war with an enhanced reputation for stability and producing a new generation of world leadership. This nation of world immigrants displayed a remarkable degree of national cultural unity, based on the dominance of the English language and on a Eurocentric, Caucasian, and male-dominated historical inheritance and social structure. Finally, historic assumptions of endless space, resources, and abundance on the vast American landscape were unquestioned. The national optimism about an unlimited American bounty was reinforced by demographic projections that the nation's population would gradually stabilize at 160 million persons at the end of one more generation.

Strains Within the Grand Alliance

Although close observers thought that President Roosevelt looked ill during the campaign of 1944, only a few persons knew that he had been suffering from cardiovascular disease for several years. By an effort of will he displayed enough physical vigor to reassure the electorate, but his doctors and friends knew that his health was rapidly declining. In early 1945, Roosevelt faced a set of decisions that would affect the postwar world, decisions he had delayed as long as possible. One decision had to do with the new weapons being prepared by the U.S. Army's Manhattan Project. Roosevelt had committed $2 billion to a secret research project designed to produce an atomic weapon; if the project succeeded, the weapon promised to revolutionize both warfare and international politics. Roosevelt was advised by Nobel Prize-winning physicist Niels Bohr and others to share the news of the progress with our ally, the U.S.S.R., but in the autumn of 1944 the president agreed with British Prime Minister Winston Churchill's counsel to continue the policy of secrecy.

Other matters required immediate discussion with the Soviets, so in February Roosevelt and Churchill traveled to the Black Sea resort of Yalta to meet with Marshal Joseph Stalin of the U.S.S.R. The agenda at Yalta addressed questions that had been glossed over or avoided at the 1943 "Big Three" meeting at Tehran—Soviet participation in the war against Japan, the future of Germany, the formation of a postwar organization of nations, and, above all, the territorial and political future of nations liberated from Nazi occupation. The Soviets readily agreed to join the war against Japan and cooperate in a United Nations organization. Their intentions toward liberated countries were unclear, with strong indications of a continuing Soviet presence. Churchill predicted conflict with the Soviets and pressed for strong Anglo-American support for a Declaration on Liberated Peoples, which would commit the U.S.S.R. to allow complete self-determination in eastern and central Europe. As the three leaders met, reports came of political oppression behind the Soviet armies as they swept through Rumania, Bulgaria, and Poland.

Roosevelt chose to delay a confrontation. On the one hand, as he had told Stalin, he "did not intend to go to war" over Soviet handling of eastern Europe. On the other hand, he faced potential political difficulties at home if postwar settlements allowed Soviet domination of formerly independent nations. Stalin produced an ambiguous promise to allow democracy in Poland, and a weary Roosevelt accepted it. The Yalta conference ended in displays of goodwill. "We really believed that this was the dawn of the new day we had all been praying for and talking about for so many years," said FDR's friend and advisor, Harry Hopkins. Later, when the Soviets prevented free elections in most of the occupied territories, it would be said that Roosevelt had given away the fruits of victory. Certainly, he was a tired and sick man at Yalta. However, with Soviet troops in control of eastern and central Europe, Roosevelt had chosen to rely on his own diplomatic skills to navigate a path of compromise between Soviet security interests and the political pressures that would have fallen on any U.S. president to press for Soviet withdrawal to prewar boundaries. Exhausted from his thirteen years as president, FDR traveled to Warm Springs, Georgia, in April. On April 12, while sitting for a portrait, he slumped forward with a cerebral hemorrhage and died. The grief and sense of loss touched even those who had been his detractors and brought millions of people to line the tracks in silence as

After Franklin D. Roosevelt died of a cerebral hemorrhage at his Warm Springs, Georgia, home on April 12, 1945, a somber Harry S Truman, with wife Bess standing by, took the oath of office, administered by Chief Justice Harlan F. Stone.
(Courtesy of Harry S Truman Library.)

a train carried his body from Georgia to his burial site in Hyde Park, New York, his ancestral home.

President Truman

Vice President Harry S Truman (formerly a senator from Missouri) was picked to be FDR's successor largely because he offended no important group. While serving as vice president, he was told almost nothing and allowed to do even less. He took the presidential oath of office with Eleanor Roosevelt and the cabinet standing helpfully by, an unpretentious man with a surprising amount of determination. Fortunately, the war in Europe required little presidential attention as it approached its end. The Japanese resistance on Okinawa was broken after bitter fighting in April and May. From Okinawa and Saipan, the Army air force could intensify the B-29 bombing of Japanese cities. An invasion of the main island was planned for November 1, 1945, and military strategists anticipated the loss of many American lives against desperate Japanese resistance.

(Military planners' estimates ranged from 63,000 to 135,000 casualties in the main invasion; after the war, Truman began to use estimates ranging from 500,000 to 1 million casualties—possibly to strengthen the case for using atomic weapons.)

Then, in July, an atomic weapon was detonated on a New Mexico desert by a team of American scientists. They witnessed its mushroom cloud with mixed feelings of elation and dread. Some exchanged hugs and shouted with joy at their technological success. As head physicist Robert Oppenheimer remembered the moment, "A few people laughed, a few people cried, most people were silent. There floated through my mind a line from the *Bhagavad Gita*, 'I am become Death, Destroyer of Worlds.' " Another scientist penned a letter to President Truman: "I beg of you sir . . . this thing must not be permitted to exist on earth."

Truman had earlier convened a committee of top officials and scientists and, after hearing the doubts about the morality of the weapon's use by scientists who had worked on it, recommended that the two available bombs be used on Japanese targets at once. Like Roosevelt before him, Truman assumed that the bomb was developed to be used, and he seriously considered only options concerning the appropriate place and timing. The president sailed to Europe in July

The Boeing B-29 "Enola Gay" returns from its historic mission of August 6, 1945. The atomic bomb attack on Japan ushered in the nuclear age. *(UPI/Bettmann)*

to attend the Potsdam conference, where he told Marshal Stalin offhandedly that the United States had developed a new weapon but supplying no further details to his ally. Truman then ordered the bomb to be dropped on Japan. Hiroshima was devastated on August 6 and Nagasaki on August 9. One hundred thousand people died in those blinding moments, and thousands more suffered dreadful burns and radiation illness. After an intense struggle inside the Japanese government, Emperor Hirohito forced his military officials to submit to surrender terms on August 14.

The costliest war in history was over. An incredible 38.5 million civilians had perished worldwide, with military deaths reaching 14.9 million—13.6 million of these were Soviets, 3.3 million Germans, 1.1 million Japanese, and 292,131 Americans. The civilian population of the United States, spared direct bombardment after Pearl Harbor, could hardly comprehend the devastation—not only industrial and urban infrastructure but also historic and cultural treasures were reduced to rubble in Berlin, Dresden, London, Leningrad, Warsaw, Budapest, and Rotterdam. (By good luck, much of historic Paris, Rome, Athens, Florence, Venice, Amsterdam, Oxford, Cambridge, and Edinburgh were spared.)

More lightly touched than any other combatant society, the generation of Americans who passed through the war would have mixed memories. They would remember the spirit of unity and social sacrifice with a sense of regret that it could not continue, and they would look back with nostalgia for the rest of their lives as they recalled the heroism and exhilaration of the war years. However, the war also had been a harrowing and dangerous time for American society, as well as a fatal occasion for nearly one third of a million of its population. More than twice that number of Americans were seriously wounded, and the direct dollar cost of the conflict for the United States was estimated at $288 billion. That sum would continue to rise for years as veterans' benefits and interest on wartime borrowing boosted the total. When war did not bring death or injury to American military personnel, it disrupted careers, families, and relationships and strained the social fabric—costs apparent to contemporaries. The war also consumed petroleum and other exhaustible mineral resources that Americans in the twenty-first century will severely miss.

THE POSTWAR AMERICAN ECONOMY

Did World War II damage or strengthen the American economy for the peacetime years ahead? Historians have emphasized the war's benefits. Wartime expansion carried the economy to more than twice its prewar size, the 1945 gross national product (GNP) reached $212 billion. Much of the industrial expansion, of course, was for war materiel. Could this expansion be converted to peacetime production, and would consumer demand match industrial capacity? Many economists feared that the weak demand of the 1930s would persist, that capitalism still contained the mysterious flaws that had crippled it since

1929. Others hoped that wartime savings, combined with New Deal income supports, would ensure demand. Certainly American science and technology had advanced greatly during the four years of economic invigoration and governmental patronage. Still, memories of the Great Depression were fresh, and the postwar economic prospect led to conflicting prophecies. Government and private economists tended to predict depression, while business publications exuded confidence in the economic future. In September 1945, *Look* magazine declared that endless opportunities lay ahead for an enterprising people: "The modern house . . . the automatic washer . . . express highways . . . television . . . the private plane . . . quick freezing."

This time, unlike in 1929, the optimists were resoundingly correct. The American economy shifted from war-time to peacetime production without major disruptions and entered an era of expansion that enabled the United States to enjoy the highest standard of living ever experienced by any society. The GNP, which most Americans accepted as a measure of social progress, mounted faster than population growth, increasing per-capita income as well. The GNP had been $213 billion at the war's end, reached $284 billion by 1950, and surpassed $500 billion by 1960. The average annual growth rate by 1965 was 2.9 percent, a figure slightly lower than that of the United States in the mid-1920s and allegedly lower than the Soviet Union's postwar rate. However, this growth was a sustained climb, which over the years spread an affluence that made the Great Depression seem a distant memory. *Look* had been right about the prospects: Sprawling suburbs allowed millions of families a newly spacious, if stylistically homogenized, shelter; households were filled with appliances, recreational equipment, abundant groceries, and television sets. By the mid-1950s the American people, 6 percent of the world's population, were consuming (and producing) one third of the world's disposable products. They were also consuming other forms of the new affluence—longer vacations, paid holidays, shorter workweeks and workdays, and a leisure time enriched by expanded air and expressway travel. All of these affluences permitted expanded recreational opportunities, both spectatorial and active.

ECONOMIC GROWTH AND THE AMERICAN FUTURE: TWO VIEWS

The postwar boom was interrupted by mild recessions in 1949–1950, 1954–1955, and 1957–1958, but over the longer term growth was sustained. America's resources were many and worth pondering by a nation that, in the 1980s, began to wonder if it had mislaid the formula. After the war, several basic industries were flourishing, leading the way in investment and job creation. Chemicals vigorously expanded the production of new products such as synthetic rubber, clothing fibers, detergents, and pesticides. Consumer electronics vaulted from the forty-ninth to the fifth largest industry between 1939 and 1956. Automobiles were larger, gaudier, more powerful, and less fuel efficient, but faced no challenge from foreign manufacturers. Neither did the steel industry, which held 50 percent of the world market. The most vigorous new industries were aircraft building and air transport, recreational equipment, and, above all, television, an industry that put 1 million sets in American homes by 1957, having started with 17,000 sets in 1946.

Whether in new or old industries, in agriculture or mining, the fundamental generator of economic advance was rising productivity per worker. Productivity gains derived chiefly from investment in labor-saving devices, such as mechanization of agriculture and mining, and in the use of computers to speed calculation, store information, and ease clerical work (20 computers in 1954 had become 35,000 by 1964). Rising demand ensured that the enhanced productive capacity led to sales and not overproduction, as it had in the 1930s. The population expanded, and the surge of buying power supplied by enforced saving during the war was supplemented by the growing use of charge accounts.

These features were the key dynamics of the private sector. Yet another set of institutions also made large contributions to postwar prosperity—government. The "built-in stabilizers" of unemployment benefits, government insurance of bank accounts and housing mortgages, farm price supports, and other measures of the New Deal era supported purchasing power. Stock market and banking regulations steadied financial institutions, and many industries were assisted by regulations that buffered them from market forces. Although some businessmen yearned for "free enterprise," support for deregulation usually ended at the portal of one's own industry. The activist state clearly lavished more aid on business groups and the middle class than on the poor. Government mortgage insurance undergirded the postwar housing boom, price supports and crop loans protected farmers from loss, tariffs shielded vulnerable industries, and one half of the nation's research and development (R&D) expenditures were advanced by Washington. Such programs, combined with the mix of monetary and fiscal policies designed to prevent major fluctuations in the business cycle, deserve a considerable share of the credit for the health of postwar American capitalism.

At least as important, government officials spurred the creation of institutions to stabilize the international economy and permit expanded trade. Believing that World War II had resulted from the economic warfare generated by depression-shrunk markets and misguided restrictive trade policies (of which the Smooth-Hawley tariff of 1930 was surely the worst offender), American officials took the lead by creating the International Monetary Fund (IMF) and the World Bank in 1944 at the Bretton Woods conference in New Hampshire. These institutions would provide financial liquidity and some measure of intergovernmental consultation. The government aggressively sponsored a pact among twenty-three nations to establish a General Agreement on Tariffs and Trade (GATT) in 1947, and successive "rounds" of multilateral trade talks within the GATT framework (seven rounds had been completed by 1995, and more than 100 nations were signatories) drove world tariffs down from an average of 40 to 5 percent. As tariff barriers fell, world trade flourished as never before, playing a key role in making the second half of the twentieth century a time of global expansion of industrialization. Unfortunately, rising environmental pollution came with this expansion.

This mix of factors launched a postwar period of economic and population expansion that lasted not quite two generations and may be seen as America's "golden age," at least in a material sense. The Great Depression had shaken national confidence in the basic American cultural assumptions of endless expansion and permanent plenty. The postwar boom restored that faith. In an editorial in *Life* magazine in February 1941, publisher Henry Luce had given an early welcome to the coming expansion of American economic power and world influence. Luce exulted that we were about to turn the twentieth century into "the American Century." American firms faced virtually no foreign competition in the vast home market, as our prewar industrial rivals, especially Germany and Great Britain, were devastated by war.

Luce's anticipation of a splendid new era of affluence along with influence was a widely shared expectation. There were fears in 1945–1946 that the Great Depression might return. When it did not, the future of our economic system seemed bright indeed.

An Early Doubter

Only a tiny handful of people raised doubts about the boom era after the war; one of them was historian Walter Prescott Webb, who reminded readers in his *The Great Frontier* (1952) that for much of history the normal lot of humankind was not abundance but daily hardship and the remorseless decline of any civilizations that man could build. Human numbers and civilized arts made only torturous headway against a hostile, resisting environment. Then there began, at about the time of the Renaissance in the West, what Webb called "the greatest boom in human history," lasting at least 400 years and benefiting principally western Europeans and their North American descendants. American school children were taught that this economic boom, which was called "progress," was produced by science and technology, by the energies released by capitalism and representative democracy, and by God's favor. At least as important, Webb pointed out, were the material bases of the boom—the discovery and exploitation of fertile lands, virgin forests, rich mineral deposits, and fossil fuels. In humanity's occupation of the planet 400 years was only a brief moment, and Webb closed the book with the thought that perhaps the boom was not entering a new phase but was coming to an end, as great industrial civilizations exploited the earth's resources at unprecedented rates.

POPULATION

Webb's book was an attempt to start a public discussion of population growth and resource issues, to move latent change into public vision where it would be visible. It was, at least, premature; Americans were not listening to people

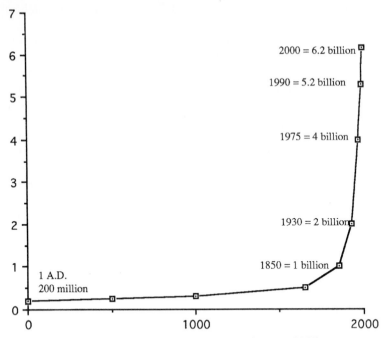

World population growth (with projections to the year 2000).
*(Statistical Abstract of the United States, Bureau of the Census, U.S.
Department of Commerce, 1983 and 1994.)*

who were offering prophecies of trouble ahead. Yet Americans in the postwar
years were participating in Webb's "population pressure on resources"
dilemma, even if they were not aware of it. The basic facts about human numbers are easily stated: Perhaps 250 million people inhabited the globe in Jesus's
time, a high-water mark of human numbers after thousands of years. Then the
growth patterns began to change. It had taken perhaps 10,000 years to accu-
mulate 250 million people, but it took only 1830 years for humanity to number
1 billion; the 2 billion mark was reached by 1930, after only 100 years! In 1945,
as the war ended, humanity was halfway to the 3 billion mark, which it
reached in 1960.

This surge of human numbers did not reflect higher fertility rates, but rather
falling death rates. The most rapid population growth came in the seventeenth,
eighteenth, and nineteenth centuries in Europe, where modernization steadily
extended life expectancy. The North American continent was transformed by
this demographic upheaval, as Europeans would not remain within the resource
and space confines of Europe. Europeans migrated, and the direction of the flow
was almost entirely westward, across the Atlantic Ocean.

In what historian Alfred Crosby has termed "the Caucasian tsunami," or
tidal wave, from 1500 to the early nineteenth century, waves of Europeans
immigrated to North America, parts of South America, and Australia. The Euro-

peans who settled in what became the United States multiplied as had their forebears and for the same reasons—Europeans had learned how to drive death rates down, yet their birth rates remained high. Population growth rates in the United States combined with continued immigration through the nineteenth century to produce an average 25 to 35 percent growth rate per decade.

The twentieth century, however, would be different. Fertility began to decline as mortality had earlier. The total fertility rate (TFR)—eventual completed family size, if women continue to have babies at the rate measured in any given year—of 1900 was perhaps 5.0 family members and dropped steadily toward 2.3 family members in the mid-1930s. This was still above the 2.1 that produces eventual population stabilization. However, migration from Europe (relatively unrestricted until 1921) and Mexico spurred further population growth. In the 1920s, the U.S. population grew by 16 percent; in the 1930s, by 7.2 percent.

These figures suggest a remarkable crossing of trend lines. At the end of World War II, world population was fifteen years from the 3 billion mark. But the U.S. story was profoundly different. Fertility rates in the United States were almost at replacement level by World War II, and immigration was negligible. If fertility rates continued to decline, population growth in America would eventually end. Demographers generally agreed on this projection, estimating the peak year as 1985, with a population of 161 million Americans.

The war was not expected to alter these trends because demographic forces move slowly—like glaciers. Death rates surprise demographers when there are plagues, but these seemed a memory of Europe's Middle Ages, and birth rates were thought to respond to deep causes and offer no surprise fluctuations. Then came the unexpected: The number of live births in America, which had averaged 2.7 million from 1909 to 1945 and never varied more than 10 percent from year to year, suddenly jumped in 1947 to 3.8 million. The figure reached 4 million in 1954 and remained there until 1964 before beginning a decline. The TFR also started a sharp rise in 1946, reaching 3.7 children by the peak Baby Boom year of 1957, and was to remain above 3.0 for eighteen consecutive years before again dropping toward the levels of the 1930s. In all, the Baby Boom generation was 72 million strong, a cohort born from 1946 to 1964 that was to shape the nation's future.

The most obvious impact was to accelerate population growth and ruin the prophecies of the demographers of the 1930s. The nation's population grew 14 percent from 1940 to 1950, to 151 million; 18.5 percent from 1950 to 1960, to 179 million; 13.4 percent in the 1960s, to 203 million; and 11.4 percent in the 1970s, to 226 million. It did not "top out" in 1985, as some had predicted. It would grow into the twenty-first century, as far as projections could be made.

Causes of the Baby Boom

Why did the women and men of the 1946–1964 period reverse fertility trends so sharply, choosing larger families than their parents had? The answer appears to lie in a combination of factors.

1. They married earlier and thus started families earlier, extending the years of childbearing and the eventual number of children. The median marriage age of women in 1955, for example, was twenty; half of those marrying were teenagers, and half of first births came within fifteen months of marriage.
2. They "calculated" (an economist would say) or "believed" (a historian or psychologist would say) that good times lay ahead, that they could afford larger families than the depression cohort had calculated or believed.
3. The women, especially, were convinced by massive cultural pressures from media, advertising, and education that all women should aspire to be mothers and to center their energies on raising children. Betty Freidan called this the "feminine mystique" in her 1963 book of that name.
4. Of people who may have calculated or believed that fewer than three (or no) children was preferable, "they didn't know how to stop," in the words of Peter Y. Landon, author of *The Baby Boom Generation*. Birth control technology was "pre-pill," and information on how to limit pregnancies was not widely diffused among women, their mates, or their doctors. Thus, some substantial part of the 72 million Baby Boomers were "unwanted children," at least inasmuch as the pregnancy had not been planned.

Raymond and Nora Baker of Joliet, Illinois, are celebrated by the media as they enjoy Thanksgiving Dinner in 1948 with their 16 children.
(*UPI/Bettmann*)

When the Baby Boom reached its peak in the 1950s, the U.S. population growth rate was boosted to 1.4 percent. This does not sound negligible when we calculate the doubling time of exponential growth.[1] A 1.4 percent growth rate will double any population in 50 years! Therefore, the United States at mid-century was not headed for a stabilized population by 1985, but for an endless growth spurt.

Almost no one cared about this latent issue. Americans in the 1940s were not interested in population numbers and lacked the elementary demographic knowledge to forecast the future population of the United States. There were some, however, who were interested in another source of change, migration patterns. Farm groups noticed with uneasiness that the long-term thinning of the rural population continued throughout the 1940s. Two other major migration patterns were evident within the nation: an accelerated move to suburban communities around the formerly dense cities and a continuing movement toward the west and southwest. A mythical "population bull's eye" had been charted by demographers, the point where the country would balance perfectly if it were a flat surface and every person on it had equal weight. This point could be called the population center of the United States, and between 1880 and 1890 it crossed the Ohio border into Indiana, by 1940 hesitated on the Illinois border one state westward, and by 1950 had traveled more than 100 miles toward Missouri.

Neither population size nor its internal distribution were public issues in postwar America. Although President Franklin Roosevelt had been much interested in both issues, as well as the issue of the adequacy of natural resources, his death took such issues out of the White House. History books provided a small, unconsulted knowledge of how the decline of ancient Chinese, Roman, and Mayan civilizations, among others, had been attributed to the population pressures and resultant exhaustion of forests and soil fertility. The premodern societies in the Tigris-Euphrates crescent and in the American southwest apparently declined primarily because their basic agricultural habits poisoned the soil with salinity from crude irrigation methods. The 151 million people living in the United States during the 1950s might not have been a significant threat to the basic ecosystem if they had been Cherokee or Sioux—that is, preindustrial, pastoral peoples. However, America was an urban, industrialized society, and its population was compiled of prodigious consumers of resources and alterers of land, water, and air. The unprecedented postwar material affluence of the United States may have seemed permanent, but the foundations of that prosperity, so robust in the short term, were insecure in the long term, when growth reached resource limits. These issues, however, were latent in the history of the era and not yet visible.

---

[1]Growth at a fixed rate over a constant time interval is exponential growth. A constant time will then be required for the growing quantity to double its size (or increase by 100 percent). If doubling time is T, and the percentage growth rate per unit time is R, then the simple formula $T = 70/R$ yields doubling time.

RESOURCES

How could North America ever lack resources? The land was vast—2 billion acres, much of it incredibly fertile. Forests covered much of the land, and on it fell nearly 2 trillion gallons of fresh water annually, to replenish streams, lakes, and groundwater. The continent was rich in minerals, wildlife, and places of natural spectacular beauty—and surely more remained to be discovered. The crucial resource for Americans of the 1950s following air, water, and soil, was fossil energy. Americans had industrialized primarily by using coal, petroleum, and natural gas to power their vehicles, industry, and their homes and gathering places.

Only a few deviant conservationists, whose prophecies of shortages often prove quite wrong, seemed to worry about the supply of these natural resources. President Theodore Roosevelt's White House Conference of Governors had received an inventory of resources from the U.S. Geological Survey in 1908, which predicted the exhaustion of petroleum by 1935 and of coal by 2027. Secretary of the Interior Franklin K. Lane had warned the public in 1915 that oil reserves would expire in 20 years. Yet these men were wrong, not merely because their data were inadequate, but because they underestimated the human ingenuity that a capitalist and technology-driven economy could unleash, finding new reserves and substitutes when present reserves were consumed. When resources were needed for wartime production, they were found—or invented, as with synthetic rubber. The modern American economy had a prodigious and growing appetite for iron ore, copper, aluminum, and zinc, and for little-known metals such as molybdenum and manganese. These, like fossil fuels, were nonrenewable resources. But surely more vast supplies than had been found in the Mesabi Range or the Rockies were yet to be found in the West, in Canada, or on other continents.

True, military demand for oil had caused some official concern about supplies of that fossil fuel (coal was known to be vastly abundant) during World War II, but this concern had to do with where the petroleum was located, not with how much of it there was. After Colonel Edwin L. Drake discovered oil in Titusville, Pennsylvania, in 1859, the United States had become the world's leading supplier of petroleum. By 1910 the United States was producing more oil than the rest of the world combined, and on the eve of World War II our own large consumption, 3.4 million barrels per day (mbpd), was still exceeded by U.S. production (3.6 mbpd), allowing a surplus for export. However, vast discoveries in the Permian Basin of the Middle East, along with increased consumption at home, changed the world oil picture. U.S. oil reserves had been 61 percent of the world total in 1938, but by 1951 had dropped to 29 percent. Arabs, not Texans, sat on top of most of the world's oil. Domestic production had jumped to 5.9 mbpd by 1950, but consumption climbed even higher, to 6.4 mbpd. A Rubicon had been crossed, unnoticed, in 1948. The United States was now, for the first time, a net importer of oil.

The vulnerability of our supply of petroleum, however, was a concern for the future. In the postwar years, oil was cheap for U.S. consumers, who did not know or care where it came from. They built their postwar life-styles around cheap petroleum. In designing cars and buildings, Americans after World War II all but ignored fuel efficiency. Cars were large and powerful, and home and office builders took little account of solar exposure or insulation. Low energy costs also influenced industrial structure in the development of "the American Ruhr," the industrial-urban belt in the colder north-northeastern section of the nation, where steel, automobiles, and chemical industries flourished beginning in the late nineteenth century. U.S. agriculture after World War II was rapidly transformed into an energy-intensive business. The labor force on farms shrank by 7 million people from 1940 to 1950, and petroleum filled the gap, driving the huge new tractors and harvesters, providing inexpensive chemical fertilizers to boost productivity. American food after World War II was produced by a shrinking input of human and animal labor and a larger input of petroleum. The same was true of industrial raw materials—wood and fiber gave way to plastics, and Dacron and nylon fibers were produced using oil.

Fossil fuels were not the only resources about which Americans were careless. Their standard of living continued to be boosted by the availability of virtual "free goods" offered by nature. Clean air flowed across the continent from west to east, carrying only moisture. Episodes of intense urban pollution, due mostly to wintertime coal burning, were regarded as local and temporary problems. Clean water could generally be assumed, at the minimal cost of a municipal piping system or, for three fourths of the population, digging a well to groundwater. In the arid West, the government (usually the Bureau of Reclamation) impounded winter runoff by damming the rivers, and pumped water hundreds of miles for irrigation or urban use, at low cost to customers.

Environment

Nature appeared to offer Americans not only mineral, woodland, and esthetic resources, but also another free good, the environment as a site for waste dumps. Americans were prodigious dumpers of waste; a 1952 study by the Paley Commission (see Chapter 2) estimated that Americans consumed more than 2.5 billion tons of materials per year—or 18 tons per capita—including 14,000 pounds of fuel and 1600 pounds of food. In 1950, the U.S. economy drew from the earth three times as much copper, twenty-six times as much natural gas, and thirty times as much oil as it had in 1900. Because matter cannot be destroyed but only transformed, what was produced and then consumed became, in time, waste material to be disposed of.

Americans, like all peoples, had long used the surrounding environment to discard wastes without cost. There was almost no cost, in a thinly populated society, to burying human feces and industrial wastes or floating them down pipes or creeks into nearby lakes or the ocean. As late as the mid-twentieth century, only a few large American cities had primary sewage treatment (which often broke down during heavy rains). Rural areas and towns dumped or buried untreated sewage. The liquid wastes of factories were pumped directly into the waterways, which also carried pesticide- and herbicide-containing runoff from fields and farms. Solid wastes were burned or buried in unregulated and foul-smelling landfills. Toxic wastes, whose volume nobody knew, were either poured into municipal sewers, transported to remote fields for surreptitious dumping, or deposited in hastily constructed and unregulated landfills, from which they seeped into rivers and aquifers. Thus, between 1942 and 1953, Hooker Chemical and Plastics Company—and possibly the U.S. Army—dumped 21,800 tons of toxic wastes in metal drums into a landfill called Love Canal, near Niagara Falls. The drums were covered with garbage and dirt, "out of sight" and thus "out of mind." Love Canal would remain for many years a latent, but not a manifest, part of our history.

Early Warnings

A handful of books warned of unprecedented global population growth and its potentially dire consequences—books such as Fairfield Osborn's *Our Plundered Planet* (1948) or William Vogt's *Road to Survival* (1948). Such books had a small readership and no immediate discernible impact; growth of population and material output were a given. Americans assumed that if resource shortages occurred—as they had during the war—solutions would be found through a free enterprise economy stabilized by government and through science and technology. Had that not been the lesson of World War II? What we had needed during the war we had produced from nature's abundance or invented in laboratories, through our new system of government-business-university cooperation. "There is almost nothing, however fantastic, that (given competent organization) a team of engineers, scientists, and administrators cannot do today," exulted David Lilienthal, chief architect of the Tennessee Valley Authority (TVA).

Science as the certain path to a prosperous future was a faith confirmed by the story of the two products of wartime inventiveness with the most apparent potential: the insecticide DDT (dichloro-diphenol-trichloroethane) and the atom bomb. Invented in a Swiss laboratory in the late 1930s, DDT was first used with spectacular success to end an insect-carried outbreak of typhus in Naples, Italy, when American troops were endangered. Here, modern chemistry was married to the war effort, and other applications soon followed. "Avenger torpedo bombers," a 1945 magazine reported,

> equipped with nozzles for spreading a spray of DDT and Diesel oil, have winged low over Pacific islands, blotting out almost entire insect populations. As a result, in one island recently wrested by the marines from the Japs, not a single case of insect-borne disease has been reported.

DDT was the "killer of killers," the "atomic bomb of the insect world." Journalists wrote, "the Army's new insect-killer has nearly every householder pawing the ground in eagerness." As early as 1946, *The New Republic* carried an article questioning the damage done by DDT and other pesticides to many beneficial insects, birds, and animals, but there was no audience for such skepticism about a quick and easy victory over insects, Japanese and Germans, and all other enemies of our technological society. On the evidence from the war record, America was now invincible in any struggle.

The atom bomb, of course, surpassed all other inventions of American science and technology in encouraging an arrogant belief in total victory over all obstacles. Two bombs, dropped by two airplanes, immediately ended the Pacific War. Japan submitted to American occupation without the expected bloody and tenacious battle for the home islands. Whether the enemies were typhus-carrying lice or armed Germans and Japanese, American science, technology, and organization had achieved total victory. It was a powerful and misleading history lesson.

CHAPTER 2

Peacetime Politics: The Truman Era

POSTWAR POLITICS

Postwar politics in America ignored trends in population growth, resources, or environmental problems. The leading concerns as the war ended centered on the restoration of a peacetime social order. Public and political leaders alike agreed on a rapid demobilization of the armed forces, but there would be disputes over whether the size and structure of U.S. military forces in the 1930s would be adequate in the postwar world. Agreement that wartime economic controls should be dismantled covered sharp disagreement over how far and where the government should yield to "free markets," and how quickly. And would restoration of peacetime conditions mean a return to the diplomatic and economic isolation of the 1920s and 1930s? President Roosevelt's position on the U.S. role in world affairs had veered from the accommodationist isolationism of the mid-1930s to a strong internationalism during the war, and the Senate ratified the United Nations Charter in July 1945 (in August 1946, the Senate confirmed U.S. membership in the International Court of Justice) with little of the fierce partisan struggles that produced the defeat of the League of Nations in 1919–1920. What should America's global economic role be, if the economic isolationism of the 1930s could be given much blame as a cause of World War II? Although all Americans wanted a return to civilian habits, bitter and protracted disputes began over the details of restoration.

At first it seemed that nothing more was at issue in the return to peacetime conditions than how soon to release wartime economic controls. Each group wanted the controls on it lifted at once but feared inflation: Farmers wished price ceilings lifted on food but not on manufactured goods; workers wished wage but not price controls scrapped; employers had the opposite priorities; owners of rental property wanted rent control lifted, but renters liked the controls. Each group expected the government, while releasing it from restraints, to hold the line on other groups to prevent rampant inflation that would wipe out all gains.

Behind the issue of economic controls lay the basic question of the role of government in the domestic and world economies.

The disagreement over reconversion exposed the reforms of the 1930s—the New Deal, and the liberal political outlook behind it—to new debate and attack.

To its proponents, New Deal liberalism meant the use of government as a compensating mechanism in an economy that chronically developed imbalances leading to recurrent economic depressions. It meant government efforts, through taxing and spending, to balance purchasing power with productive capacity so as to even out the business cycle. It meant legislation to protect the least powerful (industrial workers, farmers, consumers) from the most powerful (industrialists, bankers). It meant a new "welfare state," a federal guarantee that no American would starve or go without necessities, a commitment expressed by the New Deal's many relief and public works agencies (WPA, PWA, CCC) and the safety net of old-age pensions, unemployment insurance, and cash payments to single female heads of households that had been combined in the Social Security Act of 1935.

This cluster of ideas and programs—New Deal liberalism—faced fierce and unreconciled domestic opposition that had not yet taken on the label "conservatism." Even without a name, the opposition knew what it preferred: the concept that the "best" government "governed least"; primary reliance on free enterprise and market forces; and hostility to organized labor, to schemes for income redistribution, and to federal intervention to regulate business or preserve the natural environment.

Roosevelt to Truman

When Franklin Roosevelt died in 1945, he left New Deal liberalism leaderless, unfinished, and fiercely controversial. Liberals feared that the New Deal's enemies would try to repeal not only the wartime controls on industry but the entire New Deal structure: enforced collective bargaining; regulation of industry, agriculture, banks, and stock exchanges; compulsory social security; minimum wages; progressive taxes; conservation. Liberals also feared how the new President would react to such pressures.

Very little was known about Harry S. Truman. A farmer and haberdasher from Missouri who had served a brief stint as an artillery officer in World War I, Truman had settled into an obscure career as a county executive in Kansas City. Nominated and elected almost accidently to the U.S. Senate in 1934, he voted as a moderate New Dealer, impressing those who noticed his skillful and scrupulous chairmanship of a special Senate committee to investigate fraud and favoritism in the billions of dollars spent for defense production. Destiny selected Truman almost by default in 1944, as FDR, facing opposition over his decision to run for a fourth term, backed away from his liberal running mate of 1940, Vice President Henry Wallace. Other Democrats were better known, but Truman's credentials generated no enemies—he was a border-state moderate and was well liked in the Senate. Roosevelt barely knew him and did not consult him as World War II entered its fourth year. Then, on April 12, 1945, Truman was called to the White House, where Eleanor Roosevelt quietly told him, "Harry, the President is dead."

What leadership could come from a person reaching the presidency by such accidental byways? Educated mostly by reading history, Truman knew nothing of science, technology, or the wider world. He was short, round-faced, and bespectacled, with a Midwestern twang to his voice. Harry Truman, however, had unsuspected reserves of character, toughness, and the ability to make decisions about large matters he did not fully understand. And he intended to carry forward Roosevelt's liberal policies.

In September 1945, Truman asked Congress for what amounted to a broad expansion of the New Deal agenda—extension of social security coverage, a national health insurance program, and more river development organizations like the Tennessee Valley Authority. Truman had emerged as a New Dealer, but conservatives hoped to use the public's desire to be rid of wartime controls to cut into government programs enacted between 1933 and 1938.

Political Stalemate

Whether to modestly extend the New Deal or to sharply curtail it became the main theme of postwar politics. It was soon clear that the Congress that received Truman's 1945 proposals would not enact them. A battle over reconversion came first. Truman felt that the pent-up purchasing power of the war years— when wages and salaries had been high, and rationing and savings bonds had kept a vast amount of income from being spent—posed a potential inflationary threat if the price and rent controls of the war were dropped too quickly. Congress refused to give the president the powers he wished, passing a weak price-control bill, which he vetoed. As a result, serious inflation began in the summer of 1946, for which the parties blamed each other. The elections that year strengthened conservatives of both parties, especially Republicans, who gained control of both houses of Congress, and determined to block Truman's proposed expansion of the New Deal.

Thus almost nothing of Truman's 1945 "21-point program," soon called the "Fair Deal," would be enacted. A major battle was joined over the culminating statute of New Deal liberalism, the "Full Employment" bill of 1946. As drafted, the measure made the federal government responsible for "full employment," a role in economic planning that made the government the employer of last resort to those the private economy thrust into unemployment. Attacked by conservatives and cherished by liberals, the bill came out of Congress as the Employment (note the absence of "Full") Act of 1946, a measure that stated a mild federal commitment to maintain the health of the economy. The Fair Deal had been blocked or neutered, and conservatives trimmed sections of the structure of the New Deal back to smaller size. In June 1947, Congress passed the Taft-Hartley labor law over Truman's veto, slightly curbing union rights and, conservatives hoped, union power.

New Deal liberals recognized that a stalemate had taken shape after Roosevelt's death, and tended to blame it on Truman, who so plainly lacked FDR's communicative powers. They thought the public ready for a final round of liberal social programs, but this happy resumption of reform progress was prevented by Truman's uninspiring, perhaps half-hearted leadership. That assessment was flawed on two counts. Significant and far-reaching change in U.S. foreign economic policy came in Truman's first term. Building upon the freer-trade commitment of FDR and Secretary of State Cordell Hull, Truman used (misused, critics said) the authority of the Trade Agreements Act of 1934 to commit the United States in 1947 to the General Agreement on Tariffs and Trade (GATT), a complex set of principles and rules that would guide major trading nations (23 at the October 30, 1947, signing in Geneva; 124 at the signing of the so-called Uruguay Round in December 1993) in an almost constant series of negotiations that over the next four decades drove world tariff rates downward and helped facilitate an epochal expansion in world trade that would relentlessly tie the United States to the world economy. This was internationalist leadership of a high order, generally overlooked because of the complexity of tariff and trade policies and the decades required for impacts to be felt.

A second problem with the liberals' tendency to blame Truman for failing to engineer a postwar expansion of the New Deal was their own inability to see that the reform surge of 1933–1938 was an anomaly in American politics viewed in the long term. A stubborn centrist pattern had reestablished itself by the middle of FDR's second term. Truman seemed to sense this institutional "deadlock" (the phrase applied to American politics in 1960 by political scientist James Macgregor Burns), and, after staking out his domestic policy preferences, turned his attention increasingly to problems abroad.

ORIGINS OF A NEW GLOBAL CONFLICT

Winning wars, to Americans, meant demobilization and withdrawal from overseas responsibilities. In the autumn of 1945 there seemed no enemies on the horizon to disrupt that expectation. Events, however, were to replace war with something other than the dreams of a traditional peace and disengagement. The war against fascism had brought the United States and the U.S.S.R. together in a strained but relatively recent friendship. Lend-lease and wartime cooperation seemed to promise postwar amity. Yet conflict had a longer history. The United States had not welcomed the Bolshevik revolution, and American troops had been sent into the Soviet Union in a brief and abortive attempt to overturn the Leninist government in 1919–1920. Washington refused to recognize the U.S.S.R. until 1933, and relations thereafter were not cordial between two societies of such divergent economic and political systems and ideologies. Thus Soviet–American relations were a mixture of friendliness and suspicion as World War II came to an end. Roosevelt had bequeathed to his successor the broad promises made at Yalta and the delicate task of creating from them an acceptable postwar international order. He could not leave to Truman his experience or his charm, and it is now apparent that Truman had always viewed communism differently than FDR did. Roosevelt thought communism a much less threatening system than fascism; Truman entirely lacked any sense of their differences, and easily concluded that communists were evil and implacable enemies. East and West were on a collision course, and when Truman replaced Roosevelt the slim chances for retaining even a chilly friendship were much reduced.

Relations became strained even as Germany collapsed. The U.S.S.R., invaded by the West twice in thirty years, having lost twenty million lives and having suffered terribly during the war, was determined to achieve security. Security meant a cordon of friendly states between itself and the West, along with the permanent occupation or division of Germany. That the states in eastern Europe proposed as buffers had a deep desire for independence and were largely anticommunist meant little to the Soviets. The Red Army was master of the area, and Soviet security demanded that anticommunist elements be crushed and "friendly" governments installed. These arrangements became the center of U.S.S.R. policy as Soviet armies swept westward. There is every indication that in 1945 Soviet territorial ambitions extended no farther than a belt of states running from Finland southward to Romania and the Black Sea. It appears that Soviet goals were limited. Where those ambitions extended, however, the U.S.S.R. acted to control its buffer zone with ruthless speed and military force, or the threat of it.

American interest in eastern Europe was recent but surprisingly strong. Not only did Americans tend to sympathize with all national aspirations to independence, but also substantial ethnic groups pressured Washington to exert its influence on behalf of their European homelands as the Soviets overran them. The Yalta agreements were not followed by free elections in Poland, and while each nation within the Russian military perimeter experienced different conditions, Soviet interference in Polish political affairs was particularly blatant and objectionable. Hearing such reports, and assuming the Yalta accords to include clearer promises than they did, Truman delivered an angry rebuke to Soviet Ambassador V. M. Molotov in April 1945. Molotov complained of the harshness, to which Truman replied: "Carry out your agreements, and you won't get talked to like that."

The United States, The U.S.S.R., and Eastern Europe

Presidential rebukes had no effect on the future of Poland. There the Soviet army helped Polish communists tighten their grip over liberated Poland. The Cold War thus began in the twelve months between the spring of 1945 and the spring of 1946, as the Soviets reduced a belt of eastern European states to subservience (with curious and unaccountable exceptions; Hungary, for example, was allowed to hold free elections). In their turn, the U.S.S.R.'s former allies refused to condone what was being done.

The deteriorating relations were evident at the interminable meetings of the Council of Foreign Ministers, which began in London after the Potsdam confer-

Throughout 1948 and 1949 the Berlin Airlift broke the Soviet blockade by providing food and fuel for the people of the divided city. The blockade was lifted, but Berlin remained divided with a wall separating east from west.
(*The Bettmann Archive*)

ence in July had produced no real agreement. Treaties had to be written with the former Axis states, most of which—Hungary, Bulgaria, and large parts of Austria and Germany—were entirely or in part under Soviet occupation. The Americans and British pressed for free elections with Western observers on hand, early removal of Soviet troops, and free access for Western economic and cultural influences. The Soviets stalled and wrangled, using the delays to ship portable wealth eastward and in most cases to hamper or eliminate noncommunist political elements. The more the West urged "open" societies, the stronger became the Soviet determination to close them against outside interference, though Soviet toleration of a degree of political freedom in Czechoslovakia and Hungary hinted at either flexibility or caution.

The future of Germany was crucial. Although the United States and the Soviet Union had earlier agreed that Germany should be not only demilitarized but also fragmented, the situation in eastern Europe led the Truman administration to reverse direction, and to favor restoring German strength as a balance against the Soviets. This action the Russians rejected. Their experience with Germany had been even more painful than our own. This deadlock spread to all aspects of U.S.–Soviet relations. To the Truman administration it appeared that the Soviets were deliberately obstructing the postwar settlement in order to solidify their ideological hold over the occupied territories, perhaps as a preliminary to further expansion. The Soviets, observing that the United States excluded them from participation in the reconstruction of Japan and Italy, resented U.S. protests regarding their rule in eastern Europe, believing them to be motivated by ill will rather than altruism.

Thus almost nothing could be agreed upon in the endless discussions of reparations, territorial concessions, dispositions of colonies, and other details. Truman signed the order cutting off lend-lease aid to the U.S.S.R. in May 1945, when the need for it was still great—"a mistake," he claimed. The Soviets saw it as a move calculated to weaken and intimidate them. An American offer to share atomic secrets, presented in early 1946, fell afoul of suspicions on both sides. An early draft drawn up by an advisory group headed by Under Secretary of State Dean Acheson and Atomic Energy Commission Chair David Lilienthal was modified by a wary Truman and Bernard Baruch (who had been chosen to introduce the plan in the United Nations) to contain extra safeguards, which had the effect of permitting extensive American surveillance of the Soviet economy. The Soviets, less interested in avoiding a nuclear arms race than in preventing Western interference in their internal affairs, rejected the plan.

COLD WAR

Scholars are still untangling the record of affront and counteraffront that broke apart the wartime alliance in the first year after the war, and historians no longer blame only one side for the outcome. By the winter of 1946, leaders on both sides began to speak openly of irreconcilable animosities. He was "tired of babying the Soviets," Truman erupted: "Unless Russia is faced with an iron fist and strong language, another war is in the making." Stalin asserted a hard line in a series of speeches calling on the Soviet people for the sacrifices necessary in their confrontation with the West.

The recent prospect of Western access to Soviet archives promises to enlarge our understanding of early Cold War dynamics. American historians, with fifty years of perspective, now appear to see the Cold War through two lenses. Today, after the fall of communism, they stress that the Western alliance avoided war and mobilized the will to prevail over an authoritarian system that could not pass the tests of history. This perspective casts U.S. foreign policy and Cold War leadership in a favorable light. Yet historians during the perilous years before the Cold War came to (what now appears to be) a satisfactory end compiled a sobering record of American over-estimation of Soviet ambitions and unwillingness to exploit periodic opportunities to curb the arms race and ease superpower tensions. The question remains whether the Cold War's length, intensity, and expense were necessary and inevitable.

In any event, the differences between the blocs hardened quickly. In Fulton, Missouri, in March 1946, Winston Churchill delivered his famed "iron curtain" speech, in which he spoke of the "expansionist tendencies" of the Soviet Union and of "an iron curtain which has descended across the continent from the Balkans to the Baltic."

Formulating a Cold War Policy

Having become convinced that the U.S.S.R. intended a permanent expansion into eastern and central Europe and potentially beyond, the Truman government groped for a policy. It might conceivably have decided to grant the Soviets their sphere of influence and ignore the complaints of occupied peoples, hoping that such acquiescence would not be rewarded by further demands. This course, which a generation later would be called *detente*, was recommended by knowledgeable people, most notably former vice president Henry Wallace and the influential journalist Walter Lippmann. But the heavy Republican criticism aimed at the administration because of its agreement in December 1945 to recognize Soviet-installed governments in Romania and Bulgaria had alerted Truman to the political risks of negotiating agreements confirming a Sovietization of eastern Europe. Further, Truman and most of his advisors had themselves concluded that Soviet absorption of eastern Europe was not a limited policy but was akin to Hitler's unlimited ambitions in the late 1930s. If anything had been learned from the 1939 Allied appeasement of Adolf Hitler at Munich, they reasoned, it was that any territorial expansions must be met with prompt American resistance.

Learning such lessons from Munich and applying them to postwar Europe was a dubious use of history, but Truman saw Soviet actions in the border states not as defensive and limited but as harbingers of further expansionism. Still, it was a long step from that conclusion to the formulation of a successful counterpolicy. Truman had tried firm words, beginning with Molotov, but these had produced little apparent result. The U.S. government lacked a strategy, or an awakened nation to support it. The American public in 1946 seemed to be in no mood for suggestions that victory had not brought the opportunity to relax. Popular pressures forced the administration to remove wartime controls and demobilize the armed forces with excessive haste. Public response to Churchill's Fulton speech was unclear but was thought to be generally negative, as the speech seemed to suggest a future full of sacrifices by a people weary of tension and exertion. Throughout 1946 top officials in the administration, preoccupied with problems at home, sought a policy course more effective than rhetoric.

THE TRUMAN DOCTRINE

A crisis in Greece in the spring of 1947 brought matters to a head. A coalition of socialist-communist insurgents in that country seriously threatened the British-supported monarchist government, and Britain informed Washington that it could no longer afford to play a role in the area. Truman's advisors saw the leftist Greek rebels (of whom communists were a minority) as Moscow-dominated and -supported, which they were not. The Greek "crisis" was a civil war, rooted primarily in the corruption and ineptitude of the British-supported Greek monarchy and local rightist factions. Washington incorrectly saw Moscow behind it all, and worried over the threat to Middle Eastern oil supplies that a leftist Greek regime would pose. The president quickly went before a joint session of Congress to request an unprecedented peacetime step, military and economic aid to the governments of Greece and Turkey.

He emphasized that such action was not a temporary expedient to "save Greece," as important as that might be, but the beginning of a new Truman Doctrine of global application: "I believe that it must be the policy of the U.S.," Truman said, "to support free peoples who are resisting attempted subjugation by armed minorities or by outside pressures." Again, Truman was applying the lessons of the Hitler era, as he and his advisors understood them. Such a foreign policy was a break with the past, but the war had so undercut the isolationist argument that the appropriation passed quickly through Congress, helped by the president's tone of alarm and the conversion of a former isolationist, Republican Senator Arthur Vandenburg, who advised Truman to "scare the hell out of the country."

By 1949 American assistance had enabled the Greek government to put down the insurrection. Hundreds of U.S. military advisers had accompanied 90,000 bombs and rockets to be used by Greeks against Greeks, at an initial annual cost of $260 million. (Turkey shared in the first $400 million appropriation for military aid, and by 1962 Greece had received $1.5 billion, Turkey $2.2 billion.) The monarchy in Athens was allowed and sometimes encouraged to use repressive policy measures, including torture, prison camps, and summary executions. "Our" Greeks bore considerable resemblance to the fascists we had recently been fighting in Germany and Italy, but a Republican senator spoke the administration's mind when he said that "this fascist government through which we have to work is incidental."

In the end American support was decisive, and the rebellion was crushed. But many were worried by certain aspects of the new Truman Doctrine. The Greek government was plainly unpopular and reactionary. Was the United States to give money and arms to any government under internal pressure from a movement in which communists participated, however incompetent, corrupt, or authoritarian that government might be? Beyond this important question, some critics said that an essentially military response did not touch the economic backwardness and social injustice that lay at the root of political instability. These questions would arise again in Vietnam, the Philippines, and Central America. Could the United States come up with a foreign policy that was directed at causes, not merely symptoms?

The "Long Telegram"

An influential answer came from career diplomat George F. Kennan, in a memo written and cabled from Moscow early in 1946. Kennan, a seasoned foreign service officer deeply knowledgeable about Russian history, culture, and language, argued that Soviet territorial ambitions were potentially limitless. Yet Kennan believed that the Soviets were eager to avoid war, and he urged a policy of "long-term, patient, yet firm and vigilant containment" to confine the Soviet threat until time had moderated its leadership. Two ambiguities allowed readers of Kennan's essay to interpret it in divergent ways. Must the West merely hold the line against Soviet expansion, assuming that time was somehow inherently on our side? Or was there some way to take the initiative? Kennan's few and fleeting references to "living up to our best traditions" at home did not give clear guidance. And did "containment" mean military restraint, or were economic and diplomatic methods to receive greater emphasis? Years later, Kennan was to regret not having stressed sufficiently the nonmilitary aspects of containment. In any event his telegram, revised and published in 1947 in *Foreign Affairs* magazine under the pseudonym "Mr. X," was an influential document in the shaping of early Cold War policy.

The Truman Doctrine had been an expression of the reactive, military side of the containment concept. An opportunity soon arose to explore its other

In February 1945, worried by evidence of a militant, expansionist Soviet foreign policy, career diplomat George F. Kennan sent a long and influential telegram from Moscow to Washington, DC, and a version of it was published in 1947, signed by "Mr. X." The "long telegram" was widely accepted as the best official statement of America's Cold War strategy, but Kennan later expressed regret that he had emphasized the alarmist and defensive, rather than the optimistic and constructive, side of his analysis, which came almost as an afterthought at the end.
(George F. Kennan, "The Sources of Soviet Conduct," Foreign Affairs XXV (July 1947), pp. 566–582.)

. . . The Kremlin is under no ideological compulsion to accomplish its purposes in a hurry. . . . The very teachings of Lenin himself require great caution and flexibility in the pursuit of Communist purposes. Again, these precepts are fortified by the lessons of Russian history: of centuries of obscure battles between nomadic forces over the stretches of a vast unfortified plain. Here caution, circumspection, flexibility and deception are the valuable qualities; . . . Its political action is a fluid stream which moves constantly, wherever it is permitted to move, toward a given goal.

. . . In these circumstances it is clear that the main element of any United States policy toward the Soviet Union must be that of a long-term, patient but firm and vigilant containment of Russian expansive tendencies.

. . . In actuality the possibilities for American policy are by no means limited to holding the line and hoping for the best. It is entirely possible for the United States to influence by its actions the internal developments, both within Russia and throughout the international Communist movement. . . . This is not only a question of the modest measure of informational activity which this government can conduct in the Soviet Union and elsewhere, although that, too, is important. It is rather a question of the degree to which the United States can create among the peoples of the world generally the impression of a country which knows what it wants, which is coping successfully with the problems of its internal life and with the responsibilities of a World Power, and which has a spiritual vitality capable of holding its own among the major ideological currents of the time. . . .

thrust. Postwar Europe, west of the Iron Curtain, reached a state of near collapse during the hard winter of 1946–1947. The war-battered economies of capitalist Europe slumped into torpor, the French economy producing only 50 percent of the goods it had made in the mid-1930s, and Germany only 31 percent.
Damaged urban centers, factories, and transportation networks could not be
replaced, as domestic credit was scant and the small U.S. loans to Britain and
France were soon exhausted. Unemployment reached depression levels, millions of refugees burdened communities, and political unrest on the left shook
the foundations of every Western government. "The biggest crash since the fall
of Constantinople—the collapse of the heart of an empire—impends," declared
one alarmed observer.

THE MARSHALL PLAN

In the depression of the 1930s, the United States rebuffed suggestions for cooperative measures among Western governments and retreated into its traditional
isolationism. The result had been fascist dictatorship, and a war which eventually engulfed the United States. It was time, in 1947, for wiser responses—or so
it seemed to Washington leaders pondering the crisis across the Atlantic. In a
speech at Harvard University on June 5, 1947, Secretary of State George C. Marshall announced the administration's plan for a program of economic aid to all
European nations, the U.S.S.R. included. The plan gave form to the nonmilitary,
curative side of the containment idea. The word *communism* did not appear in
the speech. The enemy was presented as economic collapse, poverty, and the
unrest it engendered. The Marshall Plan, as it was soon called, would make
available to Europe a sum as large as $17 billion to be administered by Euro-
peans for their own economic reconstruction. The American Congress, alarmed
by the communist seizure of power in Czechoslovakia and relieved that a suspicious U.S.S.R. and its satellites refused to participate, passed the Marshall Plan
in early 1948 and eventually appropriated $13.6 billion over five years. The non-
communist countries of Europe quickly formed a Committee of European Economic Cooperation, and worked out plans for the effective use of the funds. By
1950 European economic activity was above prewar levels, a recovery which
was crucial in reducing communist voting strength in the West.

EVOLUTION OF CONTAINMENT

The American response to the problem of communism had gone beyond ver-
bal objections, to take the form of a twofold policy: military resistance and economic aid. At times the approach of the Truman Doctrine was to dominate.
When the West moved to establish a strong West German government in June
1948, the Soviets retaliated by shutting off all land traffic to isolated Berlin (the
"Berlin Wall" would be built in 1961). But Truman would neither yield nor pro-

voke war by sending in armed convoys, ordering instead an airlift of supplies to the Allied sector. The blockade was ended by spring 1949. The incident convinced conservative Europeans of the need for a military alliance against the Soviets, and in 1949 the United States took the lead in forming the North Atlantic Treaty Organization (NATO), a military alliance of twelve nations.

At other times the Marshall Plan approach was primary. In his inaugural address in January 1949, Truman appealed to Americans to come to the aid of "the more than half the people of the world living in conditions approaching misery." This was the fourth point in his program, and "Point Four" aid in the form of technical assistance to foster economic growth in underdeveloped countries commenced in 1950. The $400 million that eventually flowed out in Point-Four aid was a modest sum, and even combined with Marshall Plan funds the United States spent more on arms than on overseas economic development. If one looks only at the arms–economic assistance mix of U.S. direct aid abroad, Truman Doctrine tactics vastly outweighed Marshall Plan assumptions in most of the postwar era.

REVOLUTION IN CHINA

The containment policy did not seek a quick victory over the Soviet Union, but to limit its ability to expand and hope for moderation of its foreign as well as inter-bloc policies. It assumed that time would work to Western advantage. Such a policy, promising only slow progress and requiring great patience, would never have been received with enthusiasm in a country accustomed to quick solutions; but Truman's foreign policy in some cases failed to produce progress at any speed, so turbulent was the postwar world.

The Chinese Nationalist government of Chiang Kai-shek had received U.S. military and economic aid during and after the war, as it struggled first with Japanese invaders and then with communist forces who resumed their civil war in 1946. The communists seemed to be succeeding, and Chiang Kai-shek's hold on China weakened. After fact-finding missions by Generals George C. Marshall and Albert Wedemeyer, the Truman government judged the Nationalists' faults so great and the situation so irretrievable that it rejected an eleventh-hour proposal from Wedemeyer for the commitment of 10,000 American servicemen. This proposal for the dispatch of American troops, unlike later ones, was turned down by civilian authorities. Instead, Truman decided to continue a limited aid program and allow the Chinese to settle the future of China.

The Nationalists steadily lost ground and fled to Formosa in late 1949, leaving the mainland to the victorious communists under Mao Tse-tung. Making the doubtful assumption that more American involvement could have rescued the Nationalist regime without drawing the United States into a ground war, Republican critics attacked a containment policy that had failed to contain. A Democratic administration had "lost one quarter of the human race to communism," critics charged, and years later another Democratic president would be more receptive to military advice to intervene rather than let Asian events unfold by their own dynamics. Truman and his aides issued a report to explain their reasoning, and even took some hesitant steps toward normalization of relations with the new government of Mao Tse-tung. If there was a cold war in Asia, it was initially much less intense than the one in Europe in 1949–1950, with signs of accommodation on both sides. Few people at the time noticed the rising tensions in Korea to the north, a nation divided between communist and pro-Western governments, both armed and talking of forced unification.

AT HOME: THE ELECTION OF 1948

By 1948 the Republican Party was a study in frustration. It had tried every strategy to unseat FDR, and nothing had worked—not the conservative Alf Landon campaign of 1936, not the liberal Republican "new face" appeal of Wendell Willkie in 1940, or the moderate Republican alternative offered by New York Governor Thomas E. Dewey in 1944. Yet Harry Truman, harassed on all sides by demands for relief from taxes and inflation, wrestling with crises in Berlin and China, entered the election year of 1948 with declining prestige and slim chances. Sensing victory at last now that the invincible Roosevelt was in his grave, the Republican party convention shouted for a repeal of the New Deal, and renominated Dewey on a platform calling for a rolling back of the clock and a change at the White House. "Truman is a gone goose," exulted Republican Congresswoman Claire Boothe Luce.

On the contrary, Truman sensed that the country was in a cautious, centrist mood and wished to retain New Deal Policies. He determined to win by defending the New Deal-Fair Deal as the new center of American politics. To further cement the loyalty of two crucial blocs in the Roosevelt coalition who had welcomed the New Deal, Jews and blacks, Truman ran some risks. Over State Department and military opposition, he recognized the State of Israel on May 15, 1948, within minutes after the declaration of independence and statehood. Though certainly not a Zionist, Truman established a strongly pro-Israeli policy, over the objections of advisors who saw Arab goodwill as the key to continued access to Persian Gulf oil supplies. The decision reflected both his personal admiration for Israeli pioneering and an astute judgment on the importance of Jewish votes in pivotal urban areas.

Truman also shifted federal influence toward Negroes (the "polite" term at the time) in ways that went beyond the New Deal. His own views on race relations were a blend of the racial slurs that were conventional in conversation for his generation, and a deep commitment to fairness that eventually made him a critic of the Jim Crow system of segregation. He appointed the first presidential commission on civil rights in 1946, and its 1947 report, *To Secure These Rights*, sharply criticized American treatment of racial minorities and called for an end to segregation in the armed forces, discrimination in hiring, and interstate transportation, along with federal protection of voting rights. Truman, impressed by a memo from White House Counsel Clark Clifford pointing out the increasing political leverage of black votes, supported some of these measures in a message to Congress. A revolt at the Democratic nominating convention led by Minneapolis Mayor Hubert H. Humphrey gave Truman a stronger civil rights platform than he had asked for.

Two months before the election it seemed that Truman had miscalculated. Southern Democrats hostile to their party's new challenges to racial segregation walked out of the party convention and persuaded Governor J. Strom Thurmond of South Carolina to run on a Dixiecrat ticket. Other Democrats defected to the left to support a leading heir of New Deal liberalism, Henry A. Wallace. Wallace's Progressive Party attracted liberals who thought Truman's domestic leadership too cautious and his foreign policy too belligerent. "In our fleet of heavy bombers lies wealth and skill . . . that could have taken a million veterans out of trailer camps and chicken coops," Wallace said. "We can build new schools to rescue our children from the firetraps where they now crowd. . . . We can end the murderous tyranny of sickness and disease . . . but . . . the facts are that we spend $20 billion a year for the Cold War." Beyond a reordering of priorities, Wallace expressed views on race and gender that were far ahead of his time: "In a political, educational, and economic sense, there must be no inferior races. . . . The future must bring equal wages for equal work regardless of sex or race."

Such views made him more enemies than friends. Wallace was also hurt by charges that he was "soft" on the Soviet Union, a pattern that would be repeated many times in Cold War politics as the American right used the theme, "get tough with Russia," to tilt domestic elections. Truman's lines held. He was assisted by his image as a spunky fighter from Main Street, America (in this case, Independence, Missouri, though Truman had lived most of his adult life in Washington, D.C.). His speeches were short, aggressive, and plain-spoken, accusing the Republicans of "a real hatchet job on the New Deal" because they "stuck a pitchfork on the back of the farmers" and would "enslave totally the workingman." The public seemed to appreciate his combativeness, conveyed from the rear platform of his campaign train as it criss-crossed the country ("Give 'em hell, Harry" became the standard audience response). His feisty spirit was equally evident in private letters, such as the one to a music critic who had written unflatteringly of his daughter Margaret's singing talent: "Someday I hope I meet you. When that happens you'll need a new nose, a lot of beefsteak for black eyes, and perhaps a supporter below."

Truman and Fair Deal liberalism were closer to the political center than the Republicans. Dewey was overconfident and failed to project a clear message. The Louisville *Courier Journal* thought him "so inept that four of his major speeches can be boiled down to these historic four sentences. Agriculture is important. Our rivers are full of fish. You cannot have freedom without liberty. The future lies ahead." It was the prim, aloof Dewey's second presidential campaign, and perhaps many voters were beginning to agree with the pundit who said that "you have to know him really well to dislike him." The voters returned Truman to office by a vote of 24 to 22 million (Thurmond carried four states, Wallace

Pollsters predicted a Dewey victory over incumbent president Harry S Truman, and newspaper publishers believed them. But an energetic whistle-stop campaign, taking Truman to all parts of the United States, tipped the scales for the man from Missouri, and Truman won the election by 2 million votes. As seen in this photo, he took great pleasure in proving the headlines wrong.
(St. Louis Mercantile Library)

none). But the turnout was 1 million votes lower than in 1940, and with four candidates in the race, Truman garnered less than 50 percent of the vote.

TRUMAN'S SECOND TERM

Encouraged by the results, Truman sought after 1948 to extend the New Deal—now calling the liberal program his Fair Deal—by urging national health insurance, repeal of the Taft-Hartley act, federal aid to education and for low-income housing, broader social security provisions, and a commission on racial discrimination in employment. This moderate enlargement of the New Deal fared no better than Truman's programs of 1945–1947. No one thought Truman had received any mandate for major reform in 1948, and most congressional committees were in conservative hands. Truman had to be content with a small public housing measure in 1949, marginal enlargement of social security, and estab-lishment of the National Science Foundation to consolidate federal aid to sci-ence. Congress could not prevent him from issuing an executive order racially integrating the armed services in 1948.

Frustrated liberals were convinced that the 1949 stalemate resulted from Truman's ineptitude and lack of real commitment to his announced goals. A sounder view emphasizes the obstacles he faced in Congress and a cautious and centrist public. Truman refused to go on the defensive. His State of the Union message of January 1950 renewed his requests for all the familiar Fair Deal mea-sures, plus a new plan to shift agricultural policy toward greater benefits for small farmers and consumers. Perhaps the autumn elections in 1950 would favor the liberals and strengthen the president's hand. "I hope," Truman remarked early in 1950, "that by next January, some of the obstructionists will be removed." In domestic policy the Truman administration in 1950 hoped for an opening to the left, toward renewed liberal reforms at home. And it did not close the door on a more flexible approach to the problem of international com-munism, at least in Asia. But the Korean War ended these hopes and sharply divided the 1940s from the 1950s.

THE POSTWAR GRAND STRATEGY

By 1950 the United States had broken from its long isolationist history and led the Western allies in a series of steps amounting to a global grand strategy for avoiding another world war and strengthening the worldwide sway of capital-ism and political democracy. It is easier to see the framework of this strategy in retrospect than in the hectic postwar years when U.S. leaders were often impro-vising and the public had a sense of its government reacting defensively to events more often than shaping them. The term George Kennan devised, "con-tainment strategy," had the misleading connotation of a defensive, military-diplomatic resistance to Soviet expansionist potential, and later all forms of rev-olutionary Marxism. But this was only part of the larger strategy of promoting the growth of capitalist economies and political democracy, as the two seemed to have strong historical affiliation. The Truman Doctrine and the NATO alliance, as we have seen, were the chief building blocks of one thrust of con-tainment, the Marshall Plan representing the boldest example of a chiefly eco-nomic form of activism. The United Nations carried the older Wilsonian hopes for an apex world organization for dispute resolution and U.S.-led innovations in the arena of world trade deserved larger headlines than they received in the five years after World War II—the GATT framework for trade expansion, the World Bank, and the IMF. The "grand strategy" of containment plus interna-tional trade liberalization committed the United States to a degree of activism in sharp contrast to the nation's dominant traditions, and the strategy never lacked for domestic critics who feared it would compromise American sovereignty, lead to a perpetual war machine and swollen government, and possibly to war.

Running these risks, and dividing sharply over their wisdom and particular form, would be among the costs of the Cold War. George Kennan was asked how long it would take for containment to "win" the Cold War, and he hesitantly guessed "ten to fifteen years." It was to take nearly fifty years, making it America's longest and most costly international conflict.

LIVING WITH THE ATOM BOMB

In the early years after the atom bomb joined the human story, Americans disagreed about its meaning, as we do to this day. Some exulted when it went off at Alamagordo; some trembled.

Harry Truman's first reaction was glee: "This is the greatest thing in history," he shouted on the cruiser *Augusta* when he heard the news of Hiroshima. It was natural that Truman and his civilian and military advisors thought of the bomb as a weapon, and saw it in positive terms, as having the dual potential to compel Japanese surrender and force the Russians into a more conciliatory mood. When irritated with his burdens, Truman would sometimes commit to his diary his infrequent fantasy of bold solutions to national problems, with the bomb playing an important role. One undated entry from 1946 read:

> Declare an emergency—call out troops [to deal with the steel strike]. Start industry and put anyone to work who wants to go to work. If any leader interferes court martial him. . . . Adjourn Congress and run the country. Get plenty of Atomic Bombs on hand—drop one on Stalin . . . and eventually set up a free world.

But the bomb was not the "greatest thing on earth." In the words of Truman's biographer Robert Donovan, "it was the most ominous day in history" when the bomb joined the human story.

There were times when Truman understood this. "You have got to understand that this isn't a military weapon," the president said to his Secretary of the Army Kenneth Royall when that gentleman recommended using the bomb against Russia. Others shared that perception, and began to fear an arms race between the superpowers, whose leaders might come to believe the bomb was a weapon just like any other. Secretary of War Henry Stimson wrote Truman in September 1945, imploring the president to approach the Russians at once with the proposal to share atomic secrets:

> If the atomic bomb were merely another though more devastating military weapon to be assimilated into our pattern of international relations, it would be one thing. We could then follow the old custom of secrecy and nationalistic military superiority relying on international caution to prescribe the future use of the weapon as we did with gas. But I think the bomb instead constitutes merely a first step in a new control by man over the forces of nature too revolutionary and dangerous to fit into the old concepts. I think it really caps the climax of the race between man's growing technical power for destructiveness and his psychological power of self-control and group control—his moral

power. If so, our method of approach to the Russians is a question of the most vital importance in the evolution of human progress.

In that same year a far-sighted Yale historian of naval warfare, Bernard Brodie, wrote in his classic, *The Absolute Weapon* (1946): "Thus far the chief purpose of our military establishment has been to win wars. From now on its chief purpose must be to avert them. It can have almost no other useful purpose."

Truman occasionally pondered such thoughts on the dark side of Hiroshima, but the carefully hedged American offer to share atomic science taken to the United Nations by Bernard Baruch in 1946 was as far as Stimson's appeal would carry. There was diffuse discussion in the country about the new weapon, and much anxiety beneath the surface which occasionally broke through, as when David Bradley's *No Place to Hide* (1948), a story of radioactive fallout from the Bikini atoll tests, had strong sales, and John Hersey's *Hiroshima* (1946), a runaway bestseller, was reprinted in newspapers across the country and broadcast on the ABC radio network.

For some Americans the atomic era was just another sign of American progress, with considerable commercial potential. Apart from the high hopes for atomic-powered energy facilities, "atomic cocktails" were served in bars, "atomic earrings" were sold in stores, and an "atomic bomb" ring was available

Soldiers of the 11th Airborn Division watch as an atomic explosion mushrooms into the sky during 1951 testing maneuvers in Nevada.
(UPI/Bettmann)

to buyers of General Mills cereals. For some, even the bomb, because it was in American hands, was a splendid thing. Senator Edwin Johnson (Colorado) expressed gratitude that "God Almighty in His infinite wisdom dropped the A-bomb in our lap," and popular country/western singer Roy Acuff sang in his "Advice to Joe [Stalin],"

> You will see the lightning flashing,
> Hear atomic thunder roll,
> When Moscow lies in ashes,
> God have mercy on your soul.

The U.S. military men who were the custodians of the bomb lacked a theory of how America might use its weapon, as did their civilian superiors. Improvements in uranium processing and in weapons engineering meant that the United States had a stockpile of nine weapons in 1946, and fifty by 1948. But there were only thirty-three B-29s capable of carrying them. The military energetically stockpiled the bombs, and the president agreed to an expansion of the strategic air force. Then, a year later, in August 1949, Russian detonation of an atom bomb announced that the U.S. monopoly was over and the nuclear race was on. Despite polls showing public opinion divided between an arms build-up and negotiations, and amid conflicting scientific advice, Truman decided in early 1950 to authorize U.S. scientists to develop a "super" or hydrogen bomb (based on the fusion of hydrogen atoms rather than the fission or splitting of atoms). The weapon was successfully detonated in November 1952, but the Soviets matched the dubious achievement less than a year later. The arms race escalated, and in seven years had armed two hostile nations with weapons of such devastating power that the likely targets must include cities, not just military installations. Physicist Albert Einstein had warned, a few years earlier, that the "release of atom power has changed everything but our thinking. Thus we are drifting toward a catastrophe beyond comparison. We shall require a new manner of thinking if mankind is to survive."

BIBLIOGRAPHY FOR PART ONE

AMBROSE, STEPHEN E. *Rise to Globalism: American Foreign Policy since 1938.* Baltimore: Penguin Books, 1971.
APEROVITZ, GAR. *Atomic Diplomacy: Hiroshima and Potsdam; The Use of the Atomic Bomb and the American Confrontation with Soviet Power.* New York: Simon & Schuster, 1965.
BAILEY, STEPHEN K. *Congress Makes a Law: The Story behind the Employment Act of 1946.* New York: Columbia University Press, 1950.
BAIN, KENNETH R. *March to Zion: U.S. Policy and the Founding of Israel.* College Station: Texas A&M University Press, 1979.
BERMAN, WILLIAM C. *The Politics of Civil Rights in the Truman Administration.* Columbus: Ohio State Press, 1970.
BERNSTEIN, BARTON J., ed. *Politics and Policies of the Truman Administration.* Chicago: Quadrangle Books, 1970.

BOYER, PAUL. *By the Bomb's Early Light: American Thought and Culture at the Dawn of the Atomic Age*. New York: Pantheon, 1983.

BURNS, RICHARD DEAN. *Harry S. Truman: A Bibliography of His Times and Presidency*. Wilmington, DE: Scholarly Resources Inc., 1984.

CLEMENS, DIANE S. *Yalta*. New York: Oxford University Press, 1970.

COHEN, MICHAEL J. *Truman and Israel*. Chapel Hill: University of North Carolina Press, 1990.

CUMINGS, BRUCE. *The Origins of the Korean War: 1945–47*. Princeton, NJ: Princeton University Press, 1981.

———. *The Origins of the Korean War: The Roaring of the Cataract, 1947–1950*. Princeton, NJ: Princeton University Press, 1990.

DIGGINS, JOHN P. *The Proud Decades: America in War and Peace, 1941–1960*. New York: Norton, 1988.

DONOVAN, ROBERT J. *Conflict and Crisis: The Presidency of Harry S. Truman, 1945–1948*. New York: Norton, 1977.

———. *Tumultuous Years: The Presidency of Harry S. Truman, 1949–1953*. New York: Norton, 1982.

DRELL, SIDNEY. *In the Shadow of the Bomb: Physics and Arms Control*. New York: American Institute of Physics, 1993.

FEIS, HERBERT. *The Atomic Bomb and the End of World War II*. Princeton, NJ: Princeton University Press, 1966.

FERRELL, ROBERT H., ed. *Off the Record: Private Papers of Harry S. Truman*. New York: Harper & Row, 1980.

———. *Harry S. Truman: A Life*. Columbia, MO: University of Missouri Press, 1995.

FRANKLIN, H. BRUCE. *War Stars: The Superweapon and The American Imagination*. New York: Oxford University Press, 1988.

FREELAND, RICHARD M. *The Truman Doctrine and the Origins of McCarthyism*. New York: Knopf, 1972.

GADDIS, JOHN L. *The United States and the Origins of the Cold War*. New York: Columbia University Press, 1972.

———. *Strategies of Containment*. New York: Oxford University Press, 1982.

———. *The Long Peace: Inquiries into the History of the Cold War*. New York: Oxford University Press, 1987.

GARDNER, LLOYD C., ed. *The Origins of the Cold War*. Waltham, MA: Ginn-Blaisdell, 1970.

HAMBY, ALONZO. *Beyond the New Deal: Harry S. Truman and American Liberalism*. New York: Columbia University Press, 1973.

HARKEN, GREG. *The Winning Weapon: The Atomic Bomb in the Cold War, 1945–50*. New York: Knopf, 1980.

HARTMANN, SUSAN. *Truman and the Eightieth Congress*. Columbia: University of Missouri Press, 1971.

———. *The Home Front and Beyond: American Women in the Forties,* Boston: Twayne, 1982.

HERSEY, JOHN. *Hiroshima*. New York: Knopf, 1946.

HIXSON, WATER F. *Geroge F. Kennan*. Oxford: Oxford University Press, 1989.

HOFFMAN, STANLEY AND CHARLES MAIER, eds. *The Marshall Plan: A Retrospective*. Boulder, CO: Westview Press, 1984.

HOGAN, MICHAEL J. *The Marshall Plan: America, Britain and the Reconstruction of Western Europe*. Cambridge: Cambridge University Press, 1987.

JAMES, D. CLAYTON. *The Years of MacArthur: Triumph and Disaster, 1945–1964,* vol. 3. Boston: Houghton Mifflin, 1985.

JUNGK, ROBERT. *Brighter than a Thousand Suns: A Personal History of the Atomic Scientists*. New York: Harcourt Brace Jovanovich, 1956.

KEEGAN, JOHN. *The Second World War.* New York: Viking Press, 1990.

KENNAN, GEORGE F. *Memoirs, 1925–1950.* Boston: Little, Brown, 1967.

KIRKENDALL, RICHARD S., ed. *The Harry S. Truman Encyclopedia.* Boston: M. K. Hall, 1989.

KOLKO, GABRIEL. *The Politics of War, 1943–1945.* New York: Random House, 1969.

LACEY, MICHAEL, ed. *The Truman Presidency.* Washington, DC: Woodrow Wilson International Center for Scholars, 1989.

LAFEBER, WALTER. *America, Russia and the Cold War, 1945–1966.* New York: Wiley, 1967.

LEFFLER, MELVYN P. *A Preponderance of Power: National Security, the Truman Administration, and the Cold War.* Palo Alto, CA: Stanford University Press, 1991.

———, and DAVID PAINTER, eds. *The Origins of Cold War: An International History.* New York: Routledge, 1994.

LIEBERMAN, JOSEPH I. *The Scorpion and the Tarantula: The Struggle to Control Nuclear Atomic Weapons, 1945–1949.* Boston: Houghton Mifflin, 1970.

LIPPMAN, WALTER. *The Cold War.* New York: Harper, 1947.

LUBELL, SAMUEL. *The Future of American Politics.* New York: Harper, 1952.

MANDELBAUM, MICHAEL. *The Nuclear Question: The United States and Nuclear Weapons 1946–1976.* New York: Cambridge University Press, 1979.

MARKOWITZ, NORMAN. *The Rise and Fall of the Peoples' Century: Henry A. Wallace and American Liberalism, 1941–1948.* New York: Free Press, 1973.

MASTNY, VOJTECH. *Russia's Road to the Cold War.* New York: Columbia University Press, 1979.

McCOY, DONALD R. *The Presidency of Harry S. Truman.* Lawrence: University of Kansas Press, 1984.

McCULLOUGH, DAVID. *Truman.* New York: Simon & Schuster, 1992.

MILLER, MERLE. *Plain Speaking: An Oral Biography of Harry S. Truman.* New York: Berkeley, 1973.

PATTERSON, JAMES T. *Mr. Republican: A Biography of Robert A. Taft.* Boston: Houghton Mifflin, 1972.

PETULLA, JOSEPH M. *American Environmental History.* San Francisco: Boyd & Fraser, 1977.

PFEFFER, PAULA F. *A. Philip Randolph: Pioneer of the Civil Rights Movement.* Baton Rouge: Louisiana State University Press, 1990.

POGUE, FORREST C. *George C. Marshall: Statesman, 1945–1949.* New York: Viking, 1987.

SHERWIN, MARTIN J. *A World Destroyed: The Atomic Bomb and the Grand Alliance.* New York: Knopf, 1975.

SMITH, RICHARD NORTON. *Thomas E. Dewey and His Times.* New York: Simon & Schuster, 1982.

SMOKE, RICHARD, AND ALEX. *Deterrence in American Foreign Relations.* New York: Columbia University Press, 1974.

STUECK, WILLIAM. *Road to Confrontation: American Policy toward China and Korea.* Chapel Hill: University of North Carolina Press, 1981.

TRUMAN, HARRY S. *Memoirs.* Garden City, NY: Doubleday, 1955.

WILSON, EVAN M. *Decision on Palestine: How the United States Came to Recognize Israel.* Stanford, CA: Hoover Institution Press, 1979.

WITTNER, LAWRENCE S. *American Intervention in Greece, 1943–49.* New York: Columbia University Press, 1982.

YERGIN, DANIEL. *Shattered Peace.* Boston: Houghton Mifflin, 1977.

PART TWO

1950–1960

We travel together, passengers on a little space ship, dependent on its vulnerable supplies of air and soil . . . preserved from annihilation only by the care, the work, and I will say the love, we give our fragile craft.
—ADLAI E. STEVENSON
U.S. AMBASSADOR TO THE UNITED NATIONS, 1960–1965

CHAPTER 3

Years of Growth and Cold War

MID-CENTURY

At mid-century, the United States was the world's most dynamically evolving major economy. With good reason, the editors of *Fortune* magazine titled their 1955 book, *America: The Continuing Revolution*. Looking at the nation's economic prospects, the editors of *Fortune* found a robustly growing industrial giant viewed by all the world as a model of innovation and productivity, bringing the American people an unparalleled and rising standard of living.

Gross national product (GNP) grew from $206 billion to over $500 billion (1954 dollars) in the twenty years following 1940, representing a per-capita increase of $919. By 1955, with 6 percent of the world's population, the United States produced and consumed a third of the world's entire annual product. Several growth industries led the expansion. Some were familiar industries in which the United States had early in the century seized the lead and after World War II enjoyed global supremacy: aircraft and aerospace, electrical appliances including the dynamic television industry, chemical synthetics, lightweight metals. Foremost among these established industries reaching their zenith in the postwar years was the automobile industry, born and raised in the U.S.A. At mid-century, four fifths of the autos in the world were registered in the United States, and Japan was beginning to turn out a mere 4000 cars annually. New high-technology products won wide consumer acceptance and expanded rapidly: polaroid cameras; the photocopying machine, first built by a small company in Rochester, New York, in 1947; and the computer, first marketed by International Business Machines in 1953.

Another area of expansion came in the leisure industries. By 1963 the average industrial worker had eight paid holidays a year plus a two-week vacation and a forty-hour workweek. The proportion of families with annual incomes of

$10,000 or more crept gradually up from 9 percent of the total in 1947 to 33 percent in 1968. With more leisure time and more money, Americans spent billions on boating, bowling, golf, cameras, second cars, motorbikes, radio equipment, music systems, and television sets. Adolescents alone spent $22 billion in 1963, some of it on food and clothes, much of it on recreation—records, movies, guitars, basketballs. Television seemed to symbolize the new prosperity, with 7 million sets sold in 1953; 54 million were in operation by 1960, 90 million by 1971. Forests of antennas sprouted over suburbs, television personalities became better known than senators or scientists, and television programs reached more Americans than clergymen or teachers, launching a transformation of the habits, politics, and possibly also the values of the society.

After its material affluence, a second distinctive feature of the U.S. economy at mid-century was its relative isolation. World trade was expanding, the United States exporting $10.2 billion in goods abroad while importing $9.1 billion. Yet this represented only 6.7 percent of U.S. GNP. Americans bought American-made goods, only a few sophisticates occasionally preferring French wine, whiskey and sweaters from Ireland and Scotland, cutlery from Sweden or Spain. Japan, at the end of the U.S. occupation in 1954 producing a scant 3 percent of world manufactures and 1 percent of world exports, sold virtually nothing in the United States: "The Japanese don't make the things we want," Secretary of State John Foster Dulles said in 1954.

Optimism about the American Economy

By the mid-1950s a decade of economic expansion had made the Great Depression seem a fading memory, especially for the young. At last the formula for endless growth and mass abundance had been discovered, or so it appeared. "The fundamental problems of the industrial revolution have been solved," exulted sociologist Seymour Martin Lipset, and with per-capita income in 1960 some 35 percent higher than in 1945, few thought this a reckless comment. As *Time* magazine said: "The amazing U.S. economy could defy even the law of physics; what goes up need not necessarily come down." "The remarkable capacity of the U.S. economy," wrote economic historian Harold Vatter, "represents the crossing of a great divide in the history of humanity."

Critics of the World's Leading Economy

For twenty years after the war this was the tone of most commentary on the American economy—euphoria at its cornucopian abundance, unconstrained by visible limits; a perception of living amid a revolutionary leap beyond the old human miseries of poverty, disease, class conflict. Rising affluence was grasped eagerly by a people who recalled the hard times of the 1930s. A few critical voices could be heard, their major theme not the distribution of material wealth nor the environmental costs of producing and disposing of it, but rather the cultural impacts of mass consumption.

Americans might be better fed, housed, and entertained than before, but concern was expressed by writers such as David Riesman (in *The Lonely Crowd*, 1950) and William H. Whyte, Jr. (in *The Organizational Man*, 1956) about a stifling conformity that was both dull and a threat to creative ideas. When critics took aim at the economy itself, the complaint was that it did not grow fast enough. Democratic politicians, unable to complain about the low inflation rates produced by Eisenhower's tight monetary and fiscal policies, pointed to the trade-off paid in substantial unemployment. The economic growth rate, though it averaged 3 percent through the 1950s (which includes the Korean War mobilization), was reported to be lower than that of the U.S.S.R. and also our defeated rivals, Germany and Japan. The nation's population expanded by 28 million between 1950 and 1960, and 25,000 Americans, on average, entered the workforce weekly. The rate of economic expansion was not high enough to provide them all with jobs, and unemployment mounted to 6.8 percent of the workforce by 1958 and climbed toward 8 percent by the end of 1960. Democrats such as Senators John F. Kennedy and Paul Douglas argued that the economy ought to be made to grow more quickly—in their view, a federal responsibility.

This was not so much a critique of the economy as of its federal managers. A different criticism which reached a wide audience came from Harvard economist John Kenneth Galbraith. In his *The Affluent Society* (1958), Galbraith, writing with such wit and irony as to disqualify him among "serious" economists, questioned the balance between private and public goods in American consumption patterns. He found something fundamentally wrong with an economy which directed resources toward so much that was trivial or offensive—bubble gum and hair dye, movie magazines, hula hoops, walls of highway billboards, chrome-burdened automobiles. The American economy, Galbraith argued, should redirect much of its productive energies toward improved public goods, such as schools and hospitals, art galleries, parks, and recreation facilities. He wrote:

> The family which takes its mauve-and-cerise, air-conditioned, power-steered and power-braked automobile out for a tour passes through cities that are badly paved, made hideous by litter, blighted buildings, billboards and posts for wires that should long since have been put underground. They pass on into a countryside that has been rendered largely invisible by commercial art. . . . Just before dozing off on an air mattress beneath a nylon tent, amid the stench of decaying refuse, they may reflect vaguely on the curious unevenness of their blessings. Is this, indeed, the American genius?

In the next decade this "starvation of the public sector" argument, as well as the complaint about a high unemployment/slow growth pattern, would exert much influence in shaping political dialogue and governmental policy.

UNSEEN FLAWS

Other problems with the postwar economy went largely unnoticed in the 1940s and 1950s, since they lay deeper beneath the surface and their effects would not be seen clearly until more time had passed. The distribution of the new affluence concerned almost no one in the 1950s, given the general assumption that New Deal and wartime tax changes were redistributing income downward. This alleged redistribution, along with economic growth, was expected to eventually bring affluence to all. One noted study found that the top 5 percent of income earners took 26 percent of the national income in 1929 but only 16 percent by 1959, prompting *Fortune* magazine to announce: "Though not a head has been raised aloft on a pikestaff, not a railway station seized, the U.S. has been for some time now in a revolution" in which antagonistic classes would merge into a great middle citizenry. As for the bottom one third, FDR's "forgotten man at the bottom of the economic pyramid," they would be lifted up either by welfare programs supported by progressive taxes, or by overall economic growth. "A rising tide lifts all boats," Senator John F. Kennedy liked to say as he ran for president in 1960.

In time it would be evident that such optimistic views were wrong. The only significant redistribution of income in modern American history had come during the period 1929–1945, most of that in the war years and all of it modest. In the postwar years until the 1980s, the distribution of income did not change significantly. This should have been no surprise, since the American tax system as a whole was not progressive but at best neutral, when regressive taxes state and local were included. Wide disparities of income and wealth remained characteristic of American society. In the words of economist Paul Samuelson: "If we made an income pyramid out of child's blocks, with each portraying $1,000 of income, the peak would be far higher than the Eiffel Tower, but almost all of us would be within a yard of the ground."

Poverty

The tide of growth was apparently not lifting all boats, after all. Campaigning in West Virginia at the end of the 1950s, Senator John Kennedy saw Americans who were caught in one of society's many "pockets of poverty," in economist Galbraith's phrase. A wealthy graduate of Harvard, Kennedy had never seen rural poverty, was genuinely shocked, and became convinced that the government should "do something." He and others learned much about the extent and causes of economic deprivation within America's affluent society by reading Michael Harrington's influential book, *The Other America* (1962). Harrington estimated the number of people living at or below the level of basic subsistence (not merely a minimal diet, but adequate shelter and clothing) at 40 to 50 million. The poor were virtually invisible to suburban Americans commuting to central business districts and back. Declining industries such as coal mining trapped many in mountainous West Virginia or Illinois coal areas; others were isolated in urban ghettos, held back from ascending the economic ladder by hotly debated and puzzling factors—some combination of nonwhite skin, old age, illness, "the culture of poverty" devoid of the middle-class commitments to education, self-discipline, and planning for the future. These were ancient human problems, but until Harrington's book many had thought the postwar American economy had somehow eradicated poverty.

LATENT TROUBLES

The distribution of income may not have been as equitable as some wished, but neither income disparities nor a residual povertied population seemed to restrain the American economy, which boomed ahead despite them. With post-war economic growth slowed only by brief recessions, and with rising levels of average family incomes, few in the 1940s and 1950s saw any fundamental flaws in the American way of wresting a living from the earth. But underlying trends contained dangers.

Population

The surge in fertility rates which launched the Baby Boom in 1946–1947 continued through the 1950s, pushing the American population toward larger numbers. Over 4 million births a year were recorded annually from 1954 to 1964, and when the Baby Boom was later charted it could be seen that 76 million Americans had been added to the nation. Fertility drove the population total up to 180 million by 1960 (a net addition of 28 million, or an 18.5 percent

A growing U.S. population and the popularity of suburban living drew more and more Americans out of the cities and into the surrounding countryside. This "suburban sprawl" continues to consume the nation's finite acreage of prime agricultural land.
(UPI/Bettmann)

increase over the decade), for death rates dropped only very gradually; immigration in the 1950s added about a quarter of a million annually to the population, a demographically minor addition. The baby-driven growth of the American population was news, and to a people unaware that each new American was also the most resource-using and pollution-producing human being born anywhere on the planet, it seemed good news. Signs in New York subways declared: "Your future is great in a growing America. Every day 11,000 babies are born in America. This means new business, new jobs, new opportunities." *Life* magazine's cover photo on June 16, 1958, displayed 23 children with the caption, "Kids: Built-in Recession Cure," followed by the story, "Rocketing Births: Business Bonanza."

Postwar internal migration patterns continued established trends. The attractions of urban life steadily drew people away from agriculture, expanding the size of urban areas. Suburbs grew twice as fast as center cities generally, as the more affluent sought the space and other amenities which the automobile made accessible. Prewar regional migration trends accelerated, with the Pacific Coast and Southwest a magnet for moving Americans and the South a net exporter of people to other regions. The southern black population was especially mobile, 1.4 million leaving the South during the 1950s to relocate in the other three regions of the nation. Philadelphia experienced a net addition of 82,000 nonwhites, Detroit 86,000, Washington, D.C., 69,000; while net losses were experienced in Knoxville, Augusta, Little Rock, Birmingham, and in many southern rural counties. Every year, 20 percent of the American people changed their residence, and out of the myriad currents of migration there continued to emerge the same pattern: a slide of the population center to the west. In 1960 the mythical center was located in Illinois, as it had been ten years before, but closer to the Mississippi River than the Indiana border.

Foreign migration patterns changed considerably after the war, however. The restrictive immigration laws of the 1920s, the Depression, and World War II had cut immigration sharply and produced thirty years of negligible foreign entry—fewer than 200,000 a year. But the war's dislocations created large refugee flows within Europe, and some of it overflowed to the United States. Annual immigration totals rose to well above 200,000 through the 1950s, with a mid-decade surge of 300,000 Hungarians fleeing the Soviet suppression of the insurrection there in 1956. But a little-known program to supply wartime farm labor from Mexico had more to do with the long-term demographic future of the United States than spasmodic refugee flows from Europe. The *Bracero* program, begun in 1942, continued through the 1950s under joint U.S.–Mexican agreements, establishing a flow of as many as 400,000 laborers annually to work in cotton, vegetable, and fruit crops in California, Texas, and other states. This annual flow of labor into the United States cut deep grooves of familiarity and expectation, drawing non-*Bracero* illegal migrants ("wetbacks") and spilling outside the controlled agricultural labor markets. The program was finally ended in 1964, but the migration flows continued, increasingly more permanent than seasonal.

Noting American birth rates, demographer Donald Bogue wrote in 1959: "The people of the U.S. are on the threshold of what looks as though it may be an era of almost runaway growth." This remark had a nervous sound to it, yet few seemed to share his concern. One exception came late in the decade, when a governmental study group sounded a note of alarm about population growth—but about growth abroad, not within the national boundaries. A report on foreign aid (called the Draper report, after task force chairman William S. Draper) reached President Eisenhower's desk in 1958, containing a section recommending U.S. assistance in the form of birth-control technology to those nations seeking aid. The president squelched the topic with the comment that he could think of nothing so inappropriate for government to concern itself with than population size. The issue was banished from the White House and the newspapers, but not for long. Eisenhower's immediate successors would return to it, and he would reverse himself on the issue by 1963, joining ex-President Harry Truman as co-chairman of Planned Parenthood World Federation.

Resources

The American appetite for natural resources, renewable and nonrenewable, domestic and imported, continued to rise in the postwar expansion. Neither in the private sector nor in government was there any measurable concern about the supply side of basic resources. The worries over soil erosion that had marked the 1930s had vanished as rainfall returned to the Great Plains in the 1940s, and increased agricultural yields were achieved through the application of fertilizer, pesticides, and herbicides. President Truman appointed a committee to study the nation's water supplies and policies, but was bored by their lengthy (and mostly alarming) report, and suppressed it. A different committee under Eisenhower announced that there were no water problems in sight. There was obviously plenty of air, and it seemed clean enough if one did not live in certain coal-dependent cities such as Pittsburgh, Pennsylvania, or Gary, Indiana. Air pollution was seen as a local issue.

The onset of the Cold War and especially the Korean War mobilization did turn some minds toward the possibility of scarcity in "strategic" minerals and metals, many of them increasingly mined abroad. Worried about the national security implications of a dependence on foreign supplies, President Truman appointed a Committee on Materials Policy, chaired by William S. Paley of the Columbia Broadcasting System. The Paley commission report, *Resources for Freedom* (1952), found "many causes for concern. In area after area we encounter soaring demands, shrinking resources. . . . As a Nation, we are threatened, but not alert . . . always more interested in sawmills than seedlings." For the United States was now "a raw materials *deficit* nation . . . the world's largest importer of copper, lead, and zinc," and increasingly an importer of petroleum and iron ore, even lumber. Projections of population increase and steadily increasing demand for materials (the commission did not choose to study food or water) forecast a doubling of energy use by 1975, with minerals consumption up 90 percent.

The few readers of the report (it sold for a quarter) could learn that the United States consumed 2.5 billion tons of materials per year—18 tons of material per capita, including 14,000 pounds per capita of fuel, and 1600 pounds of food. In 1950, Americans took out of the earth twenty-six times more natural gas than in 1900, thirty times the amount of oil. Growth, however, was not seen as a debatable option, but as a given: "We shared the belief of the American people in the principle of Growth. Granting that we cannot find any absolute reason for this belief, we admit . . . it seems preferable to any opposite, which implies stagnation and decay."

If growth must not be questioned, but dependence on overseas material resources was increasing, what should be done? The report gave the standard economists' answers: Rely upon market mechanisms, that is, rising costs would stimulate shifts toward new technologies for extraction, more efficient use and substitution.

The one resource that caused the commission some uneasiness was petroleum. "Petroleum is the great enigma of future energy supplies. . . . It took nature over 500 million years to store in the ground these stockpiles of fossil fuels which civilization is now consuming in a flash of geological time." Would petroleum supplies last long enough for industry, with government R&D support, to devise and shift to substitutes? The commission thought so in its 1952 report, and its optimism was widely shared. The United States had shifted in 1948 from net exporter to net importer of oil, but globally, petroleum was still plentiful, easily extracted and transported, and therefore cheap. Gasoline sold for around 26 cents a gallon as the 1950s ended, and cheap petroleum kept energy prices so low relative to other prices that the cost of energy from 1950 to 1970 actually decreased by 28 percent. With trillions of barrels of oil buried beneath the Arabian peninsula and in other yet unknown parts of the globe, America in the postwar era went happily on a long petroleum binge, designing its infrastructure and molding its habits around cheap energy.

This was understandable, since besides oil there were vast deposits of coal. These were being exploited in the 1950s by a new technique—strip mining by huge earth-moving machines. A few journalistic accounts of the landscape-damaging effect of strip mining in eastern Kentucky and Illinois did not generate a public response. It was a decade when the burden of proof was not on the producers of goods, but on those who would raise questions about "growth." Aubrey Wagner, chairman of the Tennessee Valley Authority, then emerging as the world's largest purchaser of strip-mined coal to supply a demand for electricity which had gone far beyond the TVA's hydroelectric output, commented:

> Strip mining, while it is going on, looks like the devil, but if you look at what these mountains were doing before this stripping, they were just growing trees that were not even being harvested.

Behind coal, the last and most abundant of the fossil fuels, lay the technology which promised to end the energy problem for all time: nuclear power. Not long after the atom bomb had been set off, presidents and policy makers had spoken of the peaceful uses of the harnessed power of the atom—in medicine, but above all as a source of energy. A prototype light-water reactor designed to produce electricity was built at Shippingport, Pennsylvania, in 1957. There was euphoria in the nuclear industry, and talk of electric power "too cheap to meter." By 1965, orders for fifty systems had been placed by public utilities. A 1963 government report predicted that nuclear power would "gather momentum" and by 1980 supply "upwards of one half—some go as far as two thirds—of all new additions to generating capacity."

The Environment

Amid such optimism about the potential of science and technology to solve humanity's problems, the American public at the mid-century mark did not seem much concerned with the sort of problems that had given rise to the earlier "conservation crusades" led by Presidents Theodore and Franklin Roosevelt. Prior to World War I, Theodore Roosevelt (TR) had carried to the White House a set of public concerns about wildlife and forest depletion and preservation of places of great natural beauty. A conservation movement of modest size was based in the east-coast Boone and Crockett Clubs, the Sierra Club headquartered in San Francisco, and the larger General Federation of Women's Clubs, with strong technical support coming from federal scientists. The two Roosevelts—Theodore (1901–1909) and Franklin (1933–1945)—led in the creation of watchdog agencies over the nation's natural resources, especially the National Park Service, the Forest Service, the Soil Conservation Service, and the TVA. Much of the second Roosevelt's achievement in conservation was personal, for the conservation "movement" had diminished in size and vigor since the progressive era. Conservation, at the end of the New Deal, was an activity planned and administered in government offices in Washington, D.C., rather than by public groups at the grass-roots level. After World War II the general public and the small number of organizations concerned with conservation of natural resources generally had confidence that these watchdog agencies would protect diminishing resources and places of unique beauty. In the 1940s, rainfall returned to the Great Plains as a wet cycle ended the Dust Bowl years, and the sense of environmental crisis eased. If there was a conservation movement at all at mid-century, it was embodied in the Sierra Club, the Wilderness Society, and the National Wildlife Federation, all organizations that were small in size, the first two just beginning to stir with new leadership willing to question the stewardship of the federal government's custodians of public lands.

In retrospect, "conservation" had been a limiting term. It was associated with a call for a more orderly, nonwasteful use of resources, while conserving forever for regulated uses certain spectacular places such as Yosemite and Yellowstone. The postwar generation of Americans was not prepared to understand that setting a few special places aside as national parks, forests, or historic sites, managed by the federal bureaucracy, was only the first step in a long battle to preserve the crown jewels of national endowment. Still less were they aware of the threat posed to the natural environment by everyday human activities much closer to them than any national park. Americans' growing abilities to reach and use nature were outstripping the few controls placed between humans and the environment during the conservation crusades of the two Roosevelts.

Americans had a strong outdoor heritage, and loved to hunt the fields and forests, to fish and camp along the waterways, although the increasingly urban population had only limited access to such areas. No one anticipated that the vast expansion of auto ownership and the construction of a national network of interstate freeways after World War II would so dramatically increase public use of formerly remote landscapes. In ever-increasing numbers, especially on weekends, holidays, and during summer vacations, Americans motored to the edges of state and national forests and parks, or to the seashore, always leaving behind their litter, and leaving the meadows and beaches trampled by crowds of vacationing humans.

However, it was during the week that Americans had their primary transactions with their environment, as they worked in factories whose wastes were emitted into waterways and air; as they drove their heavy automobiles with exhaust invisible behind them; as they carried their bottles, cans, and other trash to the curb, where it "went away"; as they flushed their toilets, sprayed pesticides around their houses, built structures in spaces bulldozed out of forests and citrus groves. Almost no one considered the larger environmental impact of these millions of acts. Forests were a resource for enterprising Americans to cut, oceanfronts were meant to be lined with piers and summer cottages, swamps were waiting to be drained.

Auto junk heaps like this one were testament to America's buy-up–throw-away culture.
(UPI/Bettmann)

If not all Americans were loggers, miners, or land developers, all were consumers—of Cokes, cars, radios, appliances, chewing gum, hamburgers, bourbon whiskey, toothpaste, cat food, durable consumer goods such as automobiles and refrigerators—all the products of America's fabulously productive fields, mines, factories, and laboratories. In a call for "forced consumption," a mid-1950s writer in the *New York Journal of Retailing* explained that:

> Our enormously productive economy demands that we make consumption a way of life, that we convert the buying and use of goods into rituals, that we seek our spiritual satisfactions in consumption. . . . We need things consumed, burned up, worn out, replaced, and discarded at an ever-growing rate.

When one finished consuming, one "threw away" the container—leaving behind cars rusting on hillsides, bottles lying by roadsides, old tires bobbing in the creek or smoldering behind a gas station, trash buried in landfills. The volumes were enormous and always growing. By one estimate, the period from 1949 to 1969 saw an increase in the per-capita consumption of nonreturnable beer bottles by 3778 percent, a 1024 percent increase in the consumption of plastics, a 300 percent increase in the use of detergents. There was a pattern in the figures of production and consumption over those years: new, environmentally degrading products such as plastics, detergents, and nonrenewable cans and bottles were being substituted for older, less polluting items such as lumber, wool, and returnable bottles.

Americans were marginally aware of these problems, since garbage collection and disposal were local municipal functions financed by taxes or fees, and litter offended the eye until the Boy Scouts picked it up. But the largest environmental impact of Americans came not from what they threw away as consumers, but from the synthetic chemicals used to produce what they consumed. Production of synthetic organic chemicals was 1.3 billion pounds in 1940, rose to 49 billion pounds in 1950, then to 96.7 billion pounds in 1960. Some of this volume of chemicals was added to food or drink, paint or dye, auto seats or shampoo—to things consumed. "Better things for better living through Chemistry" was the DuPont Chemical Company's slogan for the benefits that came with the ability to transform products in ways which expanded consumer choices: new fabrics, new substitutes for metal and wood, new ways to preserve foods, new medicines. The consumer assumed that the chemically altered products brought into the household or one's body were safe, since food and drug laws had been passed in 1906 and allegedly strengthened in 1938.

And what of chemical waste products, nontoxic or toxic, left over from the processes of production? Consumers never saw them, and producers followed the most rational path: They "externalized" waste from production, including mounting volumes of human-made chemicals. This usually meant dumping in nearby sewers, landfills, or waterways. In Waukegan, Illinois, the Outboard Marine Corporation, the nation's largest manufacturer of outboard motors, used polychlorinated biphenyls (PCBs) in hydraulic fluids in manufacturing. When it was finished with the fluids, the company simply flushed them into Waukegan Harbor—an unregulated and perfectly legal practice. This bit of latent history became manifest in Waukegan in the 1970s, as did other typical acts of 1950s waste disposal. James Stringfellow, an enterprising capitalist who sensed that industrialists in California had a problem externalizing their mounting chemical wastes, opened the 20-acre Stringfellow Acid Pits at a site 20 miles northwest of Riverside, California, in the 1950s. Opening the pits was an event in latent history, unnoticed by anyone but a few companies who began to deposit the 32 million gallons of dangerous chemicals that had collected by the time Stringfellow retired to Newport Beach. In the 1970s, Stringfellow's Acid Pit, and many more, became manifest history on the public agenda.

The volume of synthetic chemicals introduced into agriculture in the years after the war was smaller than that in industry, and just as little noticed. Use of pesticides in agriculture began on a large scale in the 1940s, with the first massive applications by air coming in 1949 against infestations of the cotton boll weevil. Pesticide and herbicide use rose dramatically through the subsequent decades, an elevenfold increase being measured by 1983. Cotton farmers lauded the deadly effect of DDT and related compounds on pests, but the weevil soon adapted to chlorinated hydrocarbon insecticides. The agricultural chemical industry responded with synthetic organophosphates, new toxins with a higher concentration, persistence, and killing power. Farmers of all crops learned to spray not once but as many as fifteen times a season, sometimes spraying "just to be sure." Most consumers did not know or care, although a 1959 Food and Drug Administration (FDA) ban on the entire cranberry crop for excessive pesticide residues raised the first questions about the farmers' new chemical tools. Late in the 1950s, at least one person worried about the chemical basis of the American agricultural economy, a science writer and conservationist named Rachel Carson, who worked alone in her study on a book she intended to call *The Silent Spring*.

In the larger society, the frontier experience blended with successful industrialization and the heady triumphs of wartime technology to shape the national outlook. Our cultural inheritance was an individualistic, nature-exploiting ethic, matched with a boundless optimism about expansion, and an unshakable respect for the rights of individuals to use the land as they wished in the pursuit of wealth. Few could have been found to disagree with Democratic presidential nominee Adlai Stevenson when he said in 1956: "Growth is the very order of our existence in America. We could survive, I think, almost anything except stagnation."

THE GREAT DIVIDE: WAR IN KOREA

At the start of 1950 the Truman administration had some grounds for hope that its domestic proposals would begin to move through Congress that year or the next. The president continued to urge his Fair Deal reforms, hoping that the autumn elections might strengthen his party. In foreign affairs, the Marshall Plan and NATO had apparently begun to restore the strength and confidence of the Western democracies, and the administration debated privately whether to move toward an accommodation with the Red Chinese as one way of containing Russian communism.

Then misfortune struck. The uneasy division of Korea arranged in 1945 broke down on June 24, 1950, when North Korean armed forces suddenly attacked southward across the 38th parallel. In some measure the attack was a response to U.S. policy in South Korea after the war, where the rightist government of Syngman Rhee had been staunchly supported despite repressive activities within his own half-nation. The communist forces to the north sensed Rhee's lack of popular support, and were unfortunately encouraged in their gamble by a statement early in 1950 by U.S. Secretary of State Dean Acheson that Korea lay outside the perimeter of vital U.S. interests.

The military attack speedily altered the administration's thinking. Acting quickly, Truman committed U.S. troops just five days after the outbreak of the conflict, without asking Congress for a declaration of war.

Soon the United States was joined by small contingents from twenty-one nations under U.N. auspices. For a time the South Korean-American-U.N. forces were driven rapidly toward the tip of the peninsula and apparent defeat. But

Map of the Korean War.

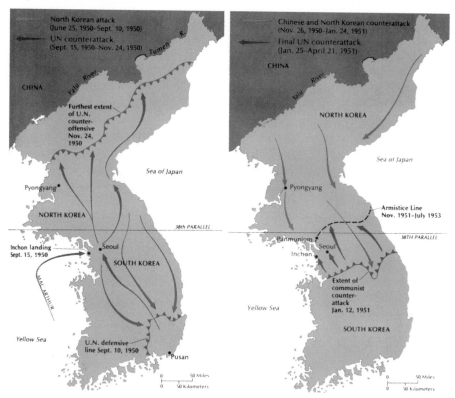

General Douglas MacArthur—a legendary military figure, commander of Allied Forces in the Pacific during World War II and commander of the Allied occupation forces in Japan—ordered a daring amphibious landing on the east coast of Korea near Inchon, in order to break out of the perimeter around the port of Pusan. The brilliant maneuver threw North Korean forces into disarray, and allied forces quickly drove them northward, inflicting heavy casualties. As they approached the 38th Parallel, Truman was faced with a difficult decision. His intention in Korea from the beginning had been to prevent the alteration of the world balance of power through force. It had been no part of initial American thinking to reunite Korea or to achieve military victory for its own sake. But as MacArthur's armies drove north, the administration became excited about the prospect of what a succeeding administration would call "rollback" or "liberation" (slogans made popular in the 1950s by Eisenhower's secretary of state, John Foster Dulles). Truman authorized an eager MacArthur to conquer North Korea; then he escalated the terms of the Cold War even further by ordering a buildup of U.S. forces in Europe, and proposing the creation of ten German divisions (over British and French protests).

When U.S. troops approached the Yalu River and began bombing across that boundary into Chinese territory, the communist government in Peking signaled its alarm by making brief attacks on MacArthur's forces and pressing for a meeting to discuss a negotiated settlement. Both Truman and MacArthur dismissed the warnings of Chinese intervention and rejected negotiations in favor of a pledge to "mop up" the war and bring "the boys home by Christmas." The Chinese then sent thousands of troops into a gap between MacArthur's advancing armies, driving the stunned Americans out of North Korea in two weeks and completely altering the military situation. The war would grind on for three more years, fought along trench lines approximately matching the original dividing line between North and South Korea.

Truman Fires MacArthur

A celebrated dispute between the president and his field commander led to Truman's firing of the popular MacArthur in April 1951, after the general had openly criticized the decision to accept a stalemated war rather than following a more aggressive and "victory-minded" policy. MacArthur openly demanded a major ground effort to reunify Korea, the "unleashing" of Chiang Kai-shek's Formosa armies for attacks on mainland China, a blockade of mainland China, and air bombardment of Chinese targets with the atomic weapon a distinct option. "There is no substitute for victory," the general wrote to a Republican House leader in a letter that was at once made public. MacArthur was challenging the very concept of "limited war," and, more seriously, the president's authority as commander-in-chief. Truman, apart from his outrage at public insubordination, had concluded that the European theater was primary and that the U.S. buildup there was hampered by diverting men and arms to Asia. The Joint Chiefs of Staff supported the president, agreeing with General Omar Bradley that an enlarged war with China would be "the wrong war, in the wrong place, at the wrong time." This military support enabled Truman to withstand a storm of denunciation for dismissing the flamboyant general, who returned to address a joint session of Congress in an emotional farewell, nursing his presidential ambitions.

NSC-68

The dramatic conflict between a president and his top military chief has obscured the main pattern of events. Truman and MacArthur did represent two divergent views in the country at large on how to deal with communism in 1950–1951. Historians have generally endorsed the president's side, seeing in it not only a defense of civilian control over military subordinates but also a prudent acceptance of limits on American power in a world threatened by nuclear war. This view exaggerates a tactical dispute and obscures the common ground on which both men stood: a fervent anticommunism backed by the conviction that there must be a military and emotional rearmament of American society. A secret and, within the top echelons of government, highly influential National Security Council report, NSC-68, spoke in vivid terms of the Soviet intention to dominate the world and foresaw a successful attack on the United States by 1954–1955, after five more years of military buildup. The paper urged that the United States enormously increase spending on armaments so as to stay decisively ahead in the race—devoting perhaps as much as 20 percent of GNP to defense. (Military spending in 1950 was 6 to 7 percent of GNP.) NSC-68 also called for enhanced internal surveillance and covert operations abroad to forward U.S. foreign policy goals, and found no methods too extreme in the perceived emergency. "The integrity of our system," the document stated, "will not be jeopardized by any measures, covert or overt, which serve the purpose of frustrating the Kremlin design."

In early 1950 Truman initialed and set aside NSC-68, apparently agreeing with its reasoning but finding its budgetary implications unacceptable. The president increased military spending in the 1951 budget only slightly, to $17 billion. NSC-68 had boldly proposed a major step toward the militarization of America, and Truman held back for fiscal reasons.

Then came the Korean War. While "restraining" MacArthur, Truman essentially embraced NSC-68 after the conflict broke out. By mid-1951 he had reintroduced the draft, sent four new divisions to Europe, doubled the number of air groups to 95, doubled the size of the army, submitted a defense budget of $50 billion, taken steps to provide the United States with the thermonuclear bomb (a decision made in March 1951), and rearmed West Germany. In Asia, defense pacts were signed with Japan and the Philippines, and American financial aid began to flow to French forces engaged in a civil uprising in a place the Europeans called Indochina. Covert operations by the CIA and intensified FBI surveillance of "security risks" at home implemented the phrase in NSC-68, "any measures, covert or overt." In the words of writer Walter Millis, circumstances and his own decision had brought Harry Truman, after initial resistance, to leave behind "an enormously expanded military establishment . . . a huge

In Korea, U.S. troops experienced bitter winters, both retreats and advances down and up the peninsula, then many months in trench warfare until the cease-fire finally came in 1953.

and apparently permanent armament industry, now wholly dependent . . . on government contracts." The arms race had broken through the few barriers that had contained it prior to the outbreak of war in Korea.

Other Impacts of the Korean War

The Korean War would eventually claim 3.5 million military casualties and perhaps as many civilian injuries and deaths, three fourths of them Korean. Decades later, it can be seen that the decision of the communist dictators Josef Stalin and Mao Tse-tung to allow North Korea's Kim Il-sung to attack South Korea was a huge blunder. Not only were the bulk of the casualties Asian, but the war spurred the rearmament of the United States and its allies, and stimulated industrial growth in capitalist Japan and—more slowly and later—in South Korea. Normalization of relations with the United States was undoubtedly in the long-term interest of China, but the North Korean attack unraveled those prospects. Two days after the opening of hostilities, Truman ordered the Seventh Fleet to protect the Chinese Nationalists on Formosa by patrolling the Formosa Strait, and any lingering hope of U.S.–China normalization was lost for a generation when the Chinese entered the war in November. Within China, the experience of military conflict with the United States hardened popular and governmental thinking into a rigid Cold War model, and encouraged repression of democratic forces.

The war's impacts on the United States were also mostly negative. A war in Asia that took 55,000 American lives and much national wealth without ending in victory served to dash Truman's hopes for domestic reforms and to harden the lines of disagreement on foreign policy. For more than twenty years the United States would build its Far Eastern diplomacy on the theory that the legitimate Chinese government was on Taiwan, not in Beijing, and on the assumption that world communism was basically monolithic and must be dealt with similarly everywhere. A nation rearmed emotionally and militarily was also asked to accept a frustrating stalemate, unending tension, danger, and expense. Understandably, such an international predicament spawned critics of those responsible for U.S. foreign policy. Most of these critics were on the right, where Harry Truman's anticommunism was seen as timid and ineffectual. Republican critics such as Senators Robert Taft, Joseph McCarthy, and William E. Jenner stepped up their attacks on an administration that had "lost" China and failed to win in Korea. The administration seemed to have few vocal supporters as Truman's second term came to an end.

POSTWAR RED SCARE

Perhaps because World War II had not been fought with the same sense of exaggerated hopes as World War I, it was not immediately followed by the same orgy of repression and vigilantism against domestic dissidents. The postwar mood may have been conservative after 1945, but it was not notably irrational, and the Truman administration included no person such as Woodrow Wilson's attorney general A. Mitchell Palmer to come forward to fan the flames of nativism or superpatriotism. Yet postwar developments placed a large strain on the public's basic optimism and sense of tolerance. Inflation followed the lifting of wartime controls; taxes did not drop to prewar levels; government regulation did not disappear; racial and ethnic divisions remained. Far more important, these years saw a series of stunning gains for communism, most notably the Soviet occupation of eastern and central Europe, and the addition of one quarter of the world's population to "the communist side" when the Chinese revolution succeeded in 1949. The tiny Communist Party of the United States worried many people, whose anxieties were understandably heightened by the convictions on charges of espionage—selling or giving atomic secrets to the U.S.S.R.—of New Dealer Alger Hiss (convicted of perjury in 1950) and of Ethel and Julius Rosenberg (convicted in 1951 and executed in 1953), along with the confession of British physicist Klaus Fuchs. Clearly, some Americans were helping our enemy–former ally, the U.S.S.R.

In twentieth-century American experience, "Red Scares" do not simply arise spontaneously out of a population anxious about foreign policy reverses, combined with news reports of treasonous disloyalty by high-placed Americans. Public worries are intensified and guided by elected and appointed officials who have careers to build, and by the news media, who have a product to sell. *Life* magazine told the public as early as 1945 that "the fellow traveler is everywhere," a message that was frequently repeated by other elements of the press and from pulpits and platforms. The Truman administration did not long remain aloof from the concern about subversion. Shaken by charges that its foreign policies were "soft on communism" and that its response to internal radicalism and espionage was feeble, the administration in 1947 instituted a new loyalty program for government employees. Attorney General Thomas Clark conducted the program with more zeal for results than respect for civil liberties, and many employees were dismissed without a fair hearing. Clark and Truman launched the program partly to head off a congressional witch hunt, but also because they shared a deep alarm about domestic communist infiltration. Truman's foreign policy rhetoric describing a world cleanly split between "free" and "captive" nations contributed to a general tendency toward oversimplification, particularly the feeling that a person who was not a fierce anticommunist must probably be a communist. The internal threat was magnified by FBI Director J. Edgar Hoover in a series of speeches and articles in the late 1940s, but even Hoover did not match the hyperbole of Attorney General J. Howard McGrath in 1950, when he declared: "There are today many communists in America. They are everywhere—in factories, offices, butcher shops, on street corners, in private business—and each carries with him the germs of death for society." Such statements contributed to a mood that was soon to be recklessly exploited by others who had even less restraint and no other business to occupy their time.

Senator Joe McCarthy

Such a person was the junior Senator from Wisconsin, Joseph R. McCarthy—a combative ex-Marine and lawyer who had slipped into the U.S. Senate by audaciously challenging Senator Robert LaFollette, Jr., in 1946 at the trough of Wisconsin voters' enthusiasm for the LaFollette brand of progressivism. After four lackluster years in the Senate and anxious about reelection, McCarthy suddenly claimed, in a speech in Wheeling, West Virginia (February 5, 1950), to have a list of 205 communists who were currently employed by the State Department. If this were true, it would neatly explain the foreign policy reverses of 1945–1950. McCarthy found that he had struck a responsive chord in national emotions. The press dutifully reported the Senator's varying charges in headlines, while finding little news value in the inconsistency of his facts and the subsequent failure of his evidence to withstand scrutiny. "McCarthy," wrote journalist Richard Rovere, "was surely the champion liar. He lied with wild abandon; he lied without evident fear; he lied in his teeth and in the teeth of truth; he lied vividly and with a bold imagination." The purpose of the fabrications was to manipulate the media for coverage, and thus to manipulate politics. The press was a willing partner, and McCarthy brought a headlong style to the

Joseph McCarthy came to power and notoriety in 1950 with a speech in Wheeling, West Virginia, and waged a campaign against communist subversion in America until his death in 1957. Here, McCarthy explains at the "Army–McCarthy Hearings" how communists had infiltrated all parts of the U.S.
(UPI/Bettmann Newsphotos)

task. In the words of historian Thomas Reeves, McCarthy "studied little, had no goals (beyond his own reelection), and thought nothing out in advance. As had long been his style, he shot from the hip, bluffed, lied, rushed to get to the plane to take him to a rally in Peoria or a parade in Cheyenne."

His base was his chairmanship of a subcommittee of the Government Operation Committee, where he was protected by the Senate's code of deference toward its members. From there McCarthy launched a series of investigations of internal subversion that was well covered by the news media. These produced headlines, polls suggesting strong public support for McCarthy, and an intimidated State Department—but no convictions of communist spies. Spurred by McCarthy, an antisubversive campaign spread to industry, schools and colleges, even churches, where people were intimidated and fired if their beliefs were found not to be appropriately "American."

It is difficult to measure the extent of this intimidation, or the resultant narrowing of the bounds of permissible speech and thought. Historian William O'Neill concludes that some 300 people lost their jobs as a result of the Hollywood blacklist and purge, and perhaps 500 state and local government employees lost their jobs to local red hunts, along with some 600 public school teachers and 150 college professors. The combined investigations of Truman's loyalty program together with the Eisenhower administration's continued efforts led to 2700 firings and 12,000 resignations from the federal bureaucracy from 1947 to 1956. Especially hard hit was the foreign service and the State Department generally, where America's Far Eastern policy was for years made timid and fearful of insufficient hostility to Chinese communism. In the universities, most of the evidence suggests, in O'Neill's words, that "freedom of thought and speech survived and even flourished," though there were many casualties.

McCarthy's support came disproportionately from the right-wing leadership within the Republican Party, from many Catholics whose church had a special animosity against "Godless communism," and from fundamentalist Protestants from rural, "Bible belt" regions, where flag and scripture had long found fervent defenders against alien challenge. While McCarthy's main target was communism and communists, he struck also at another enemy which has appeared frequently in American anxieties: a distant, arrogant, eastern financial and intellectual elite who allegedly dominated the nation's key institutions. In this sense only, McCarthy has appeared to some historians as a partial heir of the Populist tradition.

THE ELECTION OF 1952

Truman, facing a 23 percent approval rating from the public and with little party support, announced his retirement. New leadership thus came forward in both parties. The Democrats selected the eloquent governor of Illinois, Adlai E. Stevenson, who pledged to carry on with New and Fair Deal policies as well as the internationalist leadership forged since World War II. The Republicans, tired of losing presidential races, abandoned their most gifted conservative, Senator Robert Taft, and nominated the popular war hero and organizer of NATO, General Dwight D. ("Ike") Eisenhower. The genial Eisenhower endorsed a platform written by the right wing of his party and, assisted by the anticommunist rhetoric of his running mate, Congressman Richard M. Nixon, sent a signal that his election would bring some sort of end to Truman's international mistakes, domestic fumbling, and the war in Korea. Fifteen million more voters turned out than in 1948, and Ike took the votes of 12 million of them, defeating Stevenson 33.9 million votes to 27.3 million, and carrying four states of the formerly "solid" South. Republicans gained control of both houses of Congress and dreamed of a new reign as majority party. To conservatives, so long out of power, the way seemed open for a season of reform to curb two decades of governmental liberalism.

CHAPTER 4

Eisenhower: Conservative Reformer as Reluctant Centrist

IKE LEADS TO THE RIGHT

In 1953 the prospects for reform were encouraging to opponents of New Deal liberalism. Eisenhower filled his cabinet with wealthy businessmen, such as Charles Wilson from General Motors and George Humphrey from the Mark Hanna Corporation, and made clear that his philosophy of government assumed a minimal federal role in the natural workings of the economy. The administration moved at once to slash federal expenditures by approximately 10 percent in order to balance the budget, and ended federal controls adopted during the Korean War. Ike had even less interest than Truman in the federal role as protector of the environment, and he filled top positions in the great public lands agencies—the Department of the Interior, and the Forest Service of the Department of Agriculture—with men (invariably) devoted to private exploitation rather than conservation of resources. In the 1950s federal officials in the Department of the Interior and the Army Corps of Engineers pursued plans for western dams so aggressively that they awakened the slumbering conservation movement into resistance (see Chapter 5).

These prunings of the size and regulatory capacity of the federal government were achieved by executive orders and the appointing power. The administration's legislative agenda would take some time, but was expected to include critical scrutiny of New Deal landmarks such as the TVA, social security, and farm subsidies, along with a shift in the tax burden away from business. Eisenhower persuaded former President Herbert Hoover to head a second "Hoover commission" to study ways to cut governmental waste and inefficiency. A New Deal agency that actually dated back to Hoover's first year, the Reconstruction Finance Corporation (RFC), which had served as a government investment bank for more than twenty years, was targeted for abolition.

The Eisenhowers and the Nixons celebrate Ike's presidential nomination at the 1952
Republican National Convention in Chicago.
(Dwight D. Eisenhower Library)

EISENHOWER: THE REPUBLICAN AS NEW DEALER

It was not long before reality intervened to dampen Republican hopes for
sweeping changes. In principle, the Republicans wished to greatly reduce business regulation and federal aid to interest groups, while balancing the budget.
The administration's attempts to balance the budget were followed by—many
said, caused—two economic recessions (1954, 1957–1958), an experience that
baffled and discouraged many believers in a free-market economy. However,
groups whose federal assistance might be slashed became angry at the Republican reformers, and some of these were business groups. Farmers resisted cuts
in agricultural spending, influential business groups in the southeast opposed
cuts in the TVA, retired people lobbied to preserve social security.

Faced with a recession in 1954 and the political complaints it generated,
Eisenhower proved himself to be flexible, and for the remainder of the decade
pursued as best he could a moderately active federal role in the economy that
resembled the New Deal in some of its calmer years. He assumed federal
responsibility for the health of the economy, since it would apparently not take
care of itself, and fought the recession of 1954 with the usual Keynesian methods

of expansive monetary and fiscal policies. He was forced into such measures again after recession came in 1957–1958, and left office with a record of five years of deficit and three of small surplus. Federal spending, the Republicans learned, not only staved off economic slumps but was good politics, since groups that had come to depend on New Deal programs were not interested in budgetary savings at their expense. The Eisenhower administration extended social security coverage and benefits three times, continued federal housing programs at reduced levels, and inaugurated a new program of federal aid for interstate highways. Secretary of Agriculture Ezra Taft Benson, pledged to return agriculture to free-market conditions, found farm groups and their congressional allies cool to the idea, and left office in 1960 with the basic structure of federal farm subsidies intact.

In some areas the administration remained staunchly pro-business, making no concessions to New Deal liberalism. Eisenhower Republicanism meant lighter tax burdens for corporations and the wealthy. It encouraged economic development rather than the preservation of public lands under its charge.

In other respects, however, Eisenhower found himself leading his party beyond the New Deal-Fair Deal agenda. On October 4, 1957, the U.S.S.R. fired into space orbit the satellite *Sputnik,* a 184-pound sphere containing sensing devices and transmitters. One month later the Russians orbited a craft carrying a dog. It was, as journalist Clare Booth Luce stated, "an outer-space raspberry to a decade of American pretensions that the American way of life is a gilt-edged guarantee of our national superiority." The achievement came, of course, through government action, and it was quickly clear to Americans that the marketplace does not do many things, including put up space satellites or train the scientists and engineers who create them. Recognizing that aid to the nation's schools, now coping with the Baby Boom, had become a national priority as well as a local obligation, Eisenhower in 1958 signed the National Defense Education Act, which authorized federal loans to students and grants for science facilities in universities.

BLACKS AND WHITES: THE FEDERAL ROLE

The 1950s brought another expansion of the social role of government which Eisenhower did not welcome but reluctantly accepted. Of the three branches of government, the reputedly more passive and conservative one, the judiciary, enlarged the federal role in race relations beyond Harry Truman's small steps. Segregated education had come under judicial attack in a series of cases beginning in the late 1930s: In 1938 the decision of the Supreme Court in *Missouri ex rel. Gaines v. Canada* required the state of Missouri to admit a black to its publicly supported law school; in 1949 the state of Texas was told in *Sweatt v. Painter* that its recently created black law school was inadequate and that blacks must be admitted to the all-white law school of the University of Texas; in 1950, in *McLaurin v. Oklahoma State Regents,* the University of Oklahoma was enjoined from requiring a black student to sit at a separate table. These cases, all in higher education, showed that the court was moving toward the position that separate education was unequal treatment and therefore a violation of the "equal protection of the laws" clause of the Fourteenth Amendment. The Court took the big step in 1954 in the famous *Brown v. Board of Education of Topeka, et. al.,* case, ruling in a unanimous vote that "separate education was inherently unequal" and—in a subsequent ruling in 1955—that all public education facilities in the nation must now be desegregated.

The *Brown* decision was a major turning point in the battle to end Jim Crow, as it placed the authority of a unanimous Court behind the idea of racial equality and the goal of integration. As education policy, its impact was less clear than the Court's high motives. Schools were slowly integrated, but when neighborhood racial segregation limited the impact of race-blind admissions, federal judges took over many school districts and ordered elaborate school busing plans to achieve desirable racial balance. The result was years of bitter division in community school board politics, with only ambiguous gains for black students. In 1991 the Supreme Court, adopting the theory that nondiscrimination and good faith were all the Constitution required of school boards, and not necessarily racially balanced student bodies by any means necessary, essentially ended the 36-year era in which the mighty ideals of *Brown* had been entangled in judge-led engineering of many local public school systems.

The executive and legislative branches of government had been slower to join in the attack on racial discrimination. Harry Truman had asked for a commission to address job discrimination, and ordered the desegregation of the armed forces. Here his reform efforts ended, but a broader political strategy emerged among civil rights activists. Many reasoned that if the federal government would ensure voting rights for minorities, their subsequent political strength would soon bring an end to inequities in other areas of life.

When Democrats showed signs of pressing for voting-rights legislation, Eisenhower's attorney general, Herbert Brownell, convinced the president to support what became the Civil Rights Acts of 1957 and 1960. The first empowered the Justice Department to seek court injunctions against local infringements of the right to vote; the second law made bombing a federal crime and provided a very limited federal authority to register blacks when a pattern of discrimination could be shown in any locality. Eisenhower signed these weak civil rights laws, the first since the 1870s, but his view remained that race relations were somehow in that category of social mores which were and should be beyond the reach of the law. He refused to endorse the Brown decision and made no secret of his distaste for it and the role of its author, Chief Justice Earl Warren. Eisenhower would not urge local school districts to comply with the decision, and his silence emboldened groups who concluded that it might be safe to defy court orders. Governor Orval Faubus of Arkansas, after a meeting with Eisenhower in 1957 in which he heard no strong words of warning, permitted white mobs to harass the nine black school children attempting to attend Central High School in Little Rock, and then called out the state militia to close the school. Eisenhower was forced to commit troops to enforce the segregation order in Lit-

Nine black students integrated Central High School in Little Rock, Arkansas, in 1957. Here an angry white mob that surrounded the Little Rock school abusively taunts one of the "Little Rock Nine," ultimately forcing President Eisenhower—reluctantly—to mobilize the National Guard in order to protect the students and enforce the desegregation policy.
(UPI/Bettmann)

tle Rock, resulting in international embarrassment over a nationally televised event which might well have been avoided through presidential leadership.

With new voting-rights laws on the books and a judicial ban on segregated public schools, it seemed to many whites that American minorities—which in those days meant blacks, in the public mind—had made substantial gains. While this was true of formal political and constitutional rights, by the end of the 1950s it remained evident that the economic ladder toward full participation and equality was not working as well for blacks as it had for Jews and other minorities who had migrated to a predominately white Protestant society. Segregation was still the rule in all areas of life and in all parts of the country. Of the occupations in which Americans made their livelihood, only in entertainment

In Jim Crow America everything was segregated. Public accommodations of all types—restaurants, bathrooms, movie theaters, buses, classrooms—were divided between "whites" and "coloreds." Here two young American men drink from segregated water fountains.
(The Bettmann Archive)

and in organized sports were there any signs of larger opportunities for blacks, and these were painfully limited. In professional baseball, for example, brilliant athletes such as Satchel Paige, Josh Gibson, and Martin Dihigo had played out their careers in the black minor leagues (though Paige at the end of his spectacular career pitched three seasons for the Cleveland Indians), and the Baltimore Orioles once passed off a black second baseman as a Native American nicknamed Chief Tokohomah. The 1948 breakthrough made by Jackie Robinson, playing for the Brooklyn Dodgers, was only very slowly extended to others.

Even in education, where the Court had intervened, there had been little real integration. Ten years after the *Brown* decision, only 2 percent of southern blacks attended school with whites. In 1960 only 14 percent of the blacks in the south were registered to vote; in Mississippi, as few as 6 percent. Southern resistance to any change in race revelations appeared firm, and northern whites matched their disapproval of southern stubbornness with their own lack of progress in lowering barriers based on race. Perhaps more important, the postwar economic expansion had apparently produced disappointingly small change in economic disparities between the races. Although blacks earned more in 1960 than they had in 1945, whites had gained faster, and rural blacks actually seem to have lost ground economically from 1950 to 1960.

RISING MILITANCY

It is usually not disparities in condition, but unrealized expectations, which pre-cipitate dissatisfaction and movements of social protest. Migration out of the rural South, along with wartime experience and the rise of an educated and urban black middle class, gradually undermined black acquiescence in the Jim Crow order. In December 1955, in Montgomery, Alabama, a black woman named Rosa Parks, a long-time NAACP activist, refused to give up her seat on a bus to a white man, as a result of which she was arrested. The massive bus boycott by Montgomery blacks that followed showed that her defiant attitude was widely shared. The country had entered a new era in race relations. Black protest, formerly conducted by an elite of NAACP lawyers whose arena was the courts, began after Montgomery to transform itself into a mass movement

Late on a December day in 1955, Rosa Parks refused to move to the back of a Montgomery, Alabama, bus, sparking off one of the most successful civil rights demonstrations in U.S. history—a year-long bus boycott that ended in the desegregation of Montgomery's public transport. One year later, as seen in this photo taken in December of 1956, Rosa Parks was free to sit in any seat.
(UPI/Bettmann)

that exerted direct pressure in public places. The spontaneous Woolworth's lunch counter sit-ins by black college students in Greensboro, North Carolina, in early 1960 demonstrated the extent to which a new spirit of direct action had permeated the younger generation of blacks. Under the leadership of the Reverend Martin Luther King, Jr., who headed the Montgomery boycott, the new tactics of mass protest were shaped by a spirit of Christian and Gandhian nonviolence. The willingness of thousands of southern blacks to accept the physical risks of marches and sit-ins was a sign of the extent to which expectations changed more rapidly than social relationships. As the temper of the civil rights movement changed and blacks with their white allies intensified their pressure on the Jim Crow system, it was clear that political leaders had less time than they thought if they were to avert violence and more bitterness.

STILL LIVING WITH THE BOMB

Nuclear weapons, together with the airborne delivery systems developed by modern technology, represented not just another stage in the history of human armaments but an entirely new era. For the first time, humans confronted the distinct possibility that death might come to the entire human race rather than to individuals, who at least departed life with progeny behind them. A deep anxiety could be detected during the postwar years, as nuclear fear became what historian Paul Boyer has called "a shaping cultural force."

Early films that were openly critical of the arms race, such as *The Day the Earth Stood Still* (1951) and *Five* (1951), were much outnumbered by Cold War propaganda tracts such as *Bombers B-52* (1957), which conveyed admiration for America's Strategic Air Command (SAC). But a flood of science fiction was published after the 1957 Soviet launching of the *Sputnik* satellite—stories of atomic doom such as Nevil Shute's *On the Beach* (1957), Helen Clarkson's *The Last Day* (1959), Peter George's *Red Alert* (1958), Walter M. Miller, Jr.'s *A Canticle for Leibowitz* (1959), Eugene Burdick and Harvey Wheeler's *Fail-Safe* (1962). *On the Beach* became a grimly successful movie in 1959 under director Stanley Kramer, *Fail-Safe* was put on the screen in 1964 by Sidney Lumet, and George's novel became Stanley Kubrick's film, *Dr. Strangelove* (1964). Magazines, radio, and television presented skimpy coverage of the consequences of atomic war, or the genetic mutation and illness produced by radioactive fallout, but polls regularly reflected a significant level of public concern.

At the same time the public was strangely apathetic about this unique menace, gripped by feelings of powerlessness mated with evasion of reality. The bomb was in the hands of two governments, ours and the Soviets', the second beyond our direct influence and the first trusted to do the right thing behind a necessary veil of secrecy. One thing both governments did was to enlarge the stockpile of such weapons. In 1953 there were 1000 nuclear warheads in the American stockpile, and 17,000 more were added to the arsenal by 1960—virtual mass production of these weapons of annihilation.

Challenges to the U.S. government's nuclear policies, whether in the field of armaments or in nuclear applications in power generation and medicine, were few and fragile. Atomic scientists such as Leo Szilard and Robert Oppenheimer had raised moral questions about the development and deployment of nuclear weapons in an arms race with the Soviets, as had an occasional official such as Secretary of War (1940–1946) Henry Stimson. A campaign to ban atomic testing and at least morally discredit the weapon was led by the National Committee for a Sane Nuclear policy (SANE) (1957–), whose spokespersons included pediatrician Dr. Benjamin Spock, scientist Linus Pauling, union leader Walter Reuther, and politicians Norman Thomas (Socialist) and Alfred M. Landon (Republican). But the public could also read books by Henry Kissinger, who, in *Nuclear Weapons and Foreign Policy* (1957), insisted that a "limited nuclear war" was possible and should be one policy option, or Herman Kahn, whose *On Thermonuclear War* (1960) urged Americans to "think about the unthinkable," since nuclear war would be tragic but "winnable."

Facing such complex issues, the American public overwhelmingly trusted the national government, whose officials dealt with popular anxiety with a dual program of secrecy and positive public relations, including soothing reassurance, deception, and lies. The documentary movie *Atomic Cafe*, made in 1982, depicts the routine propaganda issued by Atomic Energy Commission (AEC) and civil defense officials during the 1950s. To prepare for atomic war, the public was cheerfully instructed to stockpile food and water, practice crawling under tables, and remember to avoid clogging the highways as they evacuated their cities for the serene countryside. Orderly drills taught office workers and school children how to reach nearby bomb shelters. No Soviet planes were overhead, but U.S. planes carrying nuclear weapons on training flights were indeed in American skies, where accidents would seem inevitable and could not be prevented. The government kept secret an accidental release of a hydrogen weapon from a B-36 approaching a landing in New Mexico (only the conventional explosive detonated on impact), but the news media reported another accidental atom bomb (fortunately, also with its nuclear device unarmed) release over South Carolina in 1958.

Also in the American skies was radioactive debris from nuclear weapons testing by both superpowers, and part of the public did become aroused over the issue of nuclear testing. The media reported extensive radioactive fallout after the 1954 Pacific Ocean tests by the United States brought illness and death to Japanese fishermen working 85 miles downwind from the blasts. Then deadly strontium-90 began to show up in milk and wheat in 1959 after extensive Soviet and U.S. atmospheric testing. The government managed this potential public relations problem with news releases assuring people that "there is no danger." In the late 1940s, U.S. nuclear testing of the smaller atomic weapons was removed from the Marshall Island atolls, Bikini and Eniwetok, to a site 70 miles northwest of Las Vegas, Nevada, in order to reduce costs and also Soviet opportunities for spying. (Hydrogen or thermonuclear bombs were tested in the Marshalls in 1953 and after.)

The Nevada site was chosen because "only 3682" people lived in the desert immediately downwind, and Utah towns such as St. George and Cedar City were relatively small. Between 1951 and the Test Ban Treaty of 1963, some 124 nuclear devices were tested there, with radioactive debris sifting down upon east-coast cities occasionally, and inevitably and heavily on the adjoining areas of Nevada, Utah, and Arizona. "Come out and see history being made," said an AEC invitation to local citizens prior to tests; there was no danger, they said. In 1955, local ranchers concluded that their dying sheep were too close to the testing site and sued the government, unsuccessfully. Heavy cancer rates downwind of the site produced a citizens' lawsuit which was won in a lower court in 1984 and then dismissed on appeal.

The government's casual approach to exposing its own citizens to high levels of radiation came as a shock when the extent of atmospheric pollution from weapons tests began to be disclosed in the 1980s. In the 1950s, however, the tapping of atomic energy had been seen by scientists and laity alike as almost user-friendly. The Atomic Energy Commission (AEC) created Project Plowshare in 1957 to explore civilian applications of nuclear power, and lengthy discussions were held between federal officials, scientists, and the governor of Mississippi about using atomic blasts to remove a small range of hills in Mississippi which stood in the way of the construction of the Tennessee-Tombigbee Canal linking the Tennessee River and the Gulf of Mexico. The planning went on for years before the canal builders decided to move the earth with conventional machinery, but there was no public outcry at the idea of American nuclear weapons being used for earth removal at home.

Few people questioned the government's far-flung nuclear activities. Plumes of radioactive iodine-131 were released from the Hanford Nuclear Reservation in Washington from at least 1944 to 1947, and radioactive cooling water was later released into the Columbia River. High levels of thyroid cancer in ten counties downwind of Hanford led to lawsuits in the late 1980s, but for four decades the loyal, trusting citizens of the Hanford area were grateful for the government jobs and expressed their attitudes toward a nuclear world by trading at Atomic Lawn Care or the Atomic Body Shop, and giving the local high school football team a mushroom cloud as a symbol. Unknown to the public, highly radioactive waste from production at the Hanford site of plutonium and tritium for nuclear weapons was stored until 1980 in 149 single-shell tanks, allowing possibly 750,000 gallons of this nuclear brew to drain into the ground and forming the volatile and growing stockpile of lethal wastes whose disposal would emerge in the 1980s as enormously expensive and scientifically uncertain.

EISENHOWER: CRITIC OF THE NUCLEAR ARMS RACE

No person had better access to knowledge about the threat of nuclear weapons and warfare than whoever was president of the United States, and both Truman and Eisenhower struggled, often in private, with the issue. Truman knew how many of his advisers, in secret sessions, spoke of the bomb as a weapon rather like other weapons except more effective, and indeed his diary records several occasions when he explicitly considered—sometimes with relish born of frustration—a preemptive strike on the Soviet homeland. News leaks correctly reported that the use of atomic weapons in the Korean theater was an issue of dispute between General MacArthur, who urged its use, and a more cautious Truman.

Dwight Eisenhower's eight years in office were filled with meetings with National Security Council (NSC) officials and others in which strategies for possible use of nuclear weapons were routinely discussed. When French forces in Indochina were surrounded by communist forces at Dienbienphu, the American government, which had been supporting the French war effort at a cost of $1 billion a year, engaged in weeks of intense discussions of whether and how to intervene with atomic weapons. Chairman of the Joint Chiefs of Staff Admiral Arthur Radford aggressively urged tactical strikes around Dienbienphu, either by American or French aircraft, but his goal appears to have been the larger one of legitimizing the use of the weapon so that the Chinese might be restrained. Secretary of State John Foster Dulles agreed in principle but was more cautious, telling a NATO meeting that "such weapons must now be treated as in fact having become conventional." Eisenhower agreed that the government must have contingency plans which at some point included use of atomic weapons against either the Vietnamese or the Chinese, but stubbornly and in the end successfully resisted all suggestions to use them without the consent of our allies and Congress. It was impossible to consult Congress without leaks, and both Britain and France, firmer than Ike in their objections to military use of the bomb, vetoed the idea.

Thus Eisenhower was acutely aware that atomic warfare was only a hair-trigger away, and his military experience bred skepticism that it could be put to any constructive purpose, or that either side could control a nuclear exchange. Long before writer Bernard Brodie, in *The Absolute Weapons* (1946), set out the view that the chief purpose of the military must now be not winning wars but averting them, Eisenhower wrote to a friend (1956): "We are rapidly getting to the point when no war can be *won*," and when we get to that point, "possibly we will have sense enough to meet at the conference table with the understanding that the era of armaments has ended. . . ."

Eisenhower's alarm over the arms race was genuine and sustained. When Stalin died in 1953, there seemed to be alluring prospects of a thaw in East–West relations, and Dulles's implacable hostility to any Russian leadership could not prevent Eisenhower from searching for ways to improve relations. He could not believe that international differences required the ominous and economy-sapping arms race, which seemed by now to have a life of its own. He welcomed the opportunity for a summit conference at Geneva in 1955, where a tone of conciliation prevailed. Also in 1955, security advisors brought to Eisenhower an "Open Skies" proposal for mutual arms reductions with aerial inspections, cynically designed to embarrass the Russians, who were expected to reject it and prime American public opinion to support continued defense spending. Eisenhower, however, took Open Skies seriously, softened the proposal, and was disappointed when a suspicious Soviet leadership pulled back. The Hungarian revolt and then the British-French attack on Egypt to regain control of the Suez Canal hardened U.S.–U.S.S.R. relations in 1955–1956, the latter an election year in which few major initiatives were possible from Washington.

In that year Nikita Khrushchev became increasingly dominant within the Soviet leadership group, and there was talk of "peaceful coexistence" and a twenty-year treaty with the West. In the next year the Soviets suggested a nuclear-free zone in central Europe. American national security managers, locked in a rigid cold-war outlook, easily convinced themselves that such overtures were not what they seemed, but ruses to lower the American guard. In retrospect it seems likely that the post-Stalin leadership was groping toward what would later be called *detente* with the West, prodded by the mounting tension along the Soviet–Chinese border. But the American government, gripped by the same suspicion in which the Soviets were caught, did not perceive or respond to these opportunities, which were bewilderingly interspersed with the familiar Soviet bluster and denunciation of capitalist imperialism.

If there was indeed an opportunity to avert the next big surge in the arms race, which was to begin in 1961, it was lost sometime in the mid-1950s. The arms race was driven by international rivalries and suspicions, by arms suppliers and the military on both sides, and by technology. Eisenhower opposed these forces with the rationale behind his appeal for an end to the race: Both sides had more than sufficient power to destroy the other even after an attack, so there was no need for more weapons. Hawks attacked his reasoning, and from within the administration. Intelligence spotted two new Soviet bombers in the May Day parades of 1954 and 1955 in Moscow, and national security managers at once raised fears of a surprise attack by superior forces. A "bomber gap" was said to exist as the 1950s advanced, both as to technological sophistication and numbers. The Soviets might have 600 bombers by 1960, so the United States should raise military budgets and beat them to it. Eisenhower did not believe in the bomber gap (the actual "gap" in 1960 was 600 long-range bombers for the United States and about 200 for the U.S.S.R.), and his Open Skies proposal would have allowed the inspection of mutual defense facilities which would check such intelligence frights on both sides.

Given the failure of Open Skies, what the other side did remained shrouded, and neither superpower could be sure that its retaliatory power was sufficient. Technology always seems to be a destabilizing force, and although bombers were not a new technology, missiles were. The Soviets tested their first long-range missile in August 1957 and launched the first orbital satellite, *Sputnik*, two months later. U.S. Air Force intelligence, in a fright, predicted that the Soviets could deploy a thousand intercontinental ballistic missiles (ICBMs) by 1961. Nikita Khrushchev reinforced that view with several brags, and Democratic politicians accused the Eisenhower administration of allowing a "missile gap." It was said that the Soviets had achieved a technological breakthrough and placed new weapons on line, a claim that launched a new phase in the arms race. The U.S. military and most Democrats pressed for more weapons and delivery systems. Eisenhower held to his beleaguered view that the nuclear weapons and delivery systems on both sides were sufficient for deterrence, even if one side owned more bombs.

Had he not been General Eisenhower, his attitude would have been labeled "soft on communism" and would have disqualified him from serious top-level discussion of Cold War strategy. But he was not only president, he was the former commander of Allied forces in Europe. Ike thus occupied a unique position above right-wing and Democratic "hawk" critics, and he could not be restrained from personal efforts to find more promising paths toward peace than more confrontation and larger nuclear arsenals. He pruned military defense budgets and rejected a 1958 version of NSC-68 called the Gaither report, a call for higher defense spending levels. Eisenhower responded that "we could not turn the nation into a garrison state." Even as early as 1953, in a speech to the American Society of Newspaper Editors, he had warned:

> The worst to be feared and the best to be expected [from a continuing arms race] can be simply stated. The worst is atomic war. The best would be this: a life of perpetual fear and tension; a burden of arms draining the wealth and the labor of all peoples. Every gun that is made, every warship launched, every rocket fired, signifies, in the final sense, a theft from those who hunger and are not fed, those who are cold and are not clothed.
>
> This world in arms is not spending money alone. It is spending the sweat of its laborers, the genius of its scientists, the hopes of its children. We pay for a single fighter plane with a half-million bushels of wheat. We pay for a single destroyer with new homes that could have housed more than eight thousand people.
>
> This is not a way of life at all, in any true sense. Under the cloud of threatening war, it is humanity hanging from a cross of iron.

He proposed to Soviet Secretary Khrushchev in 1958 a ban on nuclear testing, and welcomed the mercurial Khrushchev to the United States in September 1959 with high hopes for the Paris summit meeting set for May 1960. Then an American U-2 reconnaissance plane, overflying the U.S.S.R. illegally in the absence of the Open Skies agreement, was shot down over Russia. Khrushchev expressed outrage, as Eisenhower would have done if the situation had been reversed, and both the conference and Ike's hopes for a visit to Russia were ruined.

In retrospect, Ike's record of concern over the arms race and his perception of the dangers in the cold-war status quo were laudable, even though he, like the Russian leadership, often relapsed into either rigid ideology or language which suggested it. Eisenhower and Khrushchev, anxious leaders beset by hardliners and caught in tides of conflict, could not break out of the confrontational style nor interrupt the technological escalation of the nuclear cold-war rivalry. When Ike left office, the United States had deployed 18,000 nuclear weapons with more in the planning stages, and the nation was, and felt, more insecure than ever.

THE "THIRD WORLD" AND THE COLD WAR

Though American foreign policy under Eisenhower did not depart sharply from the Truman pattern, the world was changing. One of the chief results of World War II was the impetus it gave to the breakup of the old colonial empires and the emergence of "Third World" nationalism. (In the handy formulation of Mao Tse-tung, the First World was the industrialized West, the Second was the industrialized Soviet bloc, and the Third was that varied family of poorer, "underdeveloped" or "lesser developed" nations where most of humanity lived.) Britain in the years after the war withdrew, under pressure, from India, Burma, and Egypt; France was driven from Indochina, and the Netherlands from Indonesia. New states appeared almost yearly in Africa, molded out of crumbling European empires, their borders often not reflecting tribal realities. The drive toward independence was not orderly. Nationalism bred violence, even when led by nonviolent figures like Gandhi. Since the United States had little empire in the usual European pattern, independence movements should not have threatened it, especially in view of the revolutionary heritage of 1776. What complicated the American position as colonial empires collapsed was the occasional union of nationalism with communism or authoritarian socialism. Marxism possessed certain advantages over the capitalist-parliamentary democracy model in the newly emerging areas. Leftists in the poorer nations could see their countries as somehow synonymous with Marx's proletariat, and thus in the vanguard of history despite their present plight. Marxism was a creed that emphasized social discipline rather than individual liberties, and thus seemed admirably designed to serve nationalistic elites eager to regiment their pre-modern societies for the swift, difficult passage into economic modernization.

The proliferation in the Third World of new states, nationalistic and noncapitalist where not anticapitalist, was a fact of life with which American policy increasingly had to deal. Many observers, among them George F. Kennan, believed that such developments made the military-oriented containment policy obsolete. Kennan felt that underdeveloped nations experimenting with Marxism were not necessarily a threat to the United States and might be split off from the Soviet bloc by a flexible American policy. Such splitting, or "polycentrism," could be accomplished by establishing working political and economic relations with some communist states in order to detach them from others.

But the chief spokesman of American policy through much of the 1950s was John Foster Dulles, not Kennan. Dulles unshakably held a simpler vision: All communist states were part of a monolith dedicated to the destruction of the West, and it was immoral to deal with any of them. Thus the administration instinctively regarded revolutionaries such as Vietnam's Ho Chi-minh, Cuba's Fidel Castro, and Egypt's Gamal Abdel Nasser as mere puppets of the Kremlin, and saw every socialist state in the Third World as a threat to be removed if possible. Using conventional military forces as well as a new policy instrument unavailable to previous governments—the Central Intelligence Agency (CIA), set up in 1949 and developing an aggressive "covert operations" capacity during the Eisenhower years—the U.S. government intervened repeatedly to shape the internal affairs of foreign states (while keeping files and spying upon American citizens). Open military force was used when Lebanon was invaded in 1958, and was contemplated and narrowly rejected as the French regime collapsed in Indochina in 1954. The CIA channeled American arms and funds to the rightist military elements who overthrew the reform-oriented Guzman government in Guatemala in 1954, perhaps the most successful of many CIA-led clandestine operations abroad. When fifty-five American hostages were seized by Iranian revolutionaries in 1980, Americans would be rudely reminded of resentments going back to the CIA-engineered replacement of the elected, reformist-nationalist Mohammed Mossadegh regime in 1953 with a government under young Shah Mohammed Reza Pahlevi, known to be favorable to Western oil companies and Western culture.

Such overt and covert interventions were justified in the name of preventing the spread of communism, but they were often directed against liberal or socialist groups dedicated to democracy and land reform, and nationalization of some Western industrial facilities. In such situations and often without them, the United States frequently became aligned with repressive regimes of the right. Spain's Francisco Franco, Portugal's Antonio Salazar, and South Korea's Syngman Rhee were examples of reactionary dictators whose anticommunism was so strong that they became favorites of Washington. While the Eisenhower administration saw little alternative to such alliances and priorities, critics worried that the United States, a nation born with revolutionary ideals, seemed increasingly to be set against the aspirations of the masses of the emerging world. The Soviets and Chinese, on the other hand, had some success in appearing to be supportive of popular aspirations everywhere. When then-Vice President Richard M. Nixon was spat upon in Venezuela in 1958, Americans learned with dismay of their nation's great unpopularity in a country whose government was officially friendly.

To explain such evidence of U.S. unpopularity in the lesser developed world, it was said that, as the leading Western nation just at the time when emerging nations were revolting against centuries of imperialism, America would simply have to expect to be the target of resentments that should have been directed toward London, Paris, and Lisbon. A vocal segment of American opinion, however, was critical of the government for rigidly conforming to a military-oriented containment policy which, whatever its merits in the European theater, was proving unsuccessful in the underdeveloped world. Cold War costs, financial and psychological, were heavy, and many yearned for a more effective policy. Adlai Stevenson expressed this sentiment when the Democrats renominated him to run again against Eisenhower in 1956, but public uneasiness about Dulles-Eisenhower foreign policy was not substantial. The electorate returned Ike (35 to 26 million votes), though continued Democratic control of Congress reflected a lengthening political stalemate.

COSTS OF COLD WAR: BUILDING A
MILITARY-INDUSTRIAL COMPLEX

Few contemporaries were more concerned about the costs of the Cold War than Eisenhower himself. He was alarmed at the steady pressure exerted by military spending on the budget process, and feared that the cost of defending America might easily be allowed to ruin the very economic system on which national strength was based. At the end of his presidency he saw that these military spending pressures had become institutionalized, and would long outlast his own term in office to confront his successors. In his last State of the Union address, delivered in January 1961, the president spoke of a "conjunction of an immense military establishment and a large arms industry . . . new in American experience. The total influence—economic, political, even spiritual—is felt in every city, every statehouse, every office of the federal government. In the councils of governments, we must guard against the acquisition of unwarranted influence, whether sought or unsought, by the military-industrial complex. The potential for the disastrous rise of misplaced power exists and will persist."

It would indeed persist, for the military-industrial complex—an "iron triangle" composed of defense firms, the Defense Department, and congressional committees in charge of the national security budget—had a vested interest in its own perpetuation. A continuing Cold War, and an escalating arms race, now had powerful beneficiaries with considerable influence in Washington. One sentence in Eisenhower's message indicated that he foresaw an even larger problem, the "danger that public policy could itself become the captive of the scientific-technical elite" on whom the nation increasingly relied not only in matters of defense but in all areas where technology raced ahead of the comprehension of both the public and their elected representatives. A more obvious price of the Cold War was the continued dominance of the shallow and repressive form of anticommunism nurtured by Senator McCarthy and actively practiced by his senatorial associates Bourke Hickenlooper, Republican of Iowa, and Patrick McCarran, Democrat of Nevada. For four years, McCarthy used his Senate position to search for subversives in the State Department, the Army, and other federal agencies, never finding a single communist spy but hounding several people out of the civil service and encouraging a repressive atmosphere in the country. Eisenhower was angry at the harassment of the Army and contemptuous of McCarthy personally, but resisted suggestions that he rebuke or denounce the senator and his tactics. "McCarthy could have been stopped at any time by, say, J. Edgar Hoover, Richard Nixon, or Dwight Eisenhower," concludes McCarthy biographer Thomas Reeves, but the president and those under him in the administration ducked that confrontation. The senator eventually became too reckless even for his senatorial colleagues, and he was censured by the Senate in 1954 for his abusive treatment of witnesses. McCarthy then lapsed into ill health complicated by alcoholism, and died in 1957. It appeared that the Second Red Scare had peaked and begun to subside, that democratic institutions had survived a major demagogic challenge.

Elvis Presley fused black and white popular musical traditions into a style that was irresistible to a generation stirring with rebellion against the constraints of traditional culture. He died in 1977 after an accidental drug overdose. His home in Memphis, Tennessee—Graceland—still attracts more tourists every year than Washington's Mount Vernon.
(UPI/Bettmann)

of black music and the inventor of on-stage gyrations with strong sexual over-tones, was racially integrating music. He borrowed from black rhythm-and-blues what the music of white vocalists Perry Como and Frank Sinatra lacked, and his stupendous success expressed a remarkable new opening of Anglo culture at the youthful end of the scale to the culture of American blacks. In the 1950s, of course, the commercially acceptable merging of cultures, hillbilly and rhythm-and-blues music, had to be done by whites. But the big news was the merging, and it was consumer-driven.

THE EISENHOWER ERA ASSESSED

The first Republican administration since Herbert Hoover (1929–1933) had not led the way toward repeal of the New Deal, but had preserved its main outlines and at places even moderately extended governmental activism. Thus the larger significance of the Eisenhower presidency may be summed up as: an extended era of centrism (critics called it *deadlock*) in U.S. politics.

Many factors limited Eisenhower's conservative-reformist impulses, chief among them the opposition of the Democrats who controlled Congress after 1954, and the presence of organized economic groups who lobbied against budget cutting in domestic programs favorable to themselves. Eisenhower was never apologetic as it became clear that his presidency was turning out to be a maintaining rather than a radical reformist one. At heart he, unlike much of his party, was a moderate and a realist. He also knew that "the Republican difference" in the 1950s—in budget size and priorities, in executive branch appointments, in tax codes—had been substantial. The president, pointing also to the absence of wars small or large, thought it a successful performance. The electorate agreed in 1956, and probably would have returned him in 1960 if his health and the Twenty-Second Amendment had not barred the way.

Historians have raised questions about the voters' assessment. The years of relative calm and the absence of dramatic change in our politico-economic arrangements may have been psychologically necessary to a nation whose exertions in the 1930s and 1940s had been enormous and straining. They proved that the Republicans could govern after twenty years out of power, and brought both parties generally into agreement about the mixed capitalist order. But to those impressed by the social problems that churned up in the 1960s, a problem-solving presidency had been needed at least after 1956. Ike and the Republicans had declined to lead very far in the direction of social problem solving. To them the problems of poverty, race relations, and environment were best left to the private sector, or to the future. Despite the fact that Ike steered our politics as best he could on a cautious, slightly right-of-center course, dynamic forces were at work reshaping American society and creating problems that the private sector could not resolve alone. Some of these would be eagerly (and some reluctantly) addressed by liberal presidencies in the 1960s.

This perspective on the Eisenhower era—as one of missed opportunities for activist government—was widely adopted by journalists during his second term and endured among historians for years thereafter. Toward the end of the 1970s, however, historians began to shift somewhat toward a more favorable view. This upward trend in Eisenhower's reputation reflects some new evidence that his political skills were of a high order though exercised mostly behind the scenes. Often uninformed about details, Ike remained in firm command of the large issues. Even his fractured and sometimes bumbling syntax was a management tool, often feigned. When his Press Secretary James Hagerty worried about an upcoming press conference, Ike said: "Don't worry, Jim. If that question comes up, I'll just confuse them." When there was no need to confuse, Ike could dictate lucid memos and letters. Beyond the accumulation of evidence that Eisenhower was a strong and gifted personality, the years after Ike departed Washington saw high and damaging levels of inflation and a succession of broken presidencies which failed to match Ike's two popular terms. Time has brought a reappreciation of his tough stance on military spending and unbalanced budgets, as America has moved through a series of presidencies plagued by both.

NOSTALGIA FOR THE 1950s

Seen from the perspective of the 1960s, the leaders of the decade before had irresponsibly transmitted painful social problems to the next generation. But the 1950s look a bit different from the viewpoint of the 1990s. David Halberstam's best-selling 1993 book, *The Fifties,* was frankly nostalgic, reflecting a trend toward seeing the 1950s not as a staging ground for trouble but as an enjoyable plateau that should not be condemned: "It was a good time to be young and get on with family and career: Prices and inflation remained relatively low; and nearly everyone with a decent job could afford to own a home." The novelist John Updike wrote in 1994, "Many Americans were happy in the 1950s, but not as happy, looking back, as we should have been."

BIBLIOGRAPHY FOR PART TWO

ALEXANDER, CHARLES. *Holding the Line.* Bloomington: Indiana University Press, 1975.
AMBROSE, STEPHEN E. *Eisenhower: The President,* vol. 2. New York: Simon & Schuster, 1984.
BALL, HOWARD. *Justice Downwind: America's Atomic Testing Program in the 1950s.* New York: Oxford University Press, 1986.
BERNSTEIN, BARTON. "New Light on the Korean War." *International History Review,* April 1981, pp. 256–277.
BOYER, PAUL. "From Activism to Apathy: The American People and Nuclear Weapons, 1963–1980." *Journal of American History,* March 1984, pp. 821–844.
BROWN, SEYOM. *The Faces of Power.* New York: Columbia University Press, 1968.
CARSON, RACHEL. *Silent Spring.* Boston: Houghton, Mifflin, 1962.
CARTER, PAUL. *Another Part of the Fifties.* New York: Columbia University Press, 1983.

CHAFE, WILLIAM. *The American Woman: Her Changing Economic and Political Roles, 1920–1970.* New York: Oxford University Press, 1972.

COCRAN, THOMAS B., WILLIAM M. ARKIN, AND MILTON M. HOENIG. *Nuclear Weapons Databook,* 2 vols. Cambridge, MA: Ballinger, 1984.

COOPER, CHESTER. *Growth in America.* Westport, CT: Greenwood, 1976.

CUMINGS, BRUCE. *Child of Conflict: The Korean–American Relationship 1943–53.* Seattle: University of Washington Press, 1983.

DIGGINS, JOHN P. *The Proud Decades: America in War and Peace 1941–1960.* New York: Norton, 1988.

DIVINE, ROBERT A. *Eisenhower and the Cold War.* New York: Oxford University Press, 1981.

EAGLES, CHARLES W., ed. *The Civil Rights Movement in America.* Jackson: University Press of Mississippi, 1986.

EISENHOWER, DWIGHT. *Mandate for Change.* Garden City, NY: Doubleday, 1963.

———. *Waging Peace.* Garden City, NY: Doubleday, 1965.

FAIRCLOUGH, ADAM. *To Redeem the Soul of America: The Southern Christian Leadership Conference and Martin Luther King, Jr.* Athens: University of Georgia Press, 1987.

FRADKIN, PHILIP L. *Fallout: An American Nuclear Tragedy.* Tucson: University of Arizona Press, 1989.

FRANKLIN, H. BRUCE. *War Stars: The Superweapon and The American Imagination.* New York: Oxford University Press, 1988.

FULLER, JOHN G. *The Day We Bombed Utah.* New York: New American Library, 1984.

GALBRAITH, JOHN KENNETH. *American Capitalism.* Boston: Houghton Mifflin, 1952.

———. *The Affluent Society.* Boston: Houghton Mifflin, 1958.

GARCIA, MARIO T. *Mexican Americans: Leadership, Ideology and Identity, 1930–1960.* New Haven, CT: Yale University Press, 1989.

GARROW, DAVID J. *Bearing the Cross: Martin Luther King, Jr. and the Southern Christian Leadership Conference.* New York: William Morrow, 1986.

GOULDEN, JOSEPH C. *Korea, the Untold Story of War.* New York: Times Books, 1982.

GREENSTEIN, FRED. *The Hidden Hand Presidency.* New York: Basic Books, 1982.

GRIFFITH, ROBERT D. *The Politics of Fear: Joseph McCarthy and the Senate.* Lexington: University Press of Kentucky, 1970.

GURALNICK, PETER. *Last Train to Memphis: The Rise of Elvis Presley.* Boston: Little, Brown, 1994.

HALBERSTAM, DAVID, *The Fifties.* New York: Villard Books, 1993.

HART, JEFFREY. *When the Going Was Good: American Life in the Fifties.* New York: Crown, 1982.

HASTINGS, MAX. *The Korean War.* New York: Simon & Schuster, 1987.

HEWLETT, RICHARD G., AND JACK M. HOLL. *Atoms for Peace and War, 1953–1961: Eisenhower and the Atomic Energy Commission.* Berkeley: University of California Press, 1989.

HOOPES, TOWNSEND. *The Devil and John Foster Dulles.* Boston: Little, Brown, 1973.

JARRETT, HARRY, ed. *Perspectives on Conservation.* Baltimore: Johns Hopkins University Press, 1958.

JEROME, JOHN. *The Death of the Automobile.* New York: Norton, 1972.

KALEDIN, EUGENIA. *Mothers and More: American Women in the 1950s.* Boston: G. K. Hall, 1984.

KING, MARTIN LUTHER, JR. *Stride toward Freedom.* New York: Harper, 1958.

KLUGER, RICHARD. *Simple Justice.* New York: Knopf, 1975.

LOWE, PETER. *Origins of the Korean War.* New York: Longmans, 1986.

LYON, PETER. *Eisenhower: Portrait of the Hero.* Boston: Little, Brown, 1974.

MARTIN, JOHN B. *Adlai Stevenson of Illinois.* Garden City, NY: Doubleday, 1976.

McCoy, Donald R. *The Presidency of Harry S. Truman.* Lawrence: University Press of Kansas, 1984.

Miller, William L. *Piety along the Potomac.* Boston: Houghton Mifflin, 1964.

Mills, C. Wright. *The Power Elite.* New York: Oxford University Press, 1956.

Morris, Roger. *Richard Milhous Nixon: The Rise of an American Politician.* New York: Henry Holt, 1989.

O'Neill, William L. *American High: The Years of Confidence, 1945–1960.* New York: The Free Press, 1985.

Pach, Chester J., and Elmo Richardson. *The Presidency of Dwight D. Eisenhower.* Lawrence: University Press of Kansas, 1991.

Patterson, James T. *Mr. Republican: A Biography of Robert A. Taft.* Boston: Houghton Mifflin, 1972.

Powers, Richard Gid. *Secrecy and Power: The Life of J. Edgar Hoover.* New York: The Free Press, 1987.

Rae, John B. *The Road and the Car in American Life.* Cambridge, MA: MIT Press, 1971.

Ranelagh, John. *The Agency: The Rise and Decline of the CIA.* New York: Simon & Schuster, 1986.

Reeves, Thomas C. *The Life and Times of Joe McCarthy.* New York: Stein and Day, 1982.

Riesman, David, et al. *The Lonely Crowd.* New Haven, CT: Yale University Press, 1950.

Richardson, Elmo R. *Laws, Parks and Politics: Resource Development and Preservation in the Truman-Eisenhower Era.* Lexington: University Press of Kentucky, 1973.

Rostow, W. W. *Open Skies: Eisenhower's Proposal of July 21.* Austin: University of Texas Press, 1983.

Rovere, Richard. *Senator Joe McCarthy.* New York: Harcourt, Brace, 1959.

Siracusa, Joseph M. "NSC 68: A Reappraisal." *Naval War College Review,* November/December 1980, pp. 4–14.

Theoharis, Athan G., and John S. Cox. *The Boss: J. Edgar Hoover and the American Inquisition.* Philadelphia: Temple University Press, 1988.

Tygiel, Jules. *Baseballs Great Experiment: Jackie Robinson and His Legacy.* New York: Oxford University Press, 1983.

Whyte, William H., Jr. *The Organization Man.* New York: Simon & Schuster, 1956.

PART THREE

1960–1968

America is now sauntering through her resources and through the mazes of her politics with easy nonchalance; but presently there will come a time when she will be surprised to find herself grown old,—a country crowded, strained, perplexed, —when she will be obliged . . . to pull herself together, adopt a new regimen of life, husband her resources, concentrate her strength, steady her methods, sober her views, restrict her vagaries, trust her best, not her average, members. That will be the time of change.

—WOODROW WILSON, "Bryce's *American Commonwealth:* A Review."
Political Science Quarterly, March 1889.

CHAPTER 5

John F. Kennedy's 1960s

1960: JUST ANOTHER ELECTION?

The Democratic nomination in 1960 went to the energetic, attractive forty-two-year-old senator from Massachusetts, John F. Kennedy. He won it by combining hard work, good organization, an affluent and well-connected family, and a growing reputation for intelligence and a special flair for politics in the television era. At the time of his nomination, however, his political opinions were not clear. The son of a rich financier, Senator Kennedy's voting record had been neither liberal nor conservative with any consistency, and he headed a party of diverse political components and serious internal divisions.

During the primaries Kennedy had sensed that the country was eager for change, at least of leadership style and perhaps also of substance. He listened attentively to the arguments of an aide, historian Arthur Schlesinger, Jr., that the conservative cycle had run its course and that a new period of liberal reform was in the making. Kennedy's opponent, Vice President Richard M. Nixon, was also a young man, but his identification with the previous eight years and his basic conservatism restrained him from offering the electorate a comparable sense of new vistas.

Even so, the election was virtually a tie, an indication that the electorate remained uncertain about change, clustered around a cautious center. Kennedy had signaled clearly that he meant to lead an activist government "to get America moving again," but he had supplied few specifics. He was a more attractive political personality than was Nixon, and he mobilized support along the familiar New Deal lines combining labor, intellectuals, ethnic and racial minorities with part of the middle class. Nixon held the enthusiasm of the Republican right and was preferred by the business community, as well as by those afraid of

John F. Kennedy's children, Caroline and John Jr. (the latter seen here), were often photographed amid White House official functions, and added greatly to the President's youthful image.
(UPI/Bettmann)

Kennedy's Catholicism. The clearest issue between the candidates was economic policy, where it was assumed that Kennedy would attempt to stimulate job expansion to lower the 8 percent unemployment rate, even at the cost of some inflationary pressures. Both promised to conduct the Cold War vigorously; both ignored the race issue. Kennedy's majority (a bare 112,881 popular votes) was razor-thin. The electorate's mood was centrist. Despite the lack of a "mandate," Kennedy entered the White House in 1961 as a youthful presence and a harbinger of change.

U.S. Senators Edmund Muskie (D., Maine), Alan Cranston (D., California), and a
Coast Guard official view the efforts to contain the spread of thousands of gallons of
crude oil that leaked from Shell Oil Platform A off the coast of Santa Barbara,
California. The oil fouled forty miles of beaches and offshore waters; this
environmental disaster gave added urgency to the environmental movement in
America.
(Easton Collection, University of California–Santa Barbara, Special Collections)

words of a *New York Times* reporter. On January 28, 1969, oil bubbled up from a
ruptured casing near Union Oil platform A, just 6 miles off Santa Barbara's
white beaches, and within three weeks 800 square miles of coastline were fouled
with sticky, stinking crude oil.

Conveyed by television in all its ugliness, the Santa Barbara spill became the
symbol for many other large and sudden scars that humanity inflicted on nature
in the 1960s. Contemporaries calling it an accident still assumed that humanity's
injury to Nature was only occasional, and with reasonable care might be
avoided. The heightened environmental consciousness of these years owed more
to Rachel Carson's *Silent Spring* (1962), a book that not only described humanity's deliberate and ongoing poisoning of Nature but also added the gripping
news that Nature, in time, brought the poison back to people.

Winner of eight book awards, praised by Supreme Court Justice William O.
Douglas as "the most important chronicle of this century for the human race," a

Rachel Carson
(The Bettmann Archive)

Book-of-the-Month Club selection and a runaway bestseller, *Silent Spring* was certainly the most influential book in the postwar literature of environmentalism. Written by a scientist, it described in vivid and often poetic prose how chemical insecticides like DDT, along with powerful herbicides, entered the American environment in massive amounts as agricultural and household chemicals. Sprayed on crops, forests, and lakes to control weeds and pests, these humanity-made poisons entered the food chain and worked their way up from

... Only within the moment of time represented by the present century has one species—man—acquired significant power to alter the nature of his world.

During the past quarter century this power has not only increased to one of disturbing magnitude but it has changed in character. The most alarming of all man's assaults upon the environment is the contamination of air, earth, rivers, and sea with dangerous and even lethal materials . . . chemicals sprayed on croplands or forests or gardens lie long in soil, entering into living organisms, passing from one to another in a chain of poisoning and death. Or they pass mysteriously by the underground streams until they emerge and, through the alchemy of air and sunlight, combine into new forms that kill vegetation, sicken cattle, and work unknown harm on those who drink from once pure wells. As Albert Schweitzer has said, "Man can hardly even recognize the devils of his own creation."

... Since the mid-1940's over 200 basic chemicals have been created for use in killing insects, weeds, rodents, and other organisms described in the modern vernacular as "pests"; and they are sold under several thousand different brand names.

These sprays, dusts, and aerosols are now applied almost universally to farms, gardens, forests, and homes—nonselective chemicals that have the power to kill every insect, the "good" and the "bad," to still the song of birds and the leaping of fish in the streams, to coat the leaves with a deadly film, and to linger on in soil—all this though the intended target may be only a few weeds or insects. Can anyone believe it is possible to lay down such a barrage of poisons on the surface of the earth without making it unfit for all life? They should not be called "insecticides," but "biocides."

Excerpt from *Silent Spring*

plankton through fish and birds and crops, ever concentrating, until they brought a range of maladies to humanity. Carson's was a story of the modern chemical industry unleashed on "pests" with an arrogant disregard for damage to ecological communities and the capacity of insects to mutate toward more resistant forms. The poisoning of the food chain reached upward to innocent human victims who never imagined that the savior insecticide DDT, and other little-known organochlorine pesticides such as aldrin and dieldrin, chlorodane and heptachlor, could return to human bodies through concentration in milk, fish, meat, and vegetables. To some readers, *Silent Spring* was a clarion call to attack a single enemy, the chemical companies that produced the 55,000 different synthetic organic chemicals in commercial use in the United States, their volume rising from 1.3 billion pounds in 1940 to 233 billion pounds in 1970. The chemical industry had told the public of "better things for better living through chemistry," before it was known that one "externality" might be cancer in the consumer. Critics pointed out then and later that the link between agricultural pesticides and human cancer was poorly documented and the health costs uncertain. Historian Donald Fleming, however, pointed out that Carson took aim at something more fundamental than the excessive use of pesticides: the arrogant assumption so virulent in modern America, nurtured by war and cold war, "the war-inflamed ideal . . . of total eradication of all enemies, boundless control and infinite mastery of the earth." She was a gentle radical.

JOHN F. KENNEDY'S NEW FRONTIER

The new president elected in 1960 had no time for these latent issues, but prepared for a more familiar set of problems headed by the long-running Cold War with the Soviet Union. Kennedy's New Frontier was largely an attempt to set a mood, to draw the citizenry away from their private pursuits to a spirit of national discipline and self-sacrifice so that the nation might attack its external and internal problems with greater energy—under government leadership, of course. As a call for new energies and social dedication, especially among the young, the New Frontier was an instant success. Kennedy drew into government service great numbers of young men and women who were glad to forsake conventional careers for an opportunity to pit themselves directly against public problems. New faces and a new spirit invaded Washington, filling old agencies like the Departments of Labor and Justice and new ones like the Peace Corps. There was allegedly an improvement in the quality of public servants and in their idealism. There was undeniably a quickening of nationalism, of the sense that the national government was again the focus of attention, almost as in wartime. In the White House, there was a young head of state with a lovely wife, and courtiers of youth and brilliance; it was "Camelot" in America, as one writer christened Kennedy's Washington. It was an open question how far the new spirit reached beyond the Kennedy circle and the bureaucracy to touch the public at large, half of whom (judging by the election returns) had apparently favored his opponent and a less active federal government.

If the New Frontier was at first and always a new mood, it was also a set of proposals for national policy. The clearest commitment was to an invigorated economy. Kennedy's promise "to get the country moving again" was understood to be condemnation of the high unemployment and sluggish growth rates that had characterized the end of the Eisenhower years. Kennedy also conveyed in general terms a reformer's dissatisfaction with the condition of American cities and educational systems, and with the overall torpor of the national cultural life. Immediately after his election he set task forces to work preparing plans to deal with unemployment, area redevelopment, regulatory reform, health care, housing, and other domestic issues. The major preoccupation would always be with external matters—freer trade, closing of "the missile gap" (which in retrospect proved to favor the United States), recapture of the initiative in the Cold War.

At first there seemed no barriers to Kennedy's new mood save apathy, and the attractive new administration intended to disperse that with enthusiasm for change. However, the legislative program met determined resistance in a Congress which felt it had received no mandate for new and expensive initiatives. A series of Kennedy measures reached Capitol Hill but became mired in committee hearings and objections. A bill to provide over $5 billion in federal aid to education was defeated in the House. A Medicare proposal which would extend public medical insurance to those over sixty-five who were covered by social security failed in the Senate by four votes. Legislation calling for a cabinet-level

Department of Housing and Urban Affairs was also defeated. Kennedy's only legislative successes in the early days of the New Frontier were a small appropriation for area redevelopment, a manpower retraining program, and an increase in the minimum wage. Most of the members of Congress clearly did not share the sense of urgency which radiated from the White House.

KENNEDY AND THE ECONOMY

Although he was interested in programs aimed at improving access to health care, housing, and employment, Kennedy shared the general view that a faster-growing economy would solve more problems more quickly than any number of separate social programs. Economists, as always, gave conflicting advice on the means to a full employment economy. Some saw unemployment as a product of inadequate demand, and urged a stimulative federal fiscal policy in the familiar Keynesian terms. This of course meant larger budgetary deficits, at least in the short run, and Kennedy recognized the political difficulties in that direction. Other economic advisors perceived unemployment as being mainly structural, a product of rapid technological change which shifted economic activity away from older industries and regions and leaving unemployed workers behind. In this view, joblessness was more a mismatch between existing vacancies and the skills of the labor force. Examples of the problem were the older textile towns of New England, or the coal-mining regions of Appalachia. The answer, to this school of thought, was federal retraining to help people alter their skills to match new job opportunities.

The New Economics

At first Kennedy seemed to favor the structural approach, asking Congress in 1961 for a federal retraining program and for targeted aid to depressed areas. In time he came to doubt that this approach alone would achieve the growth he wanted across the economy, and under the tutelage of economist Walter Heller he began to espouse the expansionary "New Economics." Heller felt that a federal budgetary deficit created early in the year would produce the needed economic stimulus for rapid expansion, and that federal revenues would soon be so increased by the growing GNP that the budget would come into balance. Deficits were thus seen as temporary medicine which would soon, like the illness of unemployment, disappear in a surge of growth. Kennedy was eventually convinced, and in January 1963 he sent Congress his proposal for an expansionary fiscal policy in the form of a budget to spend approximately $10 billion more than would be collected in taxes. The gap could have been created by lowering taxes or by increasing spending. Kennedy chose to do a bit of both, for maximum political appeal. Most of the tax cuts were given to corporations; most of the increased spending went to the military. There was some grumbling about this among the president's liberal advisors.

The New Economics was presented as a painless remedy, but many were dubious. Congressmen, especially those from districts with high unemployment, could understand retraining and redevelopment programs, and Kennedy was able to sign the Area Redevelopment Act of 1961 and the Manpower Retraining Act of 1962. But the New Economics was greeted with suspicion, and the tax-cut strategy was resisted by Congress.

Thus the administration approached the end of 1963 with its basic domestic program stalled. Increased defense expenditures threw the budget out of balance to some extent, and the larger deficits began to have the effect that Heller had predicted. The recession of 1960–1961 ended, and the economy reached a respectable growth rate of 3.5 percent by mid-1963, while unemployment edged downward from 8 percent to 5 percent.

These hopeful trends came slowly, however, and were not clearly attributed to anything Kennedy had done. He was remarkably popular, his "approval rate" in the polls in 1963 (62 percent in September) running higher than Eisenhower's in his third year. But most of what he had wished to accomplish had been blocked. As critics will do, some argued that his leadership was too cautious (citing areas such as civil rights or tax reform) and some that he asked for too much social intervention by government (citing, oddly enough, civil rights with which he had done little, or the proposals for aid to education and for Medicare). To those who pointed to the gap between promises and performance, it was rejoined that Kennedy inherited a conservative Congress, that his own election had been so close as to provide no mandate for action, and that social reform in the Cold War era was uphill work. Nowhere were these limitations more apparent than in Kennedy's difficulties in fashioning a policy to cope with the country's racial troubles.

KENNEDY AND THE RACE ISSUE

On the race issue John Kennedy tended to be sympathetic to minorities and unsympathetic with those who impeded integration, but he had no strong sense of commitment on the matter, and in any event he thought himself blocked from taking action by the hostile Southern bloc in Congress and the 49.9 percent of the voters who had preferred his opponent. He therefore sought a path between dramatic federal action on the one hand and complete inaction on the other. Although he knew that the 1957 and 1960 civil rights laws were inadequate, the president at first tried to use the powers he had in the voting rights arena rather than ask for new ones. His brother, Attorney General Robert Kennedy, increased the staff of the Civil Rights Division and brought pressure through the courts to reduce discrimination in transportation facilities and in voting. The president announced his intention to nominate a black man, Robert Weaver, as head of a department of urban affairs, if Congress would establish it. After inexplicable delay, he issued an executive order in November 1962 banning segregation in federally assisted housing.

These steps were quite limited in their effect. In late 1962 John Kennedy could not be called a strong friend of racial equality. Nonetheless, he was increasingly unpopular among white southerners, who perhaps remembered Eisenhower's even less active position on the race issue and who saw Robert Kennedy as a strong enemy of segregation. Events, not merely convictions, were to push John Kennedy toward actions which earned him even more animosity in the white South. When black student James Meredith's attempts to attend the University of Mississippi (to which he had been legally admitted) in the autumn of 1962 produced rioting among white students and townspeople, Kennedy committed federal marshals and units of the National Guard. Thirty thousand troops were used to quell riots that took two lives and injured 375 people. The president, who never encouraged the integration of any university, was simply carrying out his constitutional responsibilities, yet those who had started the violence blamed him for the entire episode, and the events at "Ole Miss" earned him an undeserved reputation as a relentless champion of racial integration.

The truth was that, as of early spring 1963, John Kennedy had not pressed hard against the nation's biracial systems and habits. To those who were more impressed with the urgency of the situation than with Kennedy's political difficulties, he seemed much too cautious. It was pointed out that he could have signed the ban on segregated housing earlier and could have worded it more strongly; that he could have supported pending legislation to remedy the defects of the voting laws of 1957 and 1960. But more effective than such criticisms in moving Kennedy to action was the acceleration of civil rights protests, intransigent and sometimes violent opposition, and the public reaction.

The Civil Rights Movement in the 1960s

The Jim Crow system of legal segregation of the races was doomed by social change, but it was deeply rooted, and it might have been defended for decades longer than 1964–1965. The end of Jim Crow was sudden and unexpected, the triumph of the civil rights movement a dramatic turn in history. How can one account for the abrupt end of Jim Crow, in 1964–1965?

A reform movement grew rapidly after World War II, but there were obstacles. Among them was the apathy of the larger white population, some of whom must be engaged as allies before reform could occur. Historians tell us that black protest impulses and movements grew steadily in the urban south in the 1950s, but rank-and-file protest without national leadership made little headway. Defenders of segregation sometimes resorted to violence, unaware that television now placed them on national and even international display. Would the civil rights movement reciprocate with violence, out of a deep frustration and an understandable sense of righteousness? The outcome was decided not only by the strength of local protests across the south, but also by the emergence of a leadership appropriate to the occasion.

Martin Luther King, Jr., entered the 1950s postwar era with formidable talents to match the demands of a burgeoning racial protest he had not started and would

An all-too-familiar scene in Birmingham, Alabama, in 1963. Southern policemen used all forms of intimidation—angry dogs, fire hoses, and physical violence—to stop civil rights demonstrations.
(*AP/Wide World Photos*)

never entirely control. King was a Southern Baptist preacher with a sonorous voice and a fine gift for language, a nonviolent philosophy capable of easing liberal white fears, and a conception of a massive national alliance which could only be held together by the right combination of tactical patience with moral urgency.

Yet King, and the Southern Christian Leadership Conference (SCLC) he formed in 1957, were never in full control of the turbulent social movement aimed at ending Jim Crow. The black college students who took seats at a Woolworth lunch counter in Greensboro, North Carolina, on February 1, 1960, refusing to move until they were served, had invented a new tactic. They launched a series of "sit-ins" at lunch counters and restaurants, soon producing a new organization, the Student Nonviolent Coordinating Committee (SNCC). SNCC was the militant wing of the civil rights movement, along with the Congress of Racial Equality (CORE) and its "freedom rides" to challenge segregation in interstate bus terminals. While King was drawn by events into a drive to win equal access to public facilities in Albany, Georgia, black and white student activists mounted a voter registration campaign in Mississippi and Georgia in the summers of 1961 and 1962. The white power structure in those states retaliated with beatings, bombings, and murders, which were increasingly reported as national news.

The Kennedy administration was inexorably drawn into the racial issue. In February 1963 the president called for another civil rights bill to strengthen voting rights, but activists in the South became increasingly alienated from the administration as FBI agents routinely refused to protect the rights of voters and appeared to look the other way when local whites resorted to violence. King knew that the FBI was worse than a neglectful friend, indeed was carrying out an unprecedented campaign of surveillance and harassment against him, driven by FBI director J. Edgar Hoover's passionate hostility toward the black leader. In the spring of 1963, when there were more than 800 demonstrations across the South, King focused the campaign on Birmingham, Alabama, an industrial city that was in many ways a southern bastion of white working-class sentiment. A giant civil rights demonstration provoked Birmingham's white leadership to respond with a harsh attack on the peaceful protestors by police forces led by a notorious segregationist, Eugene "Bull" Connor, Public Safety Commissioner and mayoral contender. Connor's police deployed clubs, dogs, and fire hoses, all vividly portrayed on national television in front of a shocked American public. These scenes of police violence against orderly ranks of college kids, priests, and ordinary citizens created the sense of urgency that Kennedy and the country at large had lacked.

In June the president addressed the nation to propose action, saying that "we face a moral crisis as a country and as a people." To make such a speech was one form of action, but laws, too, seemed required. Kennedy sent to Congress a bill empowering the Justice Department to institute suits to desegregate schools (formerly such suits had to be brought by private individuals, at their own expense), and containing a section guaranteeing equal access to public accommodations. The move to inject federal power into local customs concerning where blacks could sit, eat, or get a haircut was a large step beyond the voting rights strategy that had to this time been the heart of the "Second Reconstruction," as Washington politicians saw it.

There seemed no chance, however, that Congress would respond to the president's appeal. Black leaders agreed upon a new "March on Washington," an idea that had been successful when unionist A. Phillip Randolph had pressured FDR into action on job discrimination by threatening to lead a march

down the capital's streets in 1941. But in 1963 there was vigorous disagreement on tactics. Black militants wanted a sit-in on Capitol Hill, to try to shut down the government until demands were met. King, pressed hard by moderate allies from church and labor groups, and by the Kennedy administration, agreed to a one-day march in August 1963, and capped a stunningly successful day of songs and speeches—punctuated repeatedly by the movement's anthem, "We Shall Overcome"—with his "I Have a Dream" oration at the Lincoln Memorial. It was a brilliant appeal to the conscience and vision of both white and black America. Still the gears of change remained jammed. Two southern committee chairmen, James Eastland of Mississippi in the Senate and Howard Smith of Virginia in the House, held the bill in limbo as the president boarded his plane for Dallas in November.

THE NEW FRONTIER, BLOCKED AT HOME, REACHES UP AND OUT

While Kennedy could implement little of his domestic program, Congress was less inclined to refuse when he asked for changes in the conduct of foreign affairs. Blocked in many of his plans to direct more resources toward domestic programs, Kennedy asked for a 15 percent increase in defense spending. With the aid of a crisis in Berlin in 1961, the increase was granted. He decided that the country should race the Soviets to put a man on the moon, despite estimates that the effort would cost approximately $20 billion. Critics would point out, correctly, that such a major commitment of national resources would be better aimed at urban decay, improving health care or education, or basic scientific research. But Kennedy liked the sheer challenge of the effort to put a man on the moon, wished to stir the nation's spirit, and rightly judged that both Congress and the public would not dare great things merely for cleaner cities or better-educated children. "But why, some say, the moon?" he asked in a speech in Texas. "And they may well ask, why climb the highest mountain? . . . Why does Rice play Texas?" Congress agreed to the logic, such as it was, and after three deaths, the expenditure of $24 billion, and the diversion of much administrative and technological talent, Neil Armstrong stepped down from his *Apollo II* spacecraft onto the moon on July 20, 1969.

The March on Washington, August 28, 1963. A quarter of a million demonstrators converged on the Lincoln Memorial in Washington, D.C., to protest racial segregation in America. There were many speakers, but the day belonged to the Reverend Martin Luther King, Jr., who had emerged in the 1950s as the movement's spiritual as well as political leader. In his moving speech King proclaimed: "I have a dream that one day . . . little black boys and black girls will be able to join hands with little white boys and white girls as sisters and brothers."
(UPI/Bettmann)

John Kennedy came to office with more zest for foreign than domestic affairs, as have all presidents since FDR. Whereas domestic politics confront the chief executive with a tangle of interest groups and a Congress jealous of its pre-rogatives, in foreign affairs there is drama and more deference to the executive. Kennedy's promise of an invigorated and more effective foreign policy led nat-urally to larger arms budgets, and to at least one relatively new idea about how to spend money—the creation of an elite "Green Beret" corps within the army to permit more small military interventions than Ike's nuclear strategy had allowed. But Kennedy doubted that military preparedness alone was enough to ensure national security or to make gains in the Cold War. America must address itself to the roots of instability in the developing world, where the superpowers struggled for advantage. These roots seemed to be those social ills which were the very definition of underdevelopment: poverty, ignorance, explosive popula-tion growth. To fight these, arms were not the answer. Returning without know-ing it to an early theme from George F. Kennan's 1946 "Long Telegram" setting out the containment idea, Kennedy asked for and received in 1961 the most com-prehensive aid program since the Marshall Plan. It was called the Alliance for Progress, and it provided American and international funds (Kennedy proposed $20 billion; $3.3 billion were appropriated by 1970) for Latin America. In the same year Congress established the Peace Corps for Americans who wished to go abroad and serve as technicians and teachers of goodwill.

The main arenas of the Cold War, however, always seemed to be chosen almost by accident. When Kennedy permitted an American-supported Cuban exile force to invade Cuba at the Bay of Pigs on April 17, 1961, the landing was crushed by the communist government of Fidel Castro, resulting in damage to the American reputation for candor and judgment that could hardly be esti-mated. Almost immediately, Nikita Khrushchev chose to increase the pressure on the Western outpost in Berlin, and then took a step which to this day has never been fully explained. Middle-range Soviet SS-4 missiles were placed in Cuba, presumably to make another American invasion less likely, to enhance the Soviet reputation for protecting Third World revolutionary states, and to counter the fifteen U.S. missiles recently installed in Turkey.

Kennedy announced in a somber television address to the nation on October 22, 1962, that aerial reconnaissance had detected the missiles, and that an Amer-ican naval blockade would go into effect at once to intercept all Soviet shipments. Thus commenced perhaps the most dangerous week in world history, as Russian ships bearing more (and longer-range) missiles steamed toward a confrontation that might easily have become a general nuclear war. Kennedy himself estimated the chances of war at "somewhere between one out of three and even," and Cuban leader Fidel Castro actually urged Khrushchev to initiate a nuclear war. Only the Soviet leader's decision to recall the ships and withdraw the missiles already in Cuba secured Kennedy's secret and tacit promise not to invade the island, and possibly also to withdraw U.S. missiles from Turkey. Conflict between the two nuclear powers was averted. As Khrushchev later said, "the smell of burning was in the air. . . . If we do not show wisdom, we will come to a clash, like blind moles, and then reciprocal extermination would begin."

Fidel Castro, Cuba's charismatic young revolutionary, addresses a crowd of
supporters. Castro's communist regime became a prime target of American foreign
policy in the 1960s, but Castro and his communist government would survive for
many years to come.
(UPI/Bettmann Newsphotos)

AFTERMATH OF CRISIS: ARMS RACE OR DETENTE?

People on both sides in the Cold War were appalled at the narrowness of the escape. Khrushchev's reckless move and the duplicity preceding it were condemned everywhere outside the Soviet Union. Kennedy's willingness to risk nuclear war over missiles which did not alter the balance of power (they only matched U.S. missiles stationed in Turkey, near the Soviet border) was less widely criticized. The immediate result of the Cuban Missile Crisis was to sober the top leadership in both countries. Both Kennedy and Khrushchev had restrained the "hawks" in their own camps at crucial moments, and both felt a new urgency to search for ways to defuse the arms race, recognizing that nuclear capacity might well spread to other nations. Almost at once a thaw occurred between the two cold warring states. At American University on June 10, 1963, Kennedy made a historic speech in which he spoke of the dangers of a nuclear war and the necessity of relaxing tensions and working for a peace in which people could "live together in mutual tolerance." The Soviet Union, affected by October's near-disaster and by its widening disagreements with China, seemed genuinely interested in easing tensions. The two states had been unable to agree upon a comprehensive test ban (CTB) treaty, which would have outlawed all tests, but signed a historic atmospheric test ban treaty (the Limited Test Ban Treaty) in August 1963, and installed a "hot line" between the two heads of state to lessen the danger of nuclear accident. Any agreement at all between the two superpowers seemed a turning of the nuclear corner, and Britain's concurrence meant that atmospheric fallout from weapons testing was reduced significantly (France and China declined to sign, and continued atmospheric tests).

To contemporaries, informed only by newspaper and television reports, it appeared that John F. Kennedy, after carrying the world to the brink of nuclear disaster over a shift in the location of Soviet missiles, had seized that sobering moment to lead the United States (as the belligerent Khrushchev might lead the U.S.S.R.) away from cold war confrontations and toward some sort of arms control and reduction. Optimistic, the American public turned away from the nuclear issue in 1963. Articles on the topic declined sharply in number, and disarmament organizations lost members as the mood changed. In 1959, 64 percent of the public listed "war (especially nuclear war)" as the most urgent problem. That figure plummeted to 16 percent by 1965. "The atom bomb is a dead issue," wrote a sociologist studying student attitudes in the early 1970s.

The American public may have relaxed, or escaped from considering this complex and grisly issue to more pleasant things. But the test ban treaty and Kennedy's softening of the official U.S. attitude toward the Soviet Union were ripples on the surface of events. Beneath, the Soviet Union, which had been quite inferior to the United States in nuclear armaments, as Kennedy and Secretary of Defense Robert McNamara discovered while in office, had already launched a massive buildup of arms. The immediate stimulus was the humiliation inflicted by Kennedy on Soviet leadership over the Cuban missile crisis, a "victory" which would cost both societies dearly. Behind this was the Soviet conclusion that America was seeking and achieving a "first-strike" capability, a conclusion supported years later by former Secretary McNamara. Commenting in a 1982 interview, he candidly told a reporter that the U.S. Air Force had in fact been seeking a first-strike capability, though McNamara and the president "didn't have any thought of attaining it." He conceded, however, that "the Soviets thought we were trying to achieve a first-strike capability," and they launched a sustained effort to harden missile silos and increase the number and accuracy of weapons, an effort designed to overtake the U.S. lead by the late 1970s.

So while the American public lost interest in pressing nuclear arms control on their government, which had after all just concluded a fine-sounding treaty banning the tests which put strontium-90 into babies' milk, the arms race gathered momentum. At Kennedy's death, the United States deployed 550 land-based ICBMs, and another 175 submarines and bomber aircraft were ready to carry nuclear destruction to Soviet cities. Atmospheric tests were banned, but not underground testing, and the United States detonated more blasts in the five years after the test ban treaty than in the five years before, some of them with fifty times the destructive power of the Hiroshima bomb. And no treaty slowed the expansion of both sides' nuclear arsenal. On the U.S. side, about which we are better informed, Eisenhower's strategy of massive retaliation led to a phenomenal jump in the number of nuclear warheads and the variety of delivery systems. The all-time peak of 32,000 nuclear warheads would be reached in 1967, deployed on over 1000 land-based missiles, over 600 on submarines, the rest on or stored near aircraft. The Soviets' 100 land missiles in 1963 would grow to over a thousand by 1976, and her submarine missiles numbered over 700 as the 1970s arrived. No one argued that this was a safer world, but nowhere in sight was a vision of how to limit or reverse this race.

ASSASSINATION OF JOHN F. KENNEDY

Kennedy was assassinated in Dallas, Texas, on November 22, 1963, apparently by Lee Harvey Oswald, firing a rifle with astonishing accuracy from a warehouse on the route of the president's parade. It was a horrible act of obscure motive, and an investigative commission led by Chief Justice Earl Warren, acting quickly in the hope of reassuring the public, concluded that Oswald acted alone. The commission's twenty-six-volume report convinced very few. Discrepancies and improbabilities were ignored, or unresolved. Could one bullet have passed through Kennedy's body and still had the force to badly wound Texas Governor John Connally, riding one seat ahead? Was there a second gunman, an elaborate conspiracy? Who was Oswald and what were his motives, and why did one Jack Ruby kill Oswald as he was being escorted from the Police Department basement, thereby depriving Americans of a trial and a chance to understand Oswald's role?

Out of such questions came a vast conspiracy industry, which produced

This photo of the grim, unrehearsed ceremony in which John F. Kennedy's body was transported to the burial site in Arlington Memorial Cemetery captures the turbulence of those awful days.
(UPI/Bettmann)

hundreds of books and streams of articles, and an annual gathering of conspiracy buffs from around the country. But no book could reach the vast audience that viewed director Oliver Stone's *JFK* (1991), a film that cobbled together a plot combining the evil designs of the CIA, the Pentagon, the Mafia, Fidel Castro, and Lyndon B. Johnson himself. Kennedy had been killed, the movie told Americans, because he was on the verge of withdrawing from Vietnam, ending the Cold War, and curbing the military-industrial complex. Seven of ten Americans polled on the thirtieth anniversary of the assassination claimed to believe in some version of such a conspiracy, though professional historians find the Stone film a tapestry of distortions, and Gerald Posner's 1993 book, *Case Closed: Lee Harvey Oswald and the Assassination of JFK*, convincingly put Oswald back in the center as a Marxist sociopath and crack shot who acted alone. But conspiracy theories have a firm foundation in conflicting facts. Author William Manchester, in an interview, astutely observed:

> If you put six million dead Jews on one side of the scale and on the other side put the Nazi regime—the greatest gang of criminals ever to seize control of a modern state—you have a rough balance: greatest crime, greatest criminals. But

if you put the murdered president of the U.S. on one side of the scale and that wretched waif Oswald on the other side, it doesn't balance. You want to add something weightier to Oswald. It would invest the president's death with meaning, endowing him with martyrdom. He would have died for something.

This the Stone film supplied to an American people that had passed from the optimism of Camelot to a losing war in Vietnam, a near-presidential impeachment after Watergate, tales of CIA plots and secrecies, and a mounting sense that power was increasingly unaccountable. The assassination of JFK was in more ways than one a pivotal moment. The trauma of that senseless ending to a remarkable and promising political era was etched deeply into the national consciousness. "I think we have been suspicious ever since," said novelist Don DeLillo (author of *Libra*, a 1988 assassination novel).

KENNEDY IN HISTORY

John F. Kennedy's place in American history has been difficult to sort out. Elected by a narrow margin, his short presidency saw little of his program enacted. His foreign policy record displayed dangerous crises narrowly averted, and no decisive gains in the Cold War or alteration of its terms—though the Limited Test Ban Treaty seemed a turning point to many. One historian predicted that in fifty years JFK would be "relegated to a footnote" in our national history.

Then why did he make such a powerful impression upon contemporaries, here and abroad, and remain such a magnetic subject for books and movies well into the 1990s? In his short term in the White House he displayed high intelligence, sometimes wry humor, and a sense of generational change. He brought to the White House the lovely, cultured Jacqueline and two attractive children. There was evidence that he was learning very fast on the job, especially in the areas of race and nuclear peril, where his initial understanding had been shallow. With the passage of time his character flaws, hidden from the public during his lifetime, became clearer: He had courage and could feel compassion, but his sexual appetites in particular raise serious questions of temperance and integrity.

Still, Kennedy, who had a sharp contempt for those he termed idealists, managed to call Americans and foreigners to the standard of idealism, especially to the need to sacrifice for common goals. "Whatever one thinks of the political record or the political man," said biographer Richard Reeves in 1993, "John Kennedy was a surpassing cultural figure—an artist, like Picasso, who changed the way people looked at things. Kennedy painted with words and images and other people's lives . . . [and] focused Americans in the directions that truly mattered—toward active citizenship, toward the joy of life itself."

CHAPTER 6

Lyndon B. Johnson's 1960s

LYNDON B. JOHNSON AND THE GREAT SOCIETY

Vice President Lyndon B. Johnson took the presidential oath on an airplane returning to Washington from Texas, pledged his loyalty to Kennedy's program, and retained all of his top aides. He inherited the problems Kennedy had wrestled with so inconclusively, but the assassination had created a national mood favorable to decisive action in the directions Kennedy had wished to go. Johnson was superbly positioned to take advantage of that opening, for the southerner from Texas had been unusually effective as Senate Majority Leader in the 1950s. He moved with his usual political skill and boundless energy to exploit the mood. Legislation was Johnson's strength, rather than administration, and he was eager to make a mark approaching the scale of Franklin Roosevelt, his political model. His presidency would be known for a legislative explosion rivaling FDR's Hundred Days—and generating as much controversy.

The House in February easily passed Kennedy's civil rights legislation, outlawing segregation in state-supported facilities as well as in privately owned "public accommodations" such as restaurants, theaters, and hotels. In a surprise maneuver, the original language banning discrimination "on account of race, creed, religion and national origin" was expanded by Virginia Democrat Howard Smith to include the word "sex." He hoped to defeat the bill by going far beyond what even liberal legislators would accept, and the strategy almost worked. Segregationist southerners and women legislators favored the amendment, and most liberals opposed it. Both sides exchanged snide remarks about men being the "real minority group" since women outnumbered them. By a narrow vote, discrimination on the basis of sex entered the legislative language. The Senate began a lengthy filibuster to prevent a floor vote, but Johnson's intense lobbying and a decision by Minority Leader Everett Dirksen that the

When Roosevelt died, a very different type of man—Harry Truman—moved into the Oval Office. The same was true in 1963, when Texas rancher and career politician Lyndon B. Johnson succeeded the urbane Kennedy. Unlike Truman, however, Johnson had been an active and well-informed vice president, and before that a skilled and resourceful Senate leader who understood the workings of congressional legislation perhaps better than anyone else.
(*AP/Wide World Photos*)

party of Lincoln should not be responsible for defeating such a measure produced a 73-to-27 vote for passage on July 2, 1964. The Civil Rights Act, signed by
LBJ with Martin Luther King, Jr. looking on, also empowered the Justice Department to intervene on behalf of individuals whose civil rights had been violated,
and established a Fair Employment Practices Commission to combat discrimination in hiring. The law would have been landmark legislation in any event.
Virginia Congressman Howard Smith's too-clever tactic adding "sex" to race
and national origin greatly increased its subsequent impact on American society, without defeating the measure, as Smith had hoped.

Retaining most of Kennedy's advisors, Johnson took from them one of his
first major programs, the "War on Poverty," which the president declared in his
State of the Union address in 1964: "This administration, here and now, declares
unconditional war on poverty in America." It was a novel turn in social policy,
for there was no very great pressure from either the poor or from society at large
for special governmental attention to poverty, despite its prevalence—20 percent of the public, or 9.3 million families, fell below the "poverty line" of $3000
per year for a family of four. The idea came from the deliberations of top
bureaucrats and some academic advisors, rather than from any pressure groups
or the poor themselves, and it struck a responsive chord in a president raised in
a poor section of east Texas.

A legislative program was produced in March, an omnibus measure built
around two decisions. First, planners rejected a direct income-transfer strategy
for a "service strategy," or "a hand up instead of a handout." A range of programs would equip the poor for jobs—a Job Corps for youths, augmented job
training, a "domestic Peace Corps" called Volunteers in Service to America
(VISTA), work-study programs for students. Second, a Community Action Program (CAP) would allow "maximum feasible participation" of the poor in
designing these and other programs in localities, in the expectation that participation itself was a crucial and lacking economic skill. The "unconditional war"
came with conditions from the start, chiefly budgetary. In 1965 officials projected annual budgets rising from $1.4 billion to $10.4 billion by 1970, and even
these targets were not to be reached.

In any event, the major war against poverty, in Johnson's mind as in
Kennedy's before him, was an expanding economy. He accepted also Kennedy's
New Economics, and had more success with it than had JFK the year before.
Congress enacted a tax cut in February 1964 which had the result predicted for
it—something of a rarity in modern government. The economic expansion
which commenced under Kennedy gained strength, and the rest of the 1960s
were to be a period of uninterrupted growth.

Johnson's legislative momentum increased with every success. The Senate,
for the first time in its history, voted to cut off a southern filibuster and passed
the Civil Rights Act of 1964, built around guarantees of access to public accommodations. In that year, a determined conservative challenge was beaten down
when Johnson was elected over Republican Barry M. Goldwater by an electoral
vote of 486 to 52, Goldwater carrying six states. The outcome was somewhat
misleading. Johnson naturally saw the vote as a sign of public affection for him-

branch would show unusual zeal to reform a perceived social flaw, as when the Surgeon General of the United States, Luther Hodges, headed a study group of scientists which in January 1964 issued a report called *Tobacco and Health.* The report concluded that medical evidence was sufficient to link cigarette smoking and lung cancer causally, and suggested unspecified "remedial measures." From that day, the Public Health Service and soon afterward the Federal Trade Commission were in conflict with the powerful industries built around tobacco. Congress required a health warning label on cigarette packages in 1965.

The federal courts, led by the Supreme Court, entered an extended period of judicial activism without prompting by presidents or Congress. Upon hearing of the *Brown* decision in 1954, Dwight Eisenhower ruefully blamed himself for launching the Supreme Court on a social reform career by appointing ex-governor of California Earl Warren as chief justice in 1953. Warren believed that the court had a duty to pursue social justice vigorously by interpreting the Constitution in broad terms, and he had many like-minded colleagues during his sixteen-year leadership. After the landmark civil rights cases of the 1950s, the Warren Court struck at malapportionment of legislative districts in *Baker v. Carr*

Beginning with the Brown v. Board of Education decision in 1954, Chief Justice Earl Warren and the Supreme Court brought the nation's highest court to a new level of judicial activism.
(AP/Wide World Photos)

(1962) and *Reynolds v. Sims* (1964) and then forced local police to advise the criminally accused of their legal rights, in a line of cases from *Gideon v. Wainwright* (1963) to *Miranda v. Arizona* (1966).

By Warren's retirement in 1968, the Supreme Court had made sweeping constitutional changes in the areas of civil rights, criminal justice, and political representation. The beneficiaries were racial minorities, accused people without funds for lawyers, those denied full voting power, and some purveyors of pornographic materials whose First Amendment rights were now defended. This was hardly an influential constituency, many of them not regarded with sympathy by the larger public. While Lyndon Johnson's energetic liberalism was still popular in the mid-1960s, Earl Warren's activist Supreme Court had angered many citizens, who called for the justice's impeachment on roadside billboards and thought that "the government" had abandoned the solid middle-class citizen in favor of the shiftless and the criminal. More principled objections could also be heard: that the Warren Court had carried judicial activism to perilous lengths, legislating the liberal Justices' own social views by stretching or even abandoning entirely the language of the Constitution. Undeniably the Supreme Court majority was helping to achieve one result that neither it nor Lyndon Johnson welcomed, a growing conservative reaction building beneath the deceptive rout of conservative forces in the 1964 election.

SIDETRACKED: JOHNSON AND VIETNAM

The remarkable momentum of liberal reform in the mid-1960s brought to mind the eras of Woodrow Wilson and Franklin Roosevelt—and it was not lost on Lyndon Johnson that these earlier activist presidencies had been interrupted and ended by American involvement in foreign wars. Yet he was quickly plunged into similar circumstances, not in one of the familiar points of combustion such as Berlin, Cuba, or a rebellious Soviet-occupied satellite, but in a part of the world few Americans could have located on a map.

When the French had been driven from their colonial empire in Indochina in 1954, the United States had moved to salvage the southern half of the country. The Vietnam-wide elections scheduled by the 1954 Geneva settlement were not held, since the United States assumed a victory for the communist government led by Ho Chi Minh from Hanoi. Instead, Washington supported the formation of what it hoped might become a new nation, South Vietnam, led by the anticommunist Ngo Dinh Diem. This regime was launched with high hopes, but by 1959–1960 there were reports of indigenous armed insurrection in rural areas. President Kennedy sent high-level missions to Saigon twice to study U.S. options as guerilla forces of the National Liberation Front (NLF) widened the war against a faltering and unpopular Diem government. The president's advisers urged increased American military and economic aid, and Kennedy was torn between his combative Cold War convictions (asked about the "domino theory," Kennedy said, "I believe it; I believe it!") and a suspicion of advice which seemed to lead

Map of the Vietnam War.

toward involvement in a land war in Asia. He authorized some increase in U.S. military assistance (948 U.S. military advisers in South Vietnam grew to 2646 by 1962) and agreed to a CIA-led coup which ended in the assassination of Diem and his replacement by fresh military leadership. At Kennedy's death his intentions in Vietnam were a mixture of hints that he intended withdrawal after the 1964 elections combined with a record of cautious escalation.

The decision fell to Lyndon Johnson, who recognized its perils. "We are not about to send American boys 9 or 10,000 miles away from home to do what Asian boys ought to be doing for themselves," he told a campaign audience in October 1964, but added that "we will not permit the independent nations of the East to be swallowed up by Communist conquest." He could not long maintain that tightrope act, for the NLF forces, now clearly reinforced by supplies and encouragement from North Vietnam, were widening their control of the rural south. In August the administration announced that two U.S. warships had been attacked without provocation in international waters in the Tonkin Gulf off North Vietnam, and Congress rushed to pass the Tonkin Gulf resolution (only two Senators voted "no," and no Representatives), giving the president open-ended authority to "take all necessary measures to repel any armed attack against the forces of the United States and to prevent further aggression," which he exercised by commencing retaliatory air attacks on North Vietnamese naval bases. The resolution was Johnson's blank check, though the attacks on the two destroyers (the *Maddox* and the *C. Turner Joy*) were a combination of provocation and jittery naval nerves. The ships had been conducting surveillance inside the 12-mile limit in Vietnamese waters in order to facilitate South Vietnamese raids; the *Maddox* was fired upon, but the nervous skipper of the second destroyer "may have been shooting at whales out there," admitted Lyndon Johnson privately. Safely elected, Johnson in March 1965 announced that U.S. Marines would go ashore in Vietnam to protect the Da Nang air base, and by summer 125,000 U.S. ground troops along with American air forces were fighting rather than advising against an Asian enemy.

It was a crucial decision, largest of many turning points as America incrementally entered, waged, and then exited the "longest war," as the 1950–1975 U.S.–Vietnam conflict would eventually be called. Many causes lay behind the decision to intervene indirectly and then with direct military force: political fears among Democratic politicians that they, like Harry Truman, would be blamed and forced from office if they "lost another country" to communism; a widespread and bipartisan belief that the warfare in South Vietnam was a Chinese communist-directed test of U.S. will to resist guerilla "wars of liberation" when it was in fact a localized civil war with strong nationalist and anti-Western overtones; overconfidence in American technology and firepower; underestimation of the tenacity and commitment of Ho Chi Minh's revolutionary armed forces and the entire North Vietnamese nation; and underestimation of the domestic consequences of fighting a protracted, destructive war which would be reported vividly on the evening television news. Foreign-policy strategists and politicians of both parties shared in these views over a generation, but the person who made the most crucial decision of all, Lyndon Johnson, added an ingredient by personalizing the difficult choices: "I am not going to lose Vietnam," presidential historian James David Barber quotes LBJ. "I am not going to be the president who saw Southeast Asia go the way China went." The president who spoke of "my troops" and "my State Department" and who worried that "people would say that I was a coward, an unmanly man" felt trapped by fate to decide as he did, though he always sensed tragedy ahead.

The beliefs and assumptions on which the decision to intervene were based have come to be seen as gravely flawed. Even Defense Secretary McNamara, silent for decades after he left office, wrote in 1995 in *In Retrospect: The Tragedy and Lessons of Vietnam* that the war could and should have been avoided, that "we misjudged . . . we were wrong, terribly wrong." McNamara's confession was relished by opponents of the war, and he did not point out that being "terribly wrong" left some room for getting one or two things right. The passage of time, harsh on LBJ and McNamara's judgment about Vietnam and the Vietnamese, cast a different light on two other assumptions. "I could see it coming all right," Johnson told biographer Doris Kearns, yet "everything I knew about history told me that . . . if we let Communist aggression succeed in taking over South Vietnam, there would follow in this country an endless national debate—a mean and destructive debate—that would shatter my Presidency, kill my administration, and damage our democracy." This analysis was not tested but was surely astute. One other source of the decision to intervene militarily in Vietnam rather than follow the course chosen in 1949–1950 when Chinese communist forces threatened another established but faltering government was the conviction that a communist takeover of South Vietnam and other parts of southeast Asia would be followed by bloody purges and all of the costs of a repressive dictatorship. This reason for intervening should be separated from the others, for whatever its importance in the cluster of motives driving the decision, time has confirmed the prophecy and the wisdom of those who made it.

Thus in 1965 the war in Vietnam entered a new phase, initiating an ordeal that would dominate American public life. Things did not go well for the Johnson administration either in Vietnam or at home. With the South Vietnamese military position deteriorating rapidly, American armed forces became more numerous and aggressive, complicating the effort by U.S. civilian advisers to "win the hearts and minds of the people" by building roads, clinics, and schools, and advising on agriculture and public health. Heavy aerial bombardment along the Ho Chi Minh Trail failed to stop infiltration of troops and supplies from the North, and the price of bombing there and against North Vietnamese military and civilian targets was not only devastating human and physical damage in Vietnam but the loss of nearly 1000 U.S. planes and several hundred killed or captured pilots from 1965 to 1968. American ground troops rose to 225,000 by the end of 1966, casualties mounted, and surging costs added $24 billion to the federal budget during that year. Johnson decided to hide the war, refusing in 1966 to mobilize reserves, seek a congressional declaration of national emergency, or require a general tax increase to head off inflationary pressures. But a broad surge of public criticism of the war was building, reaching a level unknown in any other American military engagement and helping to give the 1960s their characteristic tone of conflict.

SOCIAL MOVEMENTS: THE "COMING APART"/"COMING TOGETHER" DECADE

If the 1950s could be described as a decade of American preoccupation with its enemies without, the 1960s were a time for the discovery of problems within— problems that had existed all along but that most people had ignored in the cautious, "circle the wagons" atmosphere of the early Cold War. Indeed, so many flaws were discovered in American society and so many voices of protest were raised that historian William O'Neill entitled his history of the 1960s, *Coming Apart* (1971). John Kennedy could not have suspected how prophetic would be his remark to a biographer in 1960: "The 1960s will be a terribly difficult time."

He did not live to see the full flowering of the several social movements of protest and reform that would give the 1960s their turbulent quality. The first and most influential movement—civil rights—had occupied much of John Kennedy's time in the last year of his life. Passage of the Civil Rights Act of 1964, and the Voting Rights of 1965, seemed to bring the movement to a culmination. Jim Crow was dead. Racially separate schools, bus stations, restaurants, and water fountains were illegal. The path to voting seemed open to all.

Against these legal transformations stood the stubborn persistence of the economic and social disadvantage of black skin. The leadership of the civil rights movement never intended to end their struggle when Jim Crow was outlawed, and King, as nominal leader of the movement, entered his most difficult period with the signing of the Voting Rights Act. The legal door to full participation was open. How to speed the reality? The black community in all its subdivisions churned with rising hope and resentment in the summer of 1965.

King's leadership of the civil rights movement had repeatedly been challenged by more radical elements with different strategies and ends, and these were growing in number and influence after 1965. John Lewis of SNCC had intended to make a speech just before King's Lincoln Memorial "I Have A Dream" address calling for a more confrontational tone and tactics, but he temporarily yielded to the moderates. King's theme had been integration and Christian love, but SNCC's Stokely Carmichael promoted "black power" in political participation and economic life, which did not sound like the older goal of integration into white communities. King himself moved steadily leftward during the 1960s, especially as he shifted his campaign out of the South to the Chicago–Boston arc of northern industrial cities where Jim Crow had not been the problem but great racial disparities still existed. His speeches expressed waning confidence in liberal measures such as voting rights and access to public accommodations, as he talked more of the need for more fundamental rearrangements of economic power, whatever these might be.

Black Nationalism

Whatever the evolution of King's thought toward incorporating a socialist economics, he was surely the nation's most prominent and effective spokesman for

Charismatic and controversial Black Muslim leader Malcolm X, shown here addressing a Harlem rally in 1963, rejected Martin Luther King Jr.'s policy of nonviolent resistance and proclaimed that equality and freedom must be gained "by any means necessary."
(UPI/Bettmann)

integration of the races. But other solutions to America's racial problems found powerful expression. A new element was the growth of black nationalism— themes of racial pride and a desire for an independent racial existence which had a long history in America. The West Indian black Marcus Garvey had rallied a group of followers in the urban northeast in the 1920s with a program of black separatism. Nationalism was kept alive in the 1930s and 1940s by a group of Black Muslims under Georgia-born Elijah Poole (Elijah Muhammad), who adopted African dress and Islamic religion and advocated economic and cultural separatism. The Nation of Islam was a tiny and obscure minority until the 1960s, when it produced a leader of oratorical power and personal magnetism— Malcolm X. Malcolm spoke of the need for racial pride and solidarity, preached not integration but his own brand of segregation not free of occasional racist remarks about whites, and was of course not a Christian. Urban blacks joined the Nation of Islam in significant numbers, taking on new Muslim names and a demeanor of pride and militancy. The famous professional football player Jim Brown became a Muslim, and world heavyweight boxing champion Cassius Clay changed his name to Muhammad Ali. Malcolm was assassinated in 1965, but he left a movement that had taken root among lower-class urban blacks whom the NAACP and the Urban League had never reached.

The Riots of 1965–1968

Though the civil rights movement had given way to a confusion of voices, a radicalized tone, and much talk of separatism, it could not contain the emotions of urban blacks in particular. Five days after the signing of the 1965 Voting Rights Act, a riot broke out in Watts, a black ghetto in Los Angeles, which ultimately claimed thirty-four lives and destroyed property valued at $35 million. Thereafter, during four successive summers when the cities sweltered with heat, there were outbreaks of violence as blacks erupted out of ghettoes, burning stores and assaulting whites who happened to be in the area. There were forty-three separate outbreaks in 1966, and eight major riots in 1967. Then the assassination of Martin Luther King, Jr., in April 1968 triggered riots across the country, the most severe occurring in Washington, D.C. Some 7000 fires were set in the capital during two days of rioting, and the pall of smoke, combined with the sight of army tanks and National Guard bayonets, appeared to bring the aspect of war to the very edge of the White House. By one count, 1964 to 1968 saw 329 riots in 257 cities, with 8371 injured and 220 killed.

The riots were denounced by leaders of all races as unjustified and criminal acts, but they were also said to be a cry of rage and frustration that the lives of Afro-Americans had been so little changed by the rhetoric and legislation of the past decade. As black novelist Claude Brown said of the Harlem riots of 1966 in his *Manchild in the Promised Land:* "There were too many people full of hate and bitterness crowded into a dirty, stinky, uncared-for closet-size section of a great city."

What had gone wrong? The civil rights movement had seemed to many to be close to a resolution of America's racial problems in 1963: "We shall overcome" was a coi ident, collective commitment. The legal gains the civil rights rebellion had brought, and the changed moral outlook among members of both races, were major steps forward. But few had anticipated how hard it would be to match equality before the law with equality of social and economic results. Repealing Jim Crow had required mobilization of the southern black popula-

tion, brilliantly accomplished with appropriate tools—indigenous black religious leadership to tap the strength of the black churches, nonviolent tactics,
alliance with white liberal groups and moderate opinion. But when "rights"
were won and the goal became "results," the civil rights movement raised its
sights out of the South to the national scene, and quickly fragmented into many
competing organizations, leaders, and strategists. King was apparently concluding that ending the war in Vietnam was the central tactical issue, along with
redirecting federal resources toward ending black poverty. But his assassination in 1968 closed off the faint possibility that he could reassert leadership over
the surge of black protest. SNCC was engaged in a futile attempt to translate
Stokely Carmichael's "black power" slogan into practical goals and tactics, as
was another organization that had expelled its white members and talked
vaguely of black separatism, Core. The media gave national attention to black
militants generally, most especially to the Black Panther Party, founded in 1966
in Oakland, California, by Huey Newton and Bobby Seale, soon joined by the
articulate author of *Soul on Ice*, Eldridge Cleaver.

The Panthers were a militaristic and authoritarian organization demanding
freedom for all black prisoners, reparation payments for descendants of slaves,
and a U.N.-directed plebiscite to determine if black Americans wished to form a
separate nation. Urban blacks did not rally to the Panthers in large numbers,
and the ranks of party activists were steadily depleted by quarrels, armed internal warfare, police and FBI harassment and imprisonment, and self-imposed
foreign exile. By the decade's end there was no "civil rights movement" as the
term had been understood from the Montgomery bus boycott to the Selma
movement in 1965. A sympathetic historian, Stewart Burns, could credit to the
five years after the civil rights laws of 1964–65 only "the hard-won black studies
programs that have taken hold in many colleges and universities . . . and a flowering of African-American art, literature, music, drama, and film."

The same splintering of focus was reflected in federal civil rights policy.
Lyndon Johnson delivered a major speech on race relations at Howard University in June 1965, emphasizing that the constitutional right to eat at a lunch
counter could hardly be exercised without income, clearly implying that the
civil rights movement must now enter an economic phase. Presumably the War
on Poverty was the administration's response, but the growing cost of the other,
Asian war limited the size of the domestic one. "Because of Vietnam, we cannot
do all that we should, or all that we would like to do," Johnson admitted in January 1966. The president's mind was on the Vietnam war, and, complained
Kennedy-Johnson aide Arthur Schlesinger, Jr.: "The Great Society is now, except
for token gestures, dead. The fight for equal opportunity for the Negro, the war
against poverty, the struggle to save the cities, the improvement of our
schools—all must be starved for the sake of Vietnam."

Others in the government concluded that more federal money aimed at
poverty, even if it were well aimed, was not the only or even the best policy
route. Quietly, bureaucrats within the new Equal Employment Opportunity
Commission (EEOC) and elsewhere in the executive branch, along with an
activist judiciary, gradually but persistently created a body of regulatory law

and court decisions requiring "affirmative action" in hiring and other federal benefits (see Chapter 8, pp. 199–200). Another policy tool available to federal authorities was school busing of students to achieve desired levels of racial integration, a tactic utilized vigorously across the country by federal judges interpreting their duties under the *Brown* decision.

A third idea was aired but never tried. Labor Department aide Daniel P. Moynihan in 1967 circulated a confidential report detailing a deterioration of the black family structure in the modern urban setting, marked by rising measures of out-of-wedlock births, female-headed households, and high divorce and desertion rates. The proportion of births out of wedlock among blacks rose from 22 percent in 1960 to 37 percent in 1971, and by the early 1970s the proportion of black women who were divorced had climbed to 43 percent, contrasted with 23 percent among whites. Moynihan did not "blame the victim," but attributed these signs of social pathology within the black community's core institution on slavery and the ensuing discrimination, combined with a welfare system that unintentionally encouraged family desertion. He thought that a pro-family tilt could be given to welfare and tax policies, with special benefit to blacks, but the report leaked to the press, bringing a storm of denunciation upon Moynihan for daring to imply that part of the problem was within the black community itself. Affirmative action and school busing remained federal tools, though increasingly controversial ones; family-strengthening policy had no supporters, as the concept was novel and underdeveloped.

The New Feminism

The demand for racial equality catalyzed another protest movement from a group that was numerically a majority but had its own historic grievances: women. Here the tradition of protest was much older than among the other groups mobilized during the 1960s. The first women's movement had essentially ended in 1920 when women were granted the vote. Women's suffrage, so bitterly opposed, had neither reformed society nor much altered the situation of women. The number of women in professional fields such as law, medicine, and teaching increased gradually from the 1890s through the 1920s, but then the curve flattened out. Women made few occupational gains after the onset of the Great Depression, and in some areas their opportunities narrowed. Women received 16 percent of the Ph.D. degrees granted in the 1920s, for example, but by 1960 their share had declined to 11 percent. They were treated differently under the law, favored in some ways (protective labor legislation, for example) but subordinated to men in the more important areas of property rights, marriage, and divorce.

Yet significant change was underway in the roles, and following that in the aspirations, of American women. World War II expanded employment opportunities and began to break down the informal bars to the hiring of women to do skilled, technical work. When the wartime labor crisis came to an end, the prewar patterns were never fully restored. The structure of occupational opportunities returned to prewar norms, with women typically employed as clerks, school teachers, maids, or secretaries. Segregated in such low-paying industries, women's pay at the end of the war averaged 63 percent of white men's, and that gap had not narrowed as the 1960s arrived. There was change, however, in the labor-force participation rate of women, which continued to rise, climbing from the 25 percent in 1940 (for females over sixteen) to over 50 percent by 1970. Unlike the prewar years, however, when the typical working woman was young and single, the postwar trend saw the working wife and mother become an institution. Fifteen percent of married women worked in 1940, but 30 percent did by the start of the 1970s. When a job outside the home became not a deviation from the normal female expectation but a part of it, other changes in outlook could not be far behind.

Inexorably, wider economic participation began to erode traditional views of women's role in society. In the years immediately after World War II the dominant stereotypes did not seem in jeopardy. The female was still seen as more passive and "sensitive" than the male, fitted by God for a supporting, domestic role. A college president in the Midwest told the graduating class of a woman's college in 1955 that "the college years must be a rehearsal period for the major performance of marriage," and Adlai Stevenson told the graduates of Smith College to influence American males through their "humble role of housewife." Women's magazines reinforced a domestic orientation through articles on cooking, sewing, and natural childbirth, all practiced by radiantly happy women with handsome husbands looking on approvingly.

This traditionalism did not survive the 1960s unchallenged. Betty Friedan's influential 1963 book, *The Feminine Mystique,* described women as not fulfilled by their domestic role but trapped in it. The culture told women to aspire to marriage, motherhood, and suburban consumerism, and most women accepted these goals only to experience, in Friedan's view, high levels of boredom, fatigue, and neurosis—"the problem that had no name." Friedan urged women to free themselves from the "comfortable concentration camp of the home" and to insist on access to opportunities that men had always kept for themselves.

In the 1960s many women, especially the younger and better educated, shared Friedan's analysis. Esther Peterson, named by Kennedy to head the Women's Bureau, convinced the president to appoint a Presidential Commission on the Status of Women, and the group's 1963 report recommended requirements for equal pay for comparable work, paid maternity leaves, and improved child-care services. The Equal Pay Act of 1963 was one result.

Another catalyst to the sudden emergence of a women's movement was the burgeoning crusade for racial equality, for were not women, like blacks, subjected to discrimination and narrowed opportunities on the basis of physical, inherited characteristics? Much of the subsequent leadership of the feminist revolt had been active in the civil rights movement, often in the South, as younger women joined SNCC, SCLC, and later the Students for a Democratic Society (SDS) to work for changed race relations. The experience moved most of them from a single focus on race to an awareness that gender, too, was a realm of inequality that could not be defended and should no longer be endured. Working within SNCC, wrote Sara Evans, "created the social space within which women began to develop a new sense of their own potential. A critical vanguard of the young women accumulated the tools for movement building: a language to describe oppression and justify revolt, experience in the strategy and tactics of organizing, and beginning sense of themselves collectively as objects of discrimination."

They also developed an acute and often angry awareness that "male chauvinism" was as close as their brothers in the movement, who expected the females to do the typing and clerical work, make the coffee, and, often, provide sexual relief to males who made policy decisions. ("The only position for women in SNCC is prone," Stokely Carmichael was quoted.) Two female activists, Casey Hayden and Mary King, prepared a memo for SNCC's fall retreat in 1964, charging that women's roles in the organization resembled that of token blacks in society generally—expected to stay in their place, treated with condescension, paternalism, and unfunny jokes amounting to ridicule. Like blacks, women were not "happy and contented" under such "male supremacy," and the paper expressed hope that "sometime in the future . . . the whole of the women in this movement will . . . force the rest of the movement to stop the discrimination. . . ."

In the 1960s women joined African-Americans in the fight for equality under the law. Feminist leaders such as Bella Abzug, Betty Friedan, and Gloria Steinem led marches, lobbied Congress, and helped create the National Organization for Women. In this photo Abzug and Steinem are joined by New York's Lt. Governor Maryann Krupsak as they launch the March 8, 1975, "International Women's Day March."
(UPI/Bettmann)

The reception was negative, even hostile, but if male attitudes seemed fixed, women's were fast changing. Title VII of the 1964 Civil Rights Act had banned discrimination based on sex as well as race, a provision ironically added by conservative southerners who hoped to undercut the measure's support. Adding sex to race as a protected category was "a fluke . . . born out of wedlock," said the Equal Employment Opportunity Commission's first chairman, who refused to enforce the sex discrimination clause. When the EEOC showed no interest in vigorous enforcement, what seemed to be needed was "some sort of NAACP for women," as Betty Friedan put it. Feminist leaders persuaded her to take the lead in the formation of the National Organization for Women (NOW), in 1966. NOW's main focus became an Equal Rights Amendment (ERA) to guarantee that "equal rights under the law shall not be denied or abridged by the United States on account of sex." Congress approved the amendment in 1972, and by 1976 it had been ratified by thirty-four states. But the impression of an early resolution of this knotty social issue was misleading. As with the civil rights movement, feminism in the 1960s not only spun off more angry and radical variations who saw the ERA approach as too moderate and limited, it also provoked a backlash among women and men who mounted a determined counterattack against change in the patriarchal family and the older male–female relationships. These would not fully emerge, however, until the next decade.

Rebellion on the Campuses: The New Left

Revolutionary challenges to established authority have in modern times come primarily from the working class or the military. A surprise of the 1960s in America was that radical rhetoric and political action had their base in the colleges and universities, and among the young. Prior to World War II the college population had been an insignificant portion of the nation's young people. In 1900 only 3.9 percent of those eighteen to twenty-one years old were enrolled in a college or university, and by 1940 the slow expansion of higher education had brought the proportion only to 14.5 percent. Then a dynamic period of growth in higher education followed the war, as federal funds channeled through the G.I. Bill of 1944 supported a burgeoning of public colleges and junior colleges, and more young people sought the occupational and social advantages of a college degree. By 1970, 47 percent of those aged eighteen to twenty-one were attending college, a total of 6.3 million Americans.

Until about 1964 it was assumed that college students were more numerous but no different than before, continuing to pursue athletics, sex, beer, and sometimes even academic studies, all in the relative isolation of college communities. In October 1964, the Free Speech Movement (FSM) at the University of California, Berkeley, shattered the calm. It became apparent that a new spirit of critical social engagement was stirring among some of the young. The Berkeley protest was at first directed against university rules and officialdom, generating huge rallies and periodical occupation of administration buildings. But close attention to the rhetoric of Mario Savio and other student leaders revealed that

We are people of this generation, bred in at least modest comfort, housed now in universities, looking uncomfortably to the world we inherit. . . .

As we grew, however, our comfort was penetrated by events too troubling to dismiss. First, the permeating and victimizing fact of human degradation, symbolized by the Southern struggle against racial bigotry, compelled most of us from silence to activism. Second, the enclosing fact of the Cold War, symbolized by the presence of the Bomb, brought awareness that we ourselves, and our friends, and millions of abstract "others" we knew more directly because of our common peril, might die at any time. . . .

The declaration "all men are created equal . . ." rang hollow before the facts of Negro life in the South and the big cities of the North. The proclaimed peaceful intentions of the United States contradicted its economic and military investments in the Cold War status quo. . . .

We would replace power rooted in possession, privilege, or circumstance by power and uniqueness rooted in love, reflectiveness, reason, and creativity. As a social system we seek the establishment of a democracy of individual participation, governed by two central aims: that the individual share in those social decisions determining the quality and direction of his life; that society be organized to encourage independence in men and provide the media for their common participation. . . .

A new left must consist of younger people who matured in the post-war world, and partially be directed to the recruitment of younger people. The university is an obvious beginning point. . . .

A new left must include liberals and socialists, the former for their relevance, the latter for their sense of thoroughgoing reforms in the system. The university is a more sensible place than a political party for these two traditions to begin to discuss their differences and look for political synthesis. . . .

They must make fraternal and functional contact with allies in labor, civil rights, and other liberal forces outside the campus. . . .

As students for a democratic society, we are committed to stimulating this kind of social movement, this kind of vision and program in campus and community across the country. . . .

Excerpt from The Port Huron Statement (1962)
(Source: Judith C. Albert and Stewart E. Albert, eds., The Sixties Papers: Documents of a Rebellious Decade (Praeger, 1984), pp. 177–196.)

the university was being attacked on grounds that potentially threatened economic and political institutions as well. What students claimed most to dislike about the "multiversity" was its huge size, inflexible administration, and impersonal routine, seen as relentlessly suppressing both individuality and idealism. While UC administrators and local police were prominent targets of attack, there was also criticism of more distant enemies, including large corporations and southern whites who resisted integration. The roots of the "free speech" episode were clearly in the soil of the civil rights movement, but now the spirit of protest was finding new targets.

Large student rallies and occasional shutdown of buildings or the entire campus drew media attention, as events in Berkeley first alerted the TV-watching public to the potential of the new student radicalism. But its themes had been set out two years before in the 1962 "Port Huron Manifesto" of the new organization, Students for a Democratic Society (SDS). SDS denounced the Cold War, called for black equality, attacked university and corporate bureaucracies as dehumanizing, and proposed using the universities as a base for assaults on "the system." A "New Left" was needed, said the Port Huron statement, a movement dedicated to "participatory democracy," decentralization of power, spontaneity, and community. "What appealed to me about the SDS," recalled an early recruit, quoted in Maurice Isserman's *If I Had a Hammer*, "was three things. . . . it wasn't a New York-centered group . . . where the constant problem was how do you break out? . . . It wasn't a Left group in the traditional sense . . . it was a clean slate," and "it was multi-issue, and had a good balance between wanting to do educational work and wanting to do activism."

SDS began grass-roots organizing in urban slums, with little immediate result. Then it quickly struck a vein of energy when in 1965 it organized rallies against the expanding U.S. military role in Vietnam, and found its ranks swollen by recruits. The war, military action vividly reported on television for the first time, fanned student unrest through the rest of the 1960s. Hundreds of campuses surged with rallies and marches, the most intense and violent at Columbia University in the spring of 1968, at Harvard, Yale, Cornell, and the University of California, Santa Barbara, where one riot in 1969 led to the burning of a branch office of the Bank of America. But such episodes were rare, and came toward the end of the decade. What should be remembered about the radicalism of the 1960s is the activists' confident and optimistic sense that they had, in the words of the New Deal thirty years earlier, a "rendezvous with destiny." When the folk group Peter, Paul and Mary reissued the Old Left anthem, "If I Had a Hammer," it went to the top of the hit parade in 1962. Mary Travers of that group was a protégé of Pete Seeger, a legendary Old Left balladeer, as was Bob Dylan, who vaulted to the top of folk recordings with the news that something big was "Blowin' in the Wind."

Opposition to war in Vietnam had become the central project of SDS. Though rallies, marches, and silent vigils across the country and around the capitol and White House often mobilized groups numbering from hundreds to hundreds of thousands, the actual ranks of committed activists on the New Left "included probably no more than 250,000 people . . . a minute—but intellectually gifted—fraction of a generation that has 5.2 million of its members in college," in journalist Jack Newfield's estimate. The membership of SDS itself possibly reached 100,000 by 1968, and as the Vietnam conflict intensified, young radicals rapidly became disillusioned with reasoned protest and prone to desperate acts of violence. The SDS, whose Port Huron statement of 1962 had been liberal-reformist and hopeful, removed from its charter the bar to communist membership in 1965, moved quickly leftward, and was splintered in 1969 by the emergence of the ideological influence of China's Mao Tse-tung. A "Weatherman" faction arose, convinced that violent action was now required to end the war and bring about social transformation.

By 1970, after three Weathermen were killed while preparing explosives

Mario Savio, one of the leaders of "The New Left," addresses a free speech rally on
the University of California, Berkeley campus in 1964.
(UPI/Bettmann)

in an apartment on West 11th Street in New York, the SDS was collapsing and
the New Left had essentially run its course. Tom Hayden, principal author of
the Port Huron statement, would later claim that the New Left had achieved
much success as an agent of social change, his most concrete example being
the antiwar campaign which eventually forced an end to the Vietnam conflict.
He was correct that the radicals of the 1960s played an important part along
with church groups, intellectuals and others in mobilizing a substantial middle-class resistance to the war effort, thus altering the course of American history. But the New Left collapsed sooner and produced fewer results than
imagined by its founders. The qualities that distinguished the "New" from
the "Old" Left accounted both for the appeal of 1960s-style radicalism as well
as its internal weaknesses. The stress on spontaneity and rank-and-file participation tapped many energies, but sapped organizational strength. The
New Left's disregard for doctrine, social theory, and analysis, carried in many
cases to the point of defiant antiintellectualism, seemed at first a remedy for
the endless internal disputes which had so frequently splintered American
socialist and other radical movements. But in the end a movement without
clear ideas about ends and means was vulnerable to impatience, desperation,
and loss of contact with reality. Not tied to a base in working-class America,
the youthful radicals too easily drifted toward romantic ventures in heroic
violence.

The "Counterculture"

In retrospect, the chance for a disciplined and effective youth-based radicalism in the 1960s was most undercut by the alluring presence of a cousin in the family of rebellion, the "Counterculture," in Theodore Roszak's term (*The Making of a Counter-Culture*, 1967). This current of cultural rebellion has proven difficult for historians to describe, for it was a world of private behavior where the maturing children of the Baby Boom—some of them, at least, especially those living in California, New York's Greenwich Village, and many university communities—defied the moral values of their elders. If the traditional culture valued the work ethic, deferral of gratification, competitive striving for material success, and the confinement of sexual impulses to heterosexual marriage, the Counterculture valued liberation from restraints ("Go where you want/Do what you want," sang the popular trio, Mamas and Pappas), free and frequent sex ("All you need is love, Love is all you need," was the summary of the Beatles, a British band from Liverpool which arrived in America in February 1964 to be met by a mob of 10,000 teenagers), communal experience, inner harmony, and pacifism.

At their best, the songs, phrases, and ideas of the Counterculture were an antidote to the excesses of America's competitive, materialistic, and military inheritance, the flower in the gun barrel. At worst, the Counterculture could become a life-destroying invitation to drug abuse, going beyond marijuana highs to the hallucinogenic hard drugs urged by drug guru Timothy Leary, whose invitation to "turn on, tune in, and drop out" was accepted by many young people without internal resources to repair their broken lives. ("If you can remember the Sixties," admitted hippie Abbie Hoffman, "you weren't there.") Both the worst and the best of the Counterculture could be seen, or experienced, in one of the few counterculture media events of the decade, when a youthful crowd of up to 400,000 people gathered at a farm near Woodstock, New York, in the summer of 1969, for "three days of mud, drugs, and music" from the greatest rock 'n roll musicians of the day—the Jefferson Airplane, Santana, Richie Havens, Jimi Hendrix, and folk singer Joan Baez.

Some heard in the popular folk and rock songs of the 1960s cultural messages of the most revolutionary sort, incompatible with capitalism, weaponry and war, even conventional religion. "Christianity will go," Beatle John Lennon announced in the summer of 1966: "It will vanish and shrink. I needn't argue about that, I'm right and will be proved right. We're more popular than Jesus Christ right now." But established religions as well as war and weapons would survive the Counterculture, while capitalism embraced and commodified it, marketing rock stars, beads, stylishly ragged blue jeans—and, most lucrative of all, illegal drugs, whose ability to wrench all the countercultural values into satanic channels was evident when cult leader Charles Manson led a group of self-styled hippies into a home in Hollywood Hills in 1969 to brutally murder actress Sharon Tate and six others. A movement bent upon social change, the New Left found itself operating amid this cultural rebellion and, indeed, regarding it as a parallel movement, an ally. On balance, some of the values celebrated by the Age of Aquarius would take forms more threatening to the idealistic radicals of the 1960s themselves than to the structures of power they wished to tear down.

The Rise of Environmentalism

By mid-decade, events that had been beneath the surface of public awareness just ten years before had thrust upward from latent issues to manifest ones, and generated large social reform movements—affecting race relations, women's roles and rights, foreign policy in southeast Asia. These were joined by environmental concern on a scale sufficient to become a political force, another voice for far-reaching reform. However radical the demands made on white society by nonwhites drawn into the civil rights effort, or the changes demanded of male society by feminists, or of society at large by the New Left, the underlying ideas of these insurgent efforts were traditional and hallowed—essentially, the Declaration of Independence's assertion of human equality. What was new was the notion of living up to old ideals. The situation was reversed with environmentalism. Even when its demands were modest and readily accommodated by the system—protection of air and water quality through regulations, recycling, preserving a wild river—its underlying ideas were both novel and profoundly radical. Searching for the cultural roots of Western society's nature-exploitive outlook, historian Lynn White in a *Science* article published in 1967 pointed to the Judeo-Christian tradition, an intensely anthropomorphic religious heritage which replaced an animal- and place-revering paganism. The Book of Genesis grant to man of "dominion . . . over every creeping thing that moveth upon the earth" was an early Biblical expression of that moral stance, and White urged modern man to "re-think and re-feel our nature and destiny," to follow the example of St. Francis of Assisi toward a new humility and the acceptance of all creatures as man's equal. More influential was the earlier writing of forester Aldo Leopold, who in his *Sand County Almanac* (1949) had proposed a new "land ethic" as a larger ethical framework for humanity. "The land ethic simply enlarges the boundaries of the community to include soils, waters, plants, and animals, or collectively: the land," he wrote. This recognition changes "the role of Homo Sapiens from conqueror of the land-community to plain member and citizen of it." Out of that ethic Leopold derived a new guide for human action: "A thing is right when it tends to preserve the integrity, stability, and beauty of the biotic community. It is wrong when it tends otherwise."

Such writers were proposing profound changes in the people-centered, nature-exploiting ethical orientation of Western societies. Others questioned the uncritical reverence for science and technology, for bigness, for growth itself. Within the environmental movement there was much borrowing from Asian religions of the oriental acceptance of physical limits, humility before the natural order of things, the search for inward growth rather than the multiplication of material objects. The central idea of ecological thinking was interdependence; as John Muir had written late in the nineteenth century, "when we try to pick out anything by itself, we find it hitched to everything else in the universe."

And ecologists taught that the universe was more alterable and fragile than history had thus far taught man to understand. Adlai Stevenson observed in his last speech, before his death in 1964:

> We travel together, passengers on a little space ship, dependent on its vulnerable supplies of air and soil . . . preserved from annihilation only by the care, the work, and I will say the love, we give our fragile craft.

Such ideas ran squarely against the grain of the American cultural inheritance—of frontier optimism, acquisitive individualism, reverence for the privateness of property, faith in science and technology as straight roads to progress. "The ecological revolution," said French writer Jean-Francois Revel, "is part of a moral revolution." Environmentalists were led to challenge private property rights in land, water, and resources, and were usually angry at some corporation. Environmentalist thinkers obviously did not believe that the marketplace would guide individuals toward society's long-range interests in matters of resources or pollution, and naturally turned to government intervention and often talked of social planning. Biologist Garrett Hardin, in his famous essay, "The Tragedy of the Commons," published in 1968, used the metaphor of the English commons to demonstrate that individuals, maximizing their own self-interest as Adam Smith had taught, would add livestock to the commons until by a series of individual decisions the commons was ruined for all. With common property resources, which included at least the atmosphere, oceans, and most bodies of water, there must be collective controls. Hardin called for "mutual coercion mutually agreed upon," beginning with social pressure to curb the birth rate.

Encountering such ideas, some concluded that the new movement presented a radical challenge to capitalism, individualism, and private property. A conservative member of the Sierra Club read Rachel Carson's condemnation of current pesticide/herbicide usage and pronounced it "at best negative and at the worst possibly socialistic," a charge often repeated by lobbyists for chemical corporations. In truth, the environmental movement spanned a wide political spectrum. If the central ideas of ecological thought were communalistic, skeptical of market forces and the concept of private property in resources, if they asked man to move over at the center of the universe to make room for other creatures, few in the environmental movement had followed such ideas very far by the late 1960s. Minor elements of the environmentalist coalition rejected technology, modern "progress" as conventionally defined, agreeing with economist Georgescu-Reogen that ". . . every Cadillac produced at any time means fewer lives in the future," and repudiating the idea that continued population and economic growth was either possible or desirable. But there were in the movement wealthy people (such as the Rockefeller brothers), affluent suburbanites, engineers and scientists, who believed that environmental damage could be controlled at tolerable levels by a combination of applied science, governmental regulation, and private enlightenment, without any impairment of capitalism, basic property rights, or (against all logic) continuous growth.

The environmental movement rapidly gained momentum in the late 1960s, as citizen groups across the country—with most environmental activism found in New England, Florida, California, and Oregon—engaged in legal and political battles with developers, polluting corporations, and government public works projects. There were protests against redwood cutting in northern California; citizens mobilized by an Audubon Club member won a long battle to prevent a jetport and urban complex in the everglades near Miami; the Sierra Club blocked a $35-million ski resort planned for Mineral King Valley in California. Communities in Ramapo, New York, Boulder, Colorado, and Petaluma, California, broke with traditional pro-growth attitudes and enacted ordinances to limit their size. These were scattered and uncoordinated efforts. Then a network of conservation groups came together to celebrate April 22, 1970, as "Earth Day" across the country—holding rallies, giving away organically grown food, burying automobiles or pounding them apart with sledges. Opinion polls reflected a sharp shift in outlook, with 53 percent choosing "reducing the pollution of air and water" as the government's second most important task in 1970 (just behind crime control); five years earlier it had been ranked ninth, behind highway safety.

Local battles to preserve a beach, bay, or stand of trees, or to defeat some environment-damaging development, were sometimes won and often lost, but they served to build the membership of existing environmental groups, who were eager to channel the new public activism. Older organizations such as the Sierra Club, the Wilderness Society, and the Audubon Society gained members and became more militant; new groups sprang up and joined the work of influencing public opinion—Friends of the Earth, the Environmental Fund, Worldwatch, and Zero Population Growth. By 1976 there were 3000 environmentalist organizations, the largest dozen claiming 4.3 million members.

Yet one event of 1969 should have reminded environmentalists that their movement was in for a long struggle. On Sunday, July 20, a television audience estimated at 1 billion people watched commander Neil A. Armstrong of the spacecraft *Apollo 11* step onto the surface of the Moon, 240,000 miles from Earth. The success of the *Apollo* mission was surely humanity's most stupendous technological and organizational feat. To some, including the astronauts aboard as they looked down at our small planet, it was also a time for humility about humanity's power, or for reflections on the small size of our planetary home. But to millions it was an invitation to hubris, a resounding affirmation of the power of science and technology, especially the American variety, to solve any problem and to transcend the limits of Earth.

"The Movement" and the End of the Liberal Era

Toward the end of the 1960s many spoke of "The Movement," as if the disparate protest movements challenging the status quo in the areas of race, gender, environment, foreign policy, and a bureaucratized corporate-university system added up to a unified, perhaps revolutionary challenge to the social order. There was much reason to perceive a potent coming together of social critics and reformers, whose separate agendas appeared to overlap on a common set of beliefs. Did not everyone in The Movement agree on opposition to the "imperialistic" war in Vietnam and those who had launched it? Did not all reject "corporate-bureaucratic-plastic" life-styles and structures, dictated from Madison Avenue and enthroned in the suburbs? Did not all in The Movement affirm equality for racial minorities and women, as well as life-styles that were environmentally benign, spontaneous, and centered around participatory and non-hierarchical communities? And was it not true that the civil rights revolution had spread beyond African-Americans, to other groups that might combine to become a victorious coalition to end the oppression of all minorities?

Yes, was the answer of Mexican-American activists in the 1960s, pointing to their own tradition of community organization to change the status quo. The lobbying and educational efforts of the League of United Latin American Citizens (LULAC), founded in the 1920s, had in the 1950s been augmented by grassroots movements in the southwest promoting nondiscrimination in hiring and community activism in housing and education. With the 1960s came more militant tactics, most visibly Cesar Chavez's leadership of the United Farm Workers Union (UFW) in California, bringing national visibility and much-publicized support from the AFL's Walter Reuther, and prompting a meeting between Chavez and Robert Kennedy as the latter campaigned in California in 1968. Inspired by Chavez's efforts in agriculture, "Chicano" (a term preferred over "Mexican-American" by younger activists advocating ethnic pride and some degree of separatism from the United States) activists continued the tradition of community organization, though considerable effort went toward establishing Chicano Studies programs and departments at colleges and universities as bases for political action.

The spirit and tactics animating black protest seemed also to have found a new sounding board among America's homosexuals. On a warm June night in 1969, eight uniformed policemen broke into the Stonewall Inn on Christopher Street in Greenwich Village to arrest homosexuals, and were met not with the usual resignation but with prolonged riots. That evening the "Gay Movement" entered a new era of self-conception, with a rising determination to assert its "civil rights" to be free of harassment. The event seemed to confirm the contemporary sense that the civil rights movement had become a relentlessly expanding cluster of mobilized groups—after African-Americans came women, Latinos, gays, Native Americans, critics of American foreign policy and of brutality toward nature. The impression of widely shared values across such groups promoted a sense of destiny and of revolutionary expectation. Reinforcing this perception was the growing awareness that youth-led waves of protest were surging into visibility in other countries. Sustained rioting broke out around university communities in Mexico City, Paris, Rome, Frankfurt, and even in communist Prague, Czechoslovakia, in the spring and summer of 1968.

But beneath these indications of a gathering radical transformation of society ran hidden divisions and tensions within "The Movement" itself, calling the concept into question. Some in The Movement were peaceful "flower children," full of warm feelings of human fraternity and "sisterhood," wandering with their flutes or guitars through green places, seeking and advocating inner transformation and peace. A small number were disciplined radicals, ready to use nonconventional political tactics and even, at the edge and toward the last years of the movement, violence to achieve social transformation. But even among the more politically oriented participants in The Movement there was no obedience to ideology, Marxist or otherwise, and thus no strategic program. The Movement was not controlled from anywhere; it had no center, its activists in fact were committed to the absence of organization and hierarchy. To feel its pulse, one went to campuses such as Berkeley, Santa Cruz, or Santa Barbara in the University of California system, the University of Wisconsin–Madison, to Columbia or Harvard, Bard College or Oberlin; or to communities known to shelter unconventional lifestyles, such as Berkeley, Los Angeles, Boulder, Greenwich Village in New York.

From such a partial listing, it is obvious that The Movement directly mobilized only a small and unrepresentative part of America. At large state universities in the south and most in the midwest, at smaller sectarian colleges there was less evidence of antiwar sentiment, civil rights effort, the different life-styles of the "counterculture." And even at places like Berkeley, Madison, and Columbia there were always many students who enrolled in ROTC programs, supported the war in Vietnam, and heckled the "hippies" with long hair carrying protest posters. Yet the campus disruptions, peace marches on Main Street and on the Mall in Washington received much media attention, as did the "hippie scene" in places like the Haight-Ashbury district in San Francisco. This media exposure, along with the widespread popularity of the folk music that became such a powerful hallmark of the decade—the "protest songs" of Joan Baez, Bob Dylan, and Judy Collins, lyrics such as "The Times They Are A-Changin' " echoing throughout the era—created the illusion that revolutionary changes were underway. Yet the Movement never posed the threat of a radical transformation of American society. Indeed, it was not even one movement. Each wing of it was not only internally divided, the concerns of civil rights activists working amid poverty were very different from Sierra Clubbers protesting a nuclear power plant or the draining of a marsh.

Given these divisions, and the "turn on, tune in, and drop out" invitations of the Counterculture, the reform efforts of the 1960s left intact America's basic structures of power—private enterprise and a corporation-dominated economy, universities with tests and grades, a military fearfully armed with nuclear weapons, patriarchy. Only with the passage of time would it seem to many that the 1960s launched deep cultural rebellions that in time brought radical changes in private values and behavior perhaps as far-reaching as the rebels' designs for dismantling powerful institutions.

Even viewed from the end of the 1960s, if The Movement is broken down into its loosely connected parts and measured against reform rather than revolutionary ambitions, America was substantially changed. The Jim Crow system of legal segregation was swept away, commitments to equality were written into law. Environmental protection had advanced, women's roles had come under critical scrutiny and pressure for change. And the opposition to the war brought a stunning and unexpected event, Lyndon Johnson's 1968 decision to end the U.S. troop buildup in Vietnam and to yield to an elected successor.

Napalm bombings combined with reporters' cameras brought to the world some of
the most horrifying images of the war, this one from Trang Bang, South Vietnam, in
June 1972.
(AP/Wide World Photos)

THE QUAGMIRE IN VIETNAM

The entry of U.S. ground troops into Vietnam in 1965 had brought widening
conflict, "search and destroy" missions against an elusive, tenacious NLF
guerilla force that could never be fully destroyed, massive bombing raids on
South Vietnamese targets and, beginning late in 1965, on North Vietnam military installations and cities. Bombs, napalm, and herbicides rained down on all
of Vietnam from the air, and U.S. troop numbers increased along with the government's optimistic claims of military success and eventual victory. Then, in
February 1968, Communist forces launched a massive offensive over the Tet
holidays, striking thirty-six of the forty-two provincial capitals in South Vietnam, penetrating the U.S. embassy grounds in Saigon, and holding the city of
Hue for a month. The offensive was beaten back with an estimated 32,000 Vietcong killed and 20,000 wounded, with American losses of 4000 dead. The Communists were rebuffed and their military forces seriously depleted, but a military victory of this sort came across as very bad news. An enemy able to launch
a coordinated attack on virtually every South Vietnamese urban center pos-

sessed resources and dedication which put victory for our side far out of sight, and key interpreters of the news from Vietnam, such as CBS anchorman Walter Cronkite, expressed open skepticism about the winnability of the war. The conflict was costing $2 billion a month, inflation surged in early 1968, and Great Society programs were cut further.

Public opinion, which had backed the 1965 decision to intervene directly, now polarized. The demonstrations of antiwar protestors were countered by strong support for the war from the AFL-CIO, politicians of both parties, even some religious leaders, and 70,000 marched in New York City in 1967 to "support our men in Vietnam." Johnson seemed unwavering in his determination to persist in his course, but after the Tet offensive General William Westmoreland asked for 200,000 additional troops and mobilization of reserves.

It was a crucial decision at a moment when the political winds suddenly shifted. Senator Eugene McCarthy (D., Minn.), long an opponent of the war but an isolated figure with a literary gift and unpredictable political habits, announced his candidacy for president in November. McCarthy toured snowy New Hampshire with only the help of a few thousand student volunteers from the antiwar ranks, and instead of the 5 percent of the vote originally predicted for him or the 18 percent seen in LBJ's private poll, received 42.4 percent to the president's 49.5 percent in a traditionally conservative state. Four days later Robert F. Kennedy, since 1964 a Senator from New York and for over a year a vigorous opponent of the war, entered the race for the office his brother had held. Reports from Wisconsin predicted LBJ's defeat in that Democratic primary (he did indeed lose to McCarthy, 34 to 56 percent); a Pentagon review of the situation by respected Democrat Clark Clifford, now Secretary of Defense, informed Johnson of deep pessimism among his top advisors, the ranks of hawks depleting and those of doves suddenly on the rise. Seizing a moment in which he still commanded the ability to surprise even the insiders in Washington and to shape events even in desperation, Lyndon Johnson on March 31 went on television to announce a cessation of the bombing, an invitation to peace talks with Hanoi—and that he would not be a candidate for president in 1968.

The aura of failure cast by Johnson's humiliating withdrawal complicated the assessment of a presidency that had begun with one of the most energetic and far-reaching reform programs in modern American history. LBJ drove through Congress 181 domestic laws of the 200 he proposed in the 1965–1967 Congress alone—major legislation on voting rights, medical care, education, conservation, consumer safety. Even FDR's New Deal could not match this output, and to it Johnson added energetic sponsorship of black progress. His reputation would ultimately rest on the wisdom and effectiveness of 1960s liberalism's remedies for national problems. On a personal level, admirers who were impressed with Johnson's championing of the underdog would be matched by critics who disliked his crudity and overbearing ego. Whether it is a mark of greatness or a cautionary object lesson to all those contemplating political leadership, Lyndon Johnson surpassed all of America's presidents in his determination to construct an agenda out of America's toughest social problems, with race relations at the top of the list. His legacy is in many ways the most complex of them all.

THE POLITICS OF 1968

The shocks of that year reverberated further. On April 4, 1968, Martin Luther King, Jr. was shot and killed in Memphis, Tennessee, by a white rifleman, an event that brought riots in 125 cities with forty-six deaths and a widespread outpouring of national grief. Then, two months later, on June 5 in Los Angeles, following a victory over McCarthy in the California Democratic primary, Senator Robert Kennedy was shot and killed by an assassin in the Ambassador Hotel.

Their deaths deepened the national mood of confusion, apprehension, and crisis. Coming rapidly to the end of a political era, the Democratic Party fell into warring pieces. The ebullient and likeable Vice President Hubert Humphrey defeated McCarthy for the nomination at a Chicago convention turned into a riot scene as 12,000 of Mayor Richard Daley's Chicago police, backed by units of the National Guard, FBI and Secret Service agents, turned the convention hall into a fortress and brutally dispersed large crowds of antiwar protesters with tear gas and clubs.

With the Democratic Party in an agony of divisions, and the Republicans turning without much enthusiasm to the cautious ambition of Richard M. Nixon, former Democratic Governor of Alabama George C. Wallace offered an outlet for the "backlash" passions of southern and working-class whites, mounting a campaign for president from his new American Independent Party.

American politics thus presented the voters with a president who had destroyed his own administration and declined to run, a successor nominated behind police barricades and "in a sea of blood" in Theodore White's slightly exaggerated phrase, an unlikeable Richard Nixon who stood clearly for his own survival and office holding and unclearly for anything else, and a pugnacious, somewhat crude southern governor who openly appealed to fears of race mixing and the erosion of "law and order." The principal reaction to these choices and the events of that tragic year was political apathy, with fewer than three of five eligible voters participating in an election in which a strong conservative reaction found 57 percent of the voters favoring either Nixon (43.4 percent, president by the preference of 27 percent of those eligible to vote) or Wallace (13.5 percent) over the embodiment of New Deal Liberalism, Humphrey (42.7 percent, or 26 percent of those eligible).

Beneath the voting of that autumn ran a strong undercurrent of resistance to liberal values and policies. While the media had given prominence to liberal reformers and to the radical rhetoric heard on campus or among black militants, the resurgence on the right had been underestimated. Signs called for Chief Justice Warren's impeachment, Robert Welch of the ultrarightist John Birch Society asserted that even Eisenhower had been a communist, and radio commentators such as Dan Smoot and Paul Harvey explained to anxious citizens that internal subversion threatened America's very existence. These sentiments were reported as signs of an irrational rightist fringe, but in truth the Great Society and the 1960s had stirred a far deeper and mainstream resistance to much that had taken place. The short but intense "five- or six-year period called the Sixties," in Yale President A. Bartlett Giamatti's phrase, was quickly over. Few who lived through it would not remember those days as unprecedented and unrepeatable, a volatile mix of idealism and alienation.

BIBLIOGRAPHY FOR PART THREE

ABERNATHY, RALPH DAVID. *And the Walls Came Tumbling Down*. New York: Harper and Row, 1989.

AMBROSE, STEPHEN B. *Nixon: Volume Two: The Triumph of a Politician, 1962–1972*. New York: Simon & Schuster, 1989.

BERGERUD, ERIC M. *The Dynamics of Defeat: The Vietnam War in Hau Nghia Province*. Boulder: Westview Press, 1991.

BERMAN, LARRY. *Planning a Tragedy: The Americanization of the War in Vietnam*. New York: Norton, 1982.

———. *Lyndon Johnson's War: The Road to Stalemate in Vietnam*. New York: Norton, 1989.

BERMAN, RONALD. *America in the Sixties: An Intellectual History*. New York: The Free Press, 1968.

BERNSTEIN, CARL, AND BOB WOODWARD. *All the President's Men*. New York: Simon & Schuster, 1974/1987.

BESCHLOSS, MICHAEL. *The Crisis Years: Kennedy and Khrushchev, 1960–63*. New York: Harper Collins, 1991.

BORNET, VAUGHN D. *The Presidency of Lyndon B. Johnson*. Lawrence, KA: University of Kansas Press, 1990.

BRANCH, TAYLOR. *Parting the Waters: America in the King Years 1954–63*. New York: Simon & Schuster, 1988.

BRAUER, CARL M. *John F. Kennedy and the Second Reconstruction*. New York: Columbia University Press, 1977.

BRODER, DAVID. *The Party's Over: The Failure of Politics in America*. New York: Harper & Row, 1972.

BURNER, DAVID, ROBERT D. MARCUS AND THOMAS R. WEST. *A Giant's Strength: America in the 1960s*. New York: Holt, Rinehart and Winston, 1971.

BURNS, JAMES M. *John Kennedy: A Political Profile*. New York: Harcourt, Brace & World, 1961.

———. *The Deadlock of Democracy*. Englewood Cliffs, NJ: Prentice-Hall, 1963.

CALDWELL, LYNTON. *Environment: A Challenge for Modern Society*. Garden City, NY: Natural History Press, 1970.

CARO, ROBERT A. *The Years of Lyndon Johnson: The Path to Power*. New York: Knopf, 1982.

CHAFE, WILLIAM H. *The American Woman: Her Changing Social, Economic, and Political roles, 1920–1970*. London, New York: Oxford University Press, 1972/1974.

———. *The Paradox of Change: American Women in the 20th Century*. New York: Oxford University Press, 1991.

———. *Never Stop Running: Allard Lowenstein and the Struggle to Save American Liberalism*. New York: Basic Books, 1993.

COCHRAN, THOMAS B., WILLIAM M. ARKIN, AND MILTON M. HOENIG. *Nuclear Weapons Databook*. Cambridge, MA: Ballinger, 1984/1989.

CRAWFORD, ALAN. *Thunder on the Right: The "New Right" and the Politics of Resentment*. New York: Pantheon, 1980.

DALLEK, ROBERT. *Lone Star Rising: Lyndon Johnson and His Times, 1908–1960*. New York: Oxford University Press, 1991.

DASMANN, RAYMOND F. *A Different Kind of Country.* New York: Macmillan, 1968.

DE BENEDETTI, CHARLES. *An American Ordeal: The Antiwar Movement of the Vietnam Era.* Syracuse, New York: Syracuse University Press, 1990.

DICKSTEIN, MORRIS. *Gates of Eden: American Culture in the Sixties.* New York: Penguin Books, 1989.

DIVINE, ROBERT A., ed. *Exploring the Johnson Years.* Austin: University of Texas Press, 1981.

DRUCKER, PETER F. *The Age of Discontinuity: Guidelines to Our Changing Society.* London: Heinemann, 1969.

DUBERMAN, MARTIN. *Stonewall.* New York: Dutton, 1993.

DUGGER, RONNIE. *The Politician, The Life and Times of Lyndon Johnson: The Drive for Power, from Frontier to Master of the Senate.* New York: Norton, 1982.

DYE, LEE. *Blowout at Platform A: The Crisis That Awakened a Nation.* Garden City, NY: Doubleday, 1971.

EHRLICH, PAUL. *The Population Bomb.* New York: Ballantine, 1968.

EVANS, SARA. *Personal Politics: The Roots of Women's Liberation in the Civil Rights Movement and the New Left.* New York: Knopf, 1979.

FAIRCLOUGH, ADAM. *"To Redeem the Soul of America": The Southern Christian Leadership Conference and Martin Luther King, Jr.* Athens: University of Georgia Press, 1987.

FLADER, SUSAN L. *Thinking Like a Mountain: Aldo Leopold and the Evolution of an Ecological Attitude toward Deer, Wolves and Forests.* Lincoln: University of Nebraska Press, 1974/1978.

FLEMING, DONALD. "Roots of the New Conservation Movement." *Perspectives in American History,* 6, 1972.

FOX, STEPHEN R. *The American Conservation Movement: John Muir and His Legacy.* Madison: University of Wisconsin Press, 1985.

FREEMAN, JO. *The Politics of Women's Liberation: A Case Study of an Emerging Social Movement and Its Relation to the Policy Process.* New York: McKay, 1975.

GARROW, DAVID J. *Bearing the Cross: Martin Luther King, Jr., and the Southern Christian Leadership Conference.* New York: William Morrow, 1986.

GIGLIO, JAMES N. *The Presidency of John F. Kennedy.* Lawrence, KA: University Press of Kansas, 1991.

GITLIN, TODD. 1987. *The Sixties: Years of Hope, Days of Rage.* Toronto/New York: Bantam Books, 1987.

GOLDMAN, ERIC F. *The Tragedy of Lyndon Johnson.* New York: Knopf, 1969.

GOODWIN, DORIS KEARNS. *Lyndon Johnson and the American Dream.* New York: Harper & Row, 1976.

GRAHAM, FRANK, JR. *Since Silent Spring.* Boston: Houghton-Mifflin, 1970.

GRAHAM, HUGH D., AND TED R. GURR, eds. *The History of Violence in America: Historical and Comparative Perspectives.* New York: Praeger, 1969.

————. *Civil Rights and the Presidency.* New York: Oxford University Press, 1992.

GUTIÉRREZ, DAVID. *Walls and Mirrors: Mexican Americans, Mexican Immigrants, and the Politics of Ethnicity.* Berkeley: University of California Press, 1995.

HALBERSTAM, DAVID. *The Best and the Brightest.* New York: Random House, 1972.

HARDIN, GARRETT. "The Tragedy of the Commons," *Science, December 1968.*

HARRINGTON, MICHAEL. *The Other America: Poverty in the United States.* New York: Macmillan, 1962.

HARRIS, DAVID. *Dreams Die Hard.* New York: St. Martin's, 1982.

HARRISON, CYNTHIA. *An Account of Sex: The Politics of Women's Issues, 1945–1968.* Berkeley: University of California Press, 1988.

HEATH, JIM F. *John F. Kennedy and the Business Community.* Chicago: University of Chicago Press, 1969.

HEILBRONER, ROBERT L. *An Inquiry into the Human Prospect: With "Second Thoughts" and "What Has Posterity Ever Done for Me?"* New York: Norton, 1975.

HERRING, GEORGE C. *America's Longest War: The United States and Vietnam, 1950–1975.* New York: Wiley, 1979.

HOWARD, GERALD, ed. *The Sixties.* New York: Washington Square Press, 1982.

HURT, HENRY. *Reasonable Doubt: An Investigation into the Assassination of John F. Kennedy.* New York: Holt, Rinehart and Winston, 1985–1986.

ISSERMAN, MAURICE. *If I Had a Hammer: The Death of the Old Left and the Birth of the New Left.* New York: Basic Books, 1987.

JACOBS, PAUL, AND SAUL LANDAU, eds. *The New Radicals: A Report with Documents.* New York: Random House, 1966.

JOHNSON, LYNDON B. *The Vantage Point: Perspectives of the Presidency, 1963–69.* New York: Holt, Rinehart and Winston, 1971.

KARNOW, STANLEY. *Vietnam: A History.* New York: Viking, 1991.

KELLEY, ROBERT. *The Shaping of the American Past.* Englewood Cliffs, NJ: Prentice-Hall, 1990.

KENISTON, KENNETH. *Young Radicals: Notes on Committed Youth.* New York: Harcourt, Brace & World, 1968.

KING, MARTIN LUTHER, JR. *Why We Can't Wait.* New York: Harper & Row, 1964.

KING, MARY. *Freedom Song: A Personal Story of the 1960s Civil Rights Movement.* New York: William Morrow, 1987.

KOLKO, GABRIEL. *Anatomy of a War: Vietnam, the United States, and the Modern Historical Experience.* New York: Pantheon Books, 1985.

LEMANN, NICHOLAS. *The Promised Land: The Great Back Migration and How It Changed America.* New York: Knopf, 1991.

LeMAY, MICHAEL C. *From Open Door to Dutch Door: An Analysis of U.S. Immigration Policy since 1920.* New York: Praeger, 1987.

LEOPOLD, ALDO. *A Sand County Almanac, and Sketches Here and There.* New York: Oxford University Press, 1949.

LEVY, DAVID W. *The Debate over Vietnam.* Baltimore: Johns Hopkins University Press, 1991.

LEWY, GUENTER. *America in Vietnam.* New York: Oxford University Press, 1978.

LIPSET, SEYMOUR M., AND SHELDON S. WOLIN, eds. *The Berkeley Student Revolt: Facts and Interpretations.* Garden City, NY: Anchor Books, 1965.

LIROFF, RICHARD A. *A National Policy for the Environment: NEPA and Its Aftermath.* Bloomington: Indiana University Press, 1976.

MAGNET, MYRON. *The Dream and the Nightmare: The Sixties Legacy to the Underclass.* New York: William Morrow, 1993.

MATUSOW, ALLEN J. *The Unraveling of America: A History of Liberalism in the 1960s.* New York: Harper & Row, 1984.

McLAUGHLIN, LORETTA. *The Pill, John Rock and the Church: The Biography of a Revolution.* Boston: Little, Brown, 1982.

MEIER, MATT S., AND FELICIANO RIVERA. *The Chicanos: A History of Mexican Americans.* New York: Hill & Wang, 1972.

MILLER, JAMES. *"Democracy in the Streets": From Port Huron to the Siege of Chicago.* New York: Simon & Schuster, 1987.

MILLER, TIMOTHY. *The Hippies and American Values.* Knoxville: University of Tennessee Press, 1991.

MILLETT, KATE. *Sexual Politics.* Garden City, NY: Doubleday, 1970.

MORGAN, ROBIN, ed. *Sisterhood is Powerful: An Anthology of Writings from the Women's Liberation Movement.* New York: Random House, 1970.

MORRIS, ROGER. *Richard Milhous Nixon: The Rise of an American Politician*. New York: Holt, Rinehart and Winston, 1990.

MUSE, BENJAMIN. *The American Negro Revolution: From Nonviolence to Black Power, 1963–1967*. Bloomington: Indiana University Press, 1968.

OATES, STEPHEN B. *Let the Trumpet Sound: The Life of Martin Luther King, Jr*. New York: Harper & Row, 1982.

O'NEIL, WILLIAM L. *Coming Apart: An Informal History of America in the 1960's*. Chicago: Quadrangle Books, 1971.

O'REILLY, KENNETH. *Racial Matters: The FBK's Secret File on Black America, 1960–1972*. New York: The Free Press, 1989.

OSBORNE, JOHN. *The Nixon Watch*. New York: Liveright, 1970.

PARMET, HERBERT S. *J.F.K.—The Presidency of John F. Kennedy*. New York: Dial Press, 1983.

PASSELL, PETER, AND LEONARD ROSS. *The Retreat from Riches: Affluence and Its Enemies*. New York: Viking, 1973.

POSNER, GERALD. *Case Closed: Lee Harvey Oswald and the Assassination of JFK*. New York: Random House, 1993.

REEVES, RICHARD. *President Kennedy: Profile of Power*. New York: Simon & Schuster, 1993.

REEVES, THOMAS C. *A Question of Character: A Life of John F. Kennedy*. New York: Free Press, 1991.

REICH, CHARLES. *The Greening of America: How the Youth Revolution Is Trying to Make America Livable*. New York: Random House, 1970.

ROSZAK, THEODORE. *The Making of a Counter Culture: Reflections on the Technocratic Society and Its Youthful Opposition*. Garden City, NY: Doubleday, 1969.

RUPP, LEILA, AND VERTA TAYLOR. *Survival in the Doldrums: The American Women's Rights Movement, 1945 to the 1960s*. New York: Oxford University Press, 1987.

SCHLESINGER, ARTHUR M., JR. *A Thousand Days: John F. Kennedy in the White House*. Boston: Houghton Mifflin, 1965.

———. *Robert F. Kennedy and His Times*. Boston: Houghton Mifflin, 1978.

SILBERMAN, CHARLES E. *Crisis in Black and White*. New York: Random House, 1964.

SILVER, JAMES W. *Mississippi: The Closed Society*. New York: Harcourt, Brace & World, 1964.

SORENSEN, THEODORE C. *Kennedy*. New York: Harper & Row, 1965.

SPECTOR, RONALD H. *After Tet: The Bloodiest Year in Vietnam*. New York: The Free Press, 1993.

SUMMERS, HARRY G. *On Strategy: A Critical Analysis of the Vietnam War*. Novato, CA: Presidio Press, 1982.

THEOHARIS, ATHAN G., AND JOHN STUART COX. *The Boss: J. Edgar Hoover and the American Inquisition*. Philadelphia: Temple University Press, 1988.

UNGER, IRWIN. *The Movement: The American New Left, 1959–1972*. Lanham, MD: University Press of America, 1974/1988.

WHITE, THEODORE H. *The Making of the President, 1960*. New York: Atheneum, 1961.

———. *The Making of the President, 1964*. New York: Atheneum, 1965.

———. *The Making of the President, 1968*. New York: Atheneum, 1969.

X, MALCOLM (WITH ALEX HALEY). *The Autobiography of Malcolm X*. New York: Grove Press, 1965.

YOUNG, MARILYN B. *The Vietnam Wars, 1945–1990*. New York: Harper Collins, 1991.

PART FOUR

1969–1978

A French riddle for children illustrates another aspect of exponential growth—the apparent suddenness with which it approaches a fixed limit. Suppose you own a pond on which a water lily is growing. The lily plant doubles in size each day. If the lily were allowed to grow unchecked, it would completely cover the pond in 30 days, choking off the other forms of life in the water. For a long time the lily plant seems small, and so you decide not to worry about cutting it back until it covers half the pond. On what day will that be? On the twenty-ninth day, of course. You have one day to save your pond.

—DONELLA L. MEADOWS et al, *The Limits to Growth: A Report for the Club of Rome's Project on the Predicament of Mankind*, (New York: Universe Books, 1972) p. 29.

CHAPTER 7

Pendulum (Mostly) Right— The Resurrection of Richard Nixon

THE EVE OF THE NIXON PRESIDENCY

Richard M. Nixon was to have a longer and more dramatic role in American life than anyone suspected when he defeated liberal Congressman Jerry Voorhis in 1946 to begin his public career. A California Senator and then Vice President, Nixon's defeats in the 1960 presidential race and again in a contest for governor of California in 1962 appeared to have ended a long career on the government payroll. "You won't have Nixon to kick around anymore," he bitterly told reporters after that defeat, "because, gentlemen, this is my last press conference." But Nixon's critics, always numerous and vocal, underestimated his tenacity and ambition, and the Democrats' disarray in 1968 gave him the presidency at last.

His years in the White House would surprise both friends and enemies. Opponents of liberalism expected Nixon to fulfill campaign promises to take a hard line on crime, curb government activism on civil rights, cut federal spending and taxes, and turn a skeptical eye on the war on poverty. Liberals glumly expected the same. Nixon had talked much in the campaign about "bringing Americans together again," which could be heard as a promise somehow to remove the war in Vietnam from American debate, but whether by "victory" or disengagement no one could tell.

As president Richard Nixon was more opportunistic and unpredictable than either friends or enemies anticipated. His guide had never been and would not be doctrine or ideology, but a pragmatic assessment of how to construct an electoral majority to keep him in office. His political base urgently needed broadening, in view of the scant 43 percent of the vote he had secured in 1968. An aide to Nixon's campaign, Kevin Phillips, had circulated the draft of a manuscript that would become *The Emergence of a Republican Majority* (1969), arguing that the mistakes of liberal Democrats in the 1960s now allowed Republicans to put together a new majority by attracting formerly Democratic white southerners and members of the Catholic working class, suburbanites in the Sunbelt and average middle-class Americans. These former Democrats could be split off from the New Deal coalition by reminders of their party's "softness" on crime, excessive spending, sponsorship of busing, and general drift away from mainstream values. Nixon's years in the White House are better understood in the light of this strategic ambition to combine his party's conservative minority with disaffected Democrats in order to bring reelection in 1972 than by reference to any ideology.

The issues facing the winner of the 1968 election were expected to be: How to conclude the war in Vietnam? How to restore order in the inner cities and campuses? What more could be done about racial disparities? Beneath such immediate concerns, profound changes were thrusting a new set of global issues onto the agenda.

EVOLUTION OF THE PROBLEMATIQUE: THE POPULATION DIMENSION

"Demography is destiny," some pundit has said, reminding us that population trends are indeed basic forces shaping human history. Global and American population trends were changing radically, but in different directions.

As the 1970s began, the world's human population was estimated at a historic high of 3.8 billion people, and would reach 4 billion at 7:30 in the evening on March 21, 1976 (the Population Reference Bureau's estimate was admittedly only a guess). Seventy million people were added yearly, when deaths were subtracted from births. The global population growth rate was estimated at 1.9 percent—yielding a doubling time of thirty-seven years. Of course, not all nations were growing at the same rate. Six European nations had achieved stable population size, or zero population growth. But in the developing world there were surging populations: India and China each added upwards of 10 million more births than deaths annually, nearly one third of the global total. Nicaragua had a staggering birth rate of forty-seven births per thousand, Algeria counted forty-eight, Ethiopia forty-nine—while the United States recorded a birth rate of fifteen in 1970. The planetary population of humans was exploding toward totals estimated from 8 to 12 billion before death rates and birth rates would equalize, some time in the twenty-first century.

U.S. Population Trends

In contrast to global trends, demographic behavior in the United States began to run strongly in the opposite direction. The Baby Boom subsided in 1964, when annual births again dropped below 4 million babies a year, and domestic fertility rates declined sharply. The peak postwar TFR (children per completed family) of 3.3 reached in 1959 had dropped to a historic low of 1.86 by 1971, and would remain below replacement level (2.1) through the decade.

There were many reasons for the rapid decline in domestic births: broader social knowledge of birth control methods, especially after the introduction of "the Pill" in 1960; a desire for smaller families among females who were responding to expanded occupational opportunities; and abortion. Since a large number of pregnancies (most estimates ran from one third to one half) were unwanted, abortions, estimated at 1.5 million by the end of the 1970s pushed the birth rate even lower.

These trends reflected rapidly changing attitudes toward family size. The earlier enthusiasm for large families gave way to a preference for "the two-child family." *Life* magazine, which in the 1950s had welcomed the Baby Boom as "good for the economy," ran a story in the early 1970s entitled "Squeezing into the 1970s," stressing the dangers of overcrowding. Even *Parents* magazine ran articles such as "Overpopulation: Crisis Today, Disaster Tomorrow" and "Smaller Families: A National Imperative." Paul Ehrlich was interviewed in large-circulation magazines such as *Mademoiselle* and *Playboy,* and his warnings about the costs of overpopulation appeared in widely read journals such as *Field and Stream* and *McCall's.* Bringing the meaning of crowding home to the vacationing public, officials in Sequoia and Kings Canyon National Parks in California, noting an increase in annual visitors from 8000 in 1962 to 44,000 in 1971, installed a permit system for the following year that would limit the number of visitors in light of ecological considerations.

Whatever the causes of the rapid decline in the American fertility rate, its immediate effects were widely reported and also misinterpreted. The popular press erroneously told the public that America had instantly reached "zero population growth" because of reported fertility rates dropping below ultimate replacement level. But America was far from reaching zero population growth. Even if fertility rates remained below replacement level, the American population would continue to grow for years because of the larger number of women who had yet to pass through their child-bearing years—creating "demographic momentum." The population increase between 1970 and 1980 was the second highest on record, adding 23.92 million people. The increase from 1950 to 1980 was 76.5 million, more than the entire population of the nation in 1900.

Migration and Immigration

There was much internal migration, as always, as Americans continued the 20th Century move to the Sunbelt. The south gained 3433 people a day across the decade, the west 2280, the northeast gained 21 people a day, the north-central region 620. Florida's human population was swollen by an astonishing 43.4 percent, and Texas added 2 million to become the third most densely populated state.

But internal migration trends would not prove the leading demographic force in the 1970s and beyond. While it appeared to casual observers that U.S. domestic fertility rates placed the nation on a path toward population stabi-

In 1980, the hypothetical center of population
moved across the Mississippi River for the first
time, reflecting a long-term shift of population
to the west.
(U.S. Bureau of the Census)

lization, the global population explosion began to transform American life at
home. The immigration law of 1965 both widened the gates and radically
altered the system of selection and thus the source countries of legal immigration. This reform of U.S. immigration policy came just at the moment in history when an unprecedented population explosion churned in the underdeveloped world and as improvements in communication began to convey TV
and movie visions of wealthy America to cities and villages on all continents.
The result was a steadily growing flow of legal immigrants, rising from
approximately 400,000 in the mid-1960s 650,000 by 1978 and to 819,000 by 1980.
Much of the increase came from the admission of large numbers of refugees
from Vietnam and Cambodia, Russia, Cuba, and Haiti. The largest single
nationality group came from Mexico. The pressure behind this rising tide of
immigration came from explosive population growth in poor societies with faltering economies, intensified by displacement of rural people by mechanized
agriculture. In Mexico alone, the unemployment rate was estimated to be as
high as 50 percent, and the population growth rate was so high that in 1980 the
population was projected to double from 70 to 140 million in just 23 years. Pull
factors were also potent in explaining the great surge of immigration which
began to be felt in the late 1960s: the lure of jobs at high (by contrast with what
was available at home) wages plus welfare benefits in a society whose laws did
not make it a crime to either accept or offer work to people in the country illegally, and where there were no penalties upon arrest for illegal entry but a bus
ride back to Mexico.

Thus illegal immigration expanded along with legal admissions, increasing the total numbers and augmenting U.S. population growth. Most illegal
entry came along the 2200-mile southern border with Mexico, the world's
longest border between a First and a Third World country, though a survey of
data from the nation's airports found that thousands more foreigners were
arriving than returning annually. The Border Patrol at the Mexican border was
by the mid-1970s reporting 1 million arrests of illegal aliens per year, and conceded that most entries went undetected. Estimates of the size of the illegal

alien population varied enormously, from 300,000 to 800,000 a year, and there was even more controversy about their economic and social impacts. Employers in agriculture and some urban low-wage industries argued that a fresh supply of labor was economically desirable, ignoring evidence of some job displacement and wage depression among American workers as a result of competition with illegals, impacts felt mostly among America's minorities and less educated whites. In the 1970s evidence was too scanty to determine whether illegal aliens, and refugees, cost more in social services than they paid in taxes.

By the end of the 1970s the volume of immigration to the United States, legal and illegal, was larger than at any time in American history (though not so large a proportion of total population as in the years before World War I). Immigration was contributing up to an estimated 30 to 40 percent of total U.S. population growth by the end of the 1970s, and the Population Reference Bureau projected that, at current birth and death rates, 1 million net immigrants a year would mean that the nation's population would not stabilize at 267 million in the year 2030, but instead would reach 370 million and still be rising.

This major new force in American life did not become a large public issue in the 1970s, though a small public-interest organization (FAIR, the Federation for American Immigration Reform) was founded in 1978 to begin lobbying for restriction, and an occasional voice was heard to predict that the issue must be faced: "The United States has lost one of the cardinal attributes of sovereignty," wrote journalist Theodore White. "It no longer controls its own borders. . . . The impending transformation of the Nation, its culture, and its ethnic heritage could become one of the central debates of the politics of the 1980s."

RESOURCES

The Global Picture

For most of human history the most limiting resource has been food, and it seemed in the years following World War II that humanity might at last be winning the race against hunger. World agricultural output climbed steadily upward through the 1960s, propelled by applied agricultural research, substitution of gasoline-powered machinery for human labor, and expanded use of petroleum-based fertilizers. There was also a vast expansion of agriculture onto formerly untilled prime lands, as virgin forests in the northern hemisphere and tropical rain forests near the Equator gave way to the bulldozers and axes of humans in search of tillable soil. The world fish catch mounted over the same years, as highly mechanized fleets combed the seas with formerly undreamed-of efficiency.

But limits were encountered in the early 1970s. Over the winter of 1972–1973 the world price of oil quadrupled in response to an embargo by the OPEC nations. Serious droughts in the U.S.S.R., India, Latin America, and elsewhere reduced grain harvests and led to soaring food prices and famine. The world

There is a question in the air, more sensed than seen, like the invisible approach of a distant storm. . . . "Is there hope for man?"

. . . the more immediate cause of our new-found concern . . . is the stunning discovery that economic growth carries previously unsuspected side effects whose cumulative impact may be more deleterious than the undoubted benefits that growth also brings. In the last few years we have become apprised of these side effects in a visible decline in the quality of the air and water, in a series of man-made disasters and ecological imbalance, in a mounting general alarm as to the environmental collapse that unrestricted growth could inflict. . . .

I believe the long-term solution requires nothing less than the gradual abandonment of the lethal techniques, the uncongenial lifeways, and the dangerous mentality of industrial civilization itself.

. . . If then, by the question "Is there hope for man?" we ask whether it is possible to meet the challenges of the future without the payment of a fearful price, the answer must be: No, there is no such hope.

Robert L. Heilbroner, "Initial Reflections on the Human Prospect".
Source: Robert L. Heilbroner, "Initial Reflections on the Human Prospect," from An Inquiry into the Human Prospect *(New York: W.W. Norton, 1975), pp. 13–137.*

production of mutton peaked in 1972, and the warming of waters off Peru's coast cut the anchovy catch from 12.5 to 2 million metric tons by mid-decade.

The conjunction of these trends provoked predictions of worldwide famine ahead, as in William and Paul Paddock's *Famine 1975*, predictions which underestimated the ability of world markets and especially U.S. agriculture to continue to increase grain supplies and limit, if not eliminate, pockets of starvation in Africa and the Indian subcontinent. But the anticipation of a looming world crisis larger than food shortages, arising out of population pressures on worldwide ecosystems, came in the form of widely read books such as Robert Heilbroner's quaintly titled but entirely gloomy *An Inquiry into the Human Prospect* (1975). The American economist saw the "problematique" worsening until the industrialized world would sink along with the Third World into convulsive and losing struggles with resource shortages and strangling pollution. Military-socialist governments would arise everywhere, he foresaw, to provide authoritarian discipline. There would be interminable wars, terrorism, and crowded misery.

Even more widely noted and debated was *Limits to Growth* (1973), written by U.S. scientists Donella and Dennis Meadows and sponsored by the Club of Rome. Translated into twenty-six languages and much discussed in the United States, *Limits to Growth* used a computerized model to forecast that exponentially increasingly population growth would within the next century bring humanity to a tragic global encounter with famine, pollution, and social disintegration. Critics cast doubt on the book's simplistic computer model, and pointed out that its projections omitted the possibility of corrective actions that societies might take. Of course, the purpose of the book was to stimulate such corrective actions, though it said little about what they should be.

Trends in the United States

As we have seen, the possibility that shortages of natural resources might become a serious problem for the growing postwar American economy had been given brief attention when the Paley Commission of 1952 came to optimistic conclusions. In a modern economy, human inventiveness backed by science and technology was seen as the core resource. A shortage of this or that mineral ore could be remedied by importation Foreign sources supplied 98 percent of chromium, 81 percent of tin. Or substitutes could be invented in America's corporation or university laboratories.

Thus resource shortages were typically seen as temporary, problems that our system was designed to solve. Concerning resources for which there could be no substitute, such as clean water, the remedy was also importation—to move the water from surplus to shortage areas. This had long been the solution to the expanding water needs of the burgeoning cities and the agricultural sectors of the arid and semiarid west. Twenty-five million acres of land were brought under cultivation with irrigation water in the years 1950–1975, a tripling of the nation's irrigated farmland, most of it in the west. The source of the water was a 50 percent larger draw upon distant rivers, but a 160 percent increase in groundwater pumping from aquifers whose rate of replenishment was poorly understood.

Another resource for which there seemed no substitute, either by importation from abroad or from the labs, was the American topsoil itself. In the 1930s, with black storms sweeping out of the Great Plains Dust Bowl, there had been widespread concern about soil erosion, but that problem was allegedly corrected by the New Deal's soil conservation activities and by the return of normal rainfall in the Great Plains. When on the morning of February 23, 1977, high winds whipped tons of topsoil from the western edge of the Great Plains and in forty-eight hours a huge dust storm darkened 280,000 square miles and reached the Atlantic Ocean, it seemed that part of the Great Plains had a soil erosion problem again. But the problem was more widespread, for it was a by-product of our most basic industry, agriculture.

Even when farmers cooperated with the government's limited efforts to conserve soil, American agriculture stripped away native cover and exposed soil to water and wind erosion. Estimating topsoil losses had a low priority in the Department of Agriculture, and incomplete data indicating serious annual losses were ignored by policy makers. From World War II through the 1960s the trend had been toward overall reduction of crop acreage. From 1950 to 1972, American farmers eased the pressure on the land by removing 50 million acres from cultivation, while still raising their yields 149 percent through improved seed, mechanization, and increased doses of fertilizer, pesticides, and herbicides.

Then came a dramatic turnaround. A combination of drought, crop failures, and population growth abroad created burgeoning world demand for U.S. food supplies. "We should not ship our soil fertility to other nations," Franklin Roosevelt had once said, but that is exactly what the United States did in the 1970s, on a scale never before matched. Agricultural exports boomed, especially of grains and fibers, and the U.S. farm sector became so closely tied to world markets that 30 percent of American cropland was being used for export crops. Farmers, urged by Secretary of Agriculture Earl Butz to "plant fencerow to fencerow," rapidly expanded acreage under the plow.

One result was profits for farmers and an export surplus; another was accelerated erosion. A 1977 government study estimated that an average 4.7 tons of topsoil per acre was lost annually from farmland. Some states were especially damaged, Tennessee losing 14.1 tons per acre, Missouri 10.9. For the nation, 2.8 billion tons of soil were washed or blown off croplands every year, losses 25 percent larger than in 1934, the worst year of the Dust Bowl. And prime farmland was also lost to agricultural uses through urban sprawl; potential or actual cropland was converted to freeways, subdivisions, shopping centers, power lines, and reservoirs, as humanity's habitat encroached upon the land. As the 1970s closed, the National Agricultural Lands Study estimated that potential cropland was down to only 127 million acres, and the rate of conversion of rural lands was 3 percent a year. As one writer put it, "Every hour, with 200 new Americans to feed, the U.S. loses 220 acres of food-growing farmlands to townhouses, shopping centers and coal mines. And every day, 26 square miles of U.S. topsoil wash and blow away from the farmland that is left." A growing society had glimpsed another set of limits, now the soil itself, basic resource of civilizations.

Water, nonfuel mineral, even soil shortages were a slow form of crisis gaining little public attention. Human ingenuity, after all, might somehow steer around them. But one resource long taken for granted forced itself quickly to the front of the public's mind in the 1970s: energy supplies.

Energy was still a word virtually synonymous with fossil fuels, for hydroelectric and nuclear plants generated only 4 percent of U.S. overall energy supplies. Oil (50 percent) and gas (25 percent) were three quarters of all supplies, a relatively stable proportion which concealed a dramatic if slowly moving and mostly unnoticed change. A shift of the long-term trends in domestic demand (always upward) and supply (the United States importing more oil than it exported after 1948, becoming 19 percent dependent on foreign supplies in 1970, 47 percent dependent as the decade ended) had brought the United States to a point of unprecedented vulnerability. We had built the good life around cheap and abundant petroleum. It powered our fleet of automobiles—growing by 8 million a year—heated our homes, factories, and swimming pools; generated electricity to run our hair driers, electric knives, and air conditioners; propelled the forty-seven scheduled air carriers, which carried 169 million passengers 131 billion miles in 1970. Oil was the raw material out of which our plastics and textiles, even our fertilizers, were made. Yet foreigners increasingly supplied the oil. As the 1970s arrived there seemed little reason to worry about access to foreign petroleum supplies. Experts did not agree on petroleum reserves, but earlier estimates had been wildly erratic and usually too low. Most experts guessed that world reserves of oil amounted to 650 billion barrels of proven reserves, with another 200 billion probably recoverable. But they were forced to guess: "It is conceivable that the lowest estimate is too high and that the highest estimate is too low," said one geologist in 1975. To this physicist Albert Bartlett replied that the crucial question was not supplies but rate of use. If each human on earth consumed oil as the average American did, proven reserves would be exhausted in five years and recoverable reserves in thirteen. Did this make one yearn for larger supplies? Even if the entire earth were made of oil, if humans continued to consume it at the rate of growth in demand equal to that of 1970 (7 percent), it would all be gone in 342 years!

This simple arithmetic conveyed the fundamental lesson about growth: that it could not go on forever, and the rate of growth set the limit. Making middle-range assumptions about reserves and consumption, the world might run out of oil around the year 2020, exhausting all deposits that were economically feasible to tap. Geologist M. King Hubbert, one of the earliest to call attention to the likelihood of early depletion of petroleum, commented in 1981: "Children born in the 1930s will see the U.S. consume most of its oil and gas during their lifetimes." The human race was coming to the end of the petroleum era, with the American foot heaviest on the accelerator.

Optimists were not convinced. Maybe the estimates were too low—again. And behind petroleum there was coal, the other and more abundant fossil fuel. The United States was, as some put it, "the Persian Gulf of coal," with rich deposits that might last 500 years. Yet there were mounting problems with this energy source. Most of this fuel was strip-mined (two thirds of U.S. coal was surface-mined), with either grotesque defacement and environmental damage, or extremely high costs for reclamation techniques that were not of proven effectiveness. And coal burning generated pollutants which combined in the atmosphere to produce sulfur and nitrogen dioxides. These precipitated out miles downwind as "acid rain" (or "acid deposition," since some came down as snow or dry particles), damaging aquatic life in lakes and ponds, forests and vegetation to a degree unknown. The decade of the 1970s saw the "acid rain problem" move from obscure academic journals to the news headlines, from latent to manifest. Three short paragraphs in the Council on Environmental Quality's annual report in 1979 testified to the emergence of a related problem, far larger than acid rain: "the possibility of global climate change induced by an increase of carbon dioxide in the atmosphere," a global warming or "greenhouse" effect which might raise ocean levels and cause vast disruptions in agriculture and natural habitats.

In view of such problems, energy discussions turned naturally to the promise of a "clean" energy source—nuclear power. Encouraged by government subsidies and friendly regulation, the nuclear power industry was optimistic to the point of euphoria through the 1960s, and by 1975 there were sixty active reactors on line in the United States and 146 more under construction. Utilities planned 1200 more reactors by the year 2000. But the picture became less rosy as the decade advanced. Nuclear power generation encountered a variety of unanticipated problems which clouded its future. The basic light-water reactor was prone to malfunction, and proved much more costly to put on line and keep in operation than had been expected. The problem of spent fuel disposal was mostly ignored, but suggestions of disposal at selected underground sites invariably met fierce citizen resistance in the places selected. The other nuclear energy technology, fusion (as contrasted with fission) power, remained in the research stage, posing environmental, safety, economic, and engineering problems which frustrated its development. Yet hopes ran high for the "breeder reactor" idea, and early in the 1970s government funds were committed to a prototype reactor to be built on the Clinch River in Tennessee—another troop of the "technological cavalry" Americans hoped would ride over the hill, just in time.

Given the difficulties facing fossil and nuclear fuels, much attention turned in the 1970s to the basic energy source—the sun. Solar power could not be depleted in any time frame that should worry humanity, and it gained many advocates as the only clean, nonpolluting source of energy. But solar technology was not far advanced, since governments and large corporations had not subsidized much research in the area. Costs were high for the few home-heating and electricity-generating technologies, and parts of the nation were not well supplied with abundant sunshine. Other renewable energy sources, such as biomass and geothermal systems, were equally remote from major use. A new generation of energy specialists, such as Amory Lovins, David Freeman, and Daniel Yergin, pointed out that unprecedented energy conservation measures could and must be the substitute for sources of "new" energy until solar technologies were perfected, but this was an unwelcomed message of government restrictions and higher energy prices.

THE ENVIRONMENT

The main themes of the far-flung celebrations of Earth Day, 1970, when the environmental awakening of the 1960s came together, were the need to preserve wilderness and natural areas, to recycle garbage, and to conserve energy. The political power of environmental activists had become strong enough to produce the Wilderness Act and NEPA's requirement for environmental impact reports (EIRs) before major federal projects were undertaken. The environmentalist impulse was oriented primarily toward hopes of somehow restraining water and air pollution (a Gallup poll after Earth Day showed 53 percent of those polled regarded "reducing pollution of air and water" as the most important public issue, second only to crime), and, in view of what Rachel Carson had taught in *Silent Spring*, outlawing dangerous pesticides. In the 1970s environmental awareness and the environmental movement would travel "an immense mental distance," in the words of the EPA's first administrator, William Ruckelshaus, a voyage of continuous discovery that the crisis in humanity's relationship to habitat was wider and deeper than had been thought.

Pollution, now that the American people seemed concerned about it, presented itself in two categories: things "thrown (or flushed or piped) away" and the valuable commodities (pesticides, fertilizer) deliberately distributed across the landscape as a fundamental part of the working economy. Both aspects of pollution were large, but the effluent or "garbage" problem was more visible.

The most familiar source of water pollution was sewage, human wastes whose careless disposal had long been a problem for towns and cities. This old problem was the most technologically manageable of the many components of waste disposal, but as late as the 1970s the problem was widely neglected. In 1970, 60 million people were on sewage systems that discharged raw fecal matter and whatever else came down the sewer pipe into surface waters. During rainstorms, forty-five sewer outlets spewed untreated sewage into the Potomac River as it passed Washington, D.C., so no one wanted to swim in it in 1975, the year Lyndon Johnson had set as target for cleanup.

But in the industrial era the toilet was not so threatening to water quality as the wastes of agricultural and industrial production. Factories in the 1970s discharged an estimated 2 million tons a year of organic wastes and more than a quarter of a million tons of toxic heavy metals and other toxic chemicals directly into the nation's waterways. Dead and dying waters caught media attention: Pensacola Bay became clogged with miles of dead fish; fishing in Lake Erie virtually ended, with the lake declared near death; beaches were frequently closed because of high coliform counts.

Factories and municipal storm drains and sewage outfalls were "point" sources of pollution; agriculture was the largest source of "nonpoint" pollution of America's waterways, as creeks, rivers, and bays received fertilizers and pesticides washing off from treated fields. Using 50 million pounds of synthetic insecticides in 1950, American farmers lost 7 percent of their crops to insects; thirty years later, using now 500 million pounds or at least ten times as much, the loss to insects was 13 percent—signs of a losing battle for all but the pesticide companies. America's waterways carried away the residues.

Only a part of the pollution of an industrialized economy found its way into the waterways. Solid waste, including household garbage and industrial waste products, was another familiar disposal problem that was rapidly becoming transformed in both scale and chemical toxicity. The nation's total waste load was a staggering and unknown mass of refuse, but municipalities carried most of the volume, estimated at 154 million tons annually by 1978, the equivalent of 1400 pounds per person. This massive stream of garbage was hauled to landfills and buried, burned, or in many coastal communities dumped from barges into the ocean. The Council on Environmental Quality observed that "before the 1970s the question of what to do with a city's waste was hardly ever asked." Few had read ecologist Barry Commoner's "second law of ecology": "Everything must go somewhere."[1]

But the lesson would slowly and painfully be learned, not so much because the space available for municipal landfills was steadily filling up, though this was true, but because much of the waste—56 million metric tons of the total, at the end of the 1970s—was classified as hazardous. Until the 1970s no one knew

[1] In *The Closing Circle* (1971), Commoner defined the four laws of ecology as (1) everything is connected to everything else; (2) everything must go somewhere; (3) nature knows best; (4) there is no such thing as a free lunch.

In the 1970s and 1980s the problem of solid waste—particularly household garbage—gained more attention. In 1989, *U.S. News and World Report* predicted that by the year 2000, Americans will dump 193 million tons of garbage each year—but where? Our landfills are encroaching on our most treasured places. *(Matrix)*

where it went, and early EPA studies estimated that 94,000 landfills and 1,730,000 pits or "lagoons" were receiving most of America's avalanche of toxic waste products, 90 percent of them leaky and virtually unmonitored. Other hazardous wastes were forced deep into the earth by injection wells estimated at 400,000 in number, with 5000 new wells drilled each year, without regulation.

Hazardous wastes rarely stayed "out of sight, out of mind" in these sites. A fire brought a stew of toxic chemicals into view in 1978, when a disposal site in Chester, Pennsylvania, broke into flames; toxic fumes injured forty-five firemen and forced the closing of a bridge over the Delaware River. Other toxic waste fires or leakage into community drinking water supplies were reported in New Jersey, Arkansas, Michigan, and elsewhere. But the biggest hazardous waste story of the 1970s was less dramatic than a fire. Since 75 percent of the thousands of hazardous waste dumps, active and inactive, leaked into the ground and nearby groundwater, it was only a matter of time before human illness would remind Americans that using the environment as a sink was a temporary, even deadly solution. The Hooker Chemical Company's Love Canal disposal site, near Niagara Falls, New York, received 21,000 tons of wastes between

1942 and 1952, when the site was sealed, sold, and houses along with a school were built above it. Black liquids oozed to the surface in 1976 after unusually heavy rains, and fumes seeped from cellars. Women in the area suffered 50 percent more miscarriages than would be expected, and alert residents began to document a high incidence of birth defects among children, nervous disorders, rashes, and headaches among adults, along with suspiciously high rates of cancer. More than a thousand households were evacuated, and the homes were purchased by the state. Much scientific controversy still surrounds the illnesses reported by those who lived above the Hooker dump, but the foul seepages of August 1978 made Love Canal a milestone in the public awakening to the problem of toxic wastes.

The culprit at Love Canal, it seemed clear, was a chemical company. Certainly if pollution proved to be the fault of corporations and large farmers, that would have simplified the battle lines. The 1970s were an education in the untenability of this theory. Hospitals and laboratories, associated with social service rather than private profits, produced large amounts of hazardous chemical and radioactive wastes, which usually wound up in municipal dumps. Even the military, defender of the nation, was an unsuspected saboteur. The Department of Defense was stopped only at the last moment from dumping 27,000 tons of "surplus" nerve gas and other chemical weapons in the Atlantic Ocean in May 1979, and the furor revealed that this practice had been habitual for the Navy. While the Navy was deterred by public outcry from that disposal project, it shortly after announced plans to sink old nuclear submarines in a trench off the east coast of North Carolina, continuing a naval tradition of regarding the ocean as a waste sink as well as a transportation surface.

The Department of Defense had no monopoly on the U.S. government's environmental offenses. Environmentalists had known since the 1950s that the Bureau of Reclamation was a wilderness-invading dam builder larger and more dangerous than any corporation, and that the Army Corps of Engineers engaged habitually in damming rivers and draining swamps. Even the TVA, born with a conservationist label, had emerged in the 1960s as the nation's largest purchaser of strip-mined coal and a polluter of southeastern air with fly ash and sulfur dioxide when the coal was burned. The Department of Agriculture, a tenacious defender of pesticide use by farmers, regularly sprayed Forest Service land with pesticides.

Who, then, menaced the environment? Mining, lumber, and chemical corporations? Agribusiness, the nation's huge factory-farms? The government's dam-building, wetlands-draining, pesticide-spraying agencies? All of these, but also, said the comic-strip character Pogo, "We have met the enemy, and it is us"—the guilt was spread, if not evenly, at least widely. The mass of consumers as well as America's producers were engaged in ecosystem damage—the crime of all against all. The life-style of modern Americans was built around consumption on a scale which their grandparents could not have imagined as they leafed through the old Sears-Roebuck catalog. Fuel-thirsty and exhaust-streaming automobiles rolled, 6 to 8 million new ones a year through the 1970s, onto asphalt networks leading almost anywhere one wanted to go, carrying people clothed in synthetic textiles to homes stocked with the artifacts of a chemical age—plastic tools and toys, electric aids to washing and toothbrushing and entertainment, cellophane-wrapped food which was chemically preserved and refrigerated, cola and cat food and bug sprays and cleaning fluids in containers designed to be thrown away in an endless shower of cardboard, metal, plastic, and glass. It was a society that was stupendous in its garbage, beginning to hear the unhappy news that garbage was more than paper and bottles, sewage more than human offal. Invisible at the production end of consumption were industrial and agricultural wastes. Invisible at the other end were municipal solid and liquid waste streams. It was bad enough to learn that fish were dying in Lake Erie and in Adirondack streams, that the very eggshells of seabirds were thinned to breaking by the ingestion of human-made DDT. But the news that raised environmental concern more dramatically was harm to human health, especially in postwar America where health and fitness were more highly valued than in earlier generations less endowed with leisure.

Thus citizen awareness of an environmental crisis, generated in the past by disclosures of humanity's injuries to the redwoods, Sierra valleys, and monumental sites in the west, in the 1970s gained intensity from stories of contaminated water, food supplies, or air taken in by humans and threatening health and longevity.

The core of the threat came from chemicals synthesized or altered by humanity. Industrial economies were chemical economies, caught almost by surprise by the meteoric postwar increase in the production of synthetic organic chemicals. In 1940, 1.3 billion pounds of synthetic organic chemicals were produced in America. The total mounted rapidly, to 49 billion pounds in 1950 to 233 billion pounds in 1970 to 320 billion in 1978. Apart from the chemical wastes and by-products of industrial and agricultural production, the consumer was presented with products containing some 55,000 different human-made chemicals, products which, since "everything must go somewhere," entered the environment by multiple paths—directly ingested, applied to nearby objects, and the residues "thrown away"—paints, cleaners, dyes, preservatives, brake linings, fabrics, drugs, bug-bombs, hypodermic needles. The environment absorbed them, but under mounting stress and distress reached up the food chain to humans. Central to the rising concern was an increase in the incidence of cancer, one major cause of death whose incidence rose throughout the twentieth century, as others—heart disease, influenza and pneumonia, accidents and homicides—fluctuated toward lower levels than in 1900. Dramatically increasing lung cancer rates among males had led to warning labels on cigarette packages (1966) and in advertising (1978), one measure of rising public concern with toxic agents in the immediate environment. Cancer incidence appeared to undergo a spurt upward among both males and females, making a bestseller out of Dr. Samuel Epstein's *The Politics of Cancer* (1978), a book predicting a "new epidemic" of cancer as the new synthetic chemicals produced in the course of postwar development found their way into human stomachs and lungs.

THE NIXON PRESIDENCY: CONSERVATIVE COUNTERREVOLUTION?

Worrisome population and environmental trends were on the far margin of American politics as Richard Nixon entered the White House. To his liberal enemies, especially, he was a known quantity—an anticommunist conservative Republican, friend of the business community, suspicious of activist government, a presidential nominee who chose to run with the even farther-right Spiro Agnew. Liberals expected a conservative, "rollback liberalism" regime.

Early indications confirmed these expectations. Nixon's top-level appointments to the Justice Department, beginning with Attorney General John Mitchell, were men who preferred prosecuting criminals and political radicals to monopolists or civil rights violators. Nixon during his presidency would appoint four justices to the Supreme Court (Warren E. Burger, Henry Blackmun, Lewis Powell, William Rehnquist), all of them selected for their agreement with

President Richard Nixon is shown here with three of his aides, two of whom (Robert Haldeman, left, and John Erlichman, center) were key players in the Watergate scandal that brought down the Nixon presidency and sent Haldeman and Erlichman to prison.
(Bettman)

the view that the Warren Court had usurped judicial power to impose a liberal agenda. He nominated two other judges so conservative that the Senate refused to confirm them.

Nixon also quietly ended Johnson's War on Poverty, phasing out the Office of Economic Opportunity and offering an early verdict on that idea: "We have reaped from these [Great Society] programs an ugly harvest of frustration, violence and failure across the land."

On other leading issues, Nixon took ideologically contradictory positions, and was ultimately an enigma. On civil rights, his cautious, almost issueless 1968 campaign had talked only of "moderation" and rejected the extremes of "forced busing." Once in office, he acted to delay school desegregation, proposed a constitutional amendment to end school busing, and nominated two southern racial conservatives to the Supreme Court to replace Justice Abe Fortas (both nominees were rejected). Yet he formulated voting rights proposals that were thought by civil rights leaders to be constructive if centrist, and he appalled conservatives by sponsoring a "Philadelphia Plan" for racial hiring that would require construction firms bidding on federal contracts to reserve a quota of the jobs to African-Americans.

Liberal Borrowings

This unpredictable pattern reflected Nixon's political instincts, which told him that a public that was conservative on some issues—crime, drugs, the sanctity of the flag, the work ethic, a strong defense—was also devoted to much of the liberal program structure put in place since the Great Depression. He was keenly aware that Eisenhower, recognizing this, had made his peace with social security, farm subsidies, urban infrastructure spending, business regulation. A winning Republican coalition for the 1970s must fashion an appeal that would combine these elements into a centrist majority. Drawing often on the ideas of sociologist Daniel Patrick Moynihan, a Democrat brought on board as White House aide, Nixon kept liberals off-balance by borrowing from their pantry and acting as an innovator. In 1969 Nixon proposed a reform of the welfare system that joined work to a "guaranteed annual income" concept, which offered every participant a basic cash income ($1600) while joining the work force. Nixon's liberal-conservative mix on welfare reform confused all parties and became deadlocked in political wrangling; and the president lost interest.

He surprised his liberal opposition again on the environmental issue. The last year of the 1960s had produced NEPA, sponsored by liberal Democrats who seemed to have seized the environmental issue. But Nixon would not concede environmental leadership, and devoted one third of his 1970 State of the Union address to the need for environmental protection—hoping to move ahead of his expected 1972 presidential rivals, Senators Edmund Muskie (D., Maine) and Henry Jackson (D., Washington). He further surprised environmentalists by signing NEPA in early 1970, then promptly establishing the Environmental Protection Agency (EPA) and the Council on Environmental Quality (CEQ), while tolerating the surprisingly staunch commitment to conservation of his Secretary of the Interior, Walter J. Hickel of Alaska. He signed the Clean Air Act of 1970, the Water Pollution Control Act of 1972, the coastal zone management and pesticide control acts of that year, a law protecting endangered species in 1973. Yet the administration took the lead in drafting none of these laws, and was an unreliable friend of environmental protection. After yielding to enormous pressure to stop construction of a proposed Cross-Florida Barge Canal with devastating predicted impacts on the state's Okefenokee Swamp, Nixon endorsed a plan to slash across several watersheds with a canal from the Tennessee River to the Gulf of Mexico (the Tennessee-Tombigbee Waterway), aggressively (and unsuccessfully) backed government funding for a supersonic transport plane (SST) even though studies indicated that its speed and altitudes would cause both atmospheric and surface ecological harm, and threw his weight at a decisive moment against a national land-use planning system sponsored by Senator Jackson.

NIXON AS PLANNER

Nixon's policy course disconcerted both liberals and conservatives of all types, his supporters seeing innovation where critics saw unprincipled confusion. Both were present, and historians have begun to discern in the Nixon presidency a strong leaning toward planning, surprising in a conservative politician fond of praising the virtues of an unplanned "free-enterprise system." Nixon wrote on the margin of a memo in 1970, "Government doesn't work," reflecting frustration at the government he inherited from LBJ, with its swollen agenda, uncoordinated structure, and inability to look ahead. He proved remarkably receptive to advice from White House aides Moynihan and John Ehrlichman, along with Secretary of the Treasury John Connally, that he pioneer in the necessary reforms to permit a president to anticipate events rather than merely react to them. Though he talked of the need for decentralization of social programs to state and local governments, Nixon centralized power in a streamlined White House staff, with a new Domestic Council for Policy Coordination and a National Goals Research Staff for long-range studies. His 1970 proposals for sweeping reorganization of the executive branch promised to improve the chief executive's ability to coordinate national policy. (Congress, knowing that a fragmented executive branch was easier to control, blocked the plan.) Not since FDR's day had a president shown so much interest in remedying the institutional defects of the presidency and the executive branch, which close observers knew to be serious. The administration appeared to be moving in the direction of "indicative planning" on the French model, a set of techniques for obtaining greater coherence and future-orientation in governmental policy without resorting to the "command and control" planning devices of Soviet-bloc economies.

Nixon called openly for more planning of this sort, and accepted the advice of the creative Moynihan, a former academic from Harvard, to take the lead in two areas requiring the national government's attention even though no large group of voters was demanding it. In his State of the Union Address in January

1970, Nixon endorsed a national system of land-use controls as part of something he called a "National Growth Policy" to clarify and give direction to the choices to be made as the nation continued its expansive growth.

The idea aroused some critics, stunned that a conservative Republican president was promoting a national population distribution policy, to supersede the traditional patchwork of state and local land-use regulations. More alarming, was the administration raising questions about the desirability of "growth" itself? Nixon had touched the edge of a rising controversy, for while basic questions about growth had been avoided in Washington, the desirability of slowing population growth and urban expansion was politically volatile at the state and local levels.

POPULATION POLICY

The "No-Growth Movement" in States and Localities

Several states, led by Iowa in 1972, convened conferences or task forces to project their population and environmental situation in the year 2000, studies which invariably suggested that growth should be slowed and more closely controlled. Only one state, Hawaii, seriously proposed limiting immigration in order to stabilize population, but the governor of Oregon, Tom McCall, delighted most of his state's citizens by asking Californians to visit but not to stay. In the 1970s states began for the first time to enter the field of land-use controls, traditionally left to local governments that wished to exercise them. In what has been called "the Quiet Revolution in the States," the governments of Oregon and Vermont enacted systems which amounted to partial state zoning of land, while California and Florida led the way in establishing state permitting systems for developments with large environmental impacts. By the end of the 1970s more than thirty-five states were engaged in some form of land-use controls of varying degrees of strictness.

Developers were startled to have to deal with state laws and regulations before the bulldozers could be turned loose. More radical changes came in attitudes toward population growth, housing, and commercial development at the community level. Communities as diverse as Petaluma, California, Ramapo, New York, and Boulder, Colorado, enacted ordinances that attempted to restrict housing starts, going beyond traditional zoning to devise sophisticated systems to control land use and limit population growth. Builders and real estate brokers were dumbfounded at this "no-growth" sentiment, since American communities had traditionally welcomed virtually any new building and equated increased size with prestige and achievement. The no-growth movement grew rapidly in the early 1970s, with the Urban Land Institute counting 39 municipalities restricting growth by 1973, 87 by 1974, 138 by 1975. "No growth" was a misnomer, since very few jurisdictions went so far as Boca Raton, Florida, which at one point enacted a numerical cap on population (which was abandoned as unconstitutional). Most communities wished only to slow the pace of expansion, using zoning or utility hookup controls; and since any growth prevented in one place was merely diverted to other communities, the much discussed no-growth movement did not actually prevent any growth in America. But such measures represented a remarkable reversal of local attitudes toward the prospect of having more people in one's community. A 1973 Rockefeller Brothers Task Force report, *The Uses of Land,* concluded about the new opposition to growth:

> This mood defies easy generalization because it springs from a melange of concerns—many that are unselfish and legitimate, some that are selfish and not so legitimate. The mood is both optimistic and expansive in its expectations of the future, and pessimistic and untrusting about inevitable change. . . . The new mood reflects a burgeoning sophistication on the part of citizens about the overall, long-term economic impact of development. . . . But the new attitude toward growth is not exclusively motivated by economics. It appears to be part of a rising emphasis on humanism, on the preservation of natural and cultural characteristics that make for a humanly satisfying living environment.

The growth restrictionism so evident around the nation in the 1970s was an expression of "environmentalism" only in the sense that present residents did not wish their local communities to become crowded. Ecological concerns were not much involved in the effort to close pleasant suburbs and towns to swarms of outsiders, or to prevent a nuclear or coal-fired power facility from being built nearby. (This came to be called the "NIMBY" reflex—"Not In My Back Yard.") Nixon's call for a National Growth Policy was no "radical" step, but a call for a system of land-use decision making which allowed the federal government to override local jurisdictions and force the installation of power facilities and deep-water ports.

"A Stabilized Population for the United States"

Nixon's National Growth Policy was an innovative means to a conservative, pro-growth end. Moynihan helped persuade the president to take a second step toward population-related national policy which directly, if only briefly, challenged the fundamental growth orientation of three centuries of colonial and national history. Nixon had been vice president when Dwight Eisenhower had responded to a 1959 question about whether the government should oppose population growth by saying, "I cannot imagine anything more emphatically a subject that is not a proper political or governmental activity or function or responsibility. . . . The government has no . . . program that has to do with this problem." This was untrue, of course, even under Ike. The government's policy was not neutral: It was and always had been pro-natalist, encouraging large families through tax laws that provided deductions for children, and supporting research in the area of procreation. A historic shift came in 1967 (after Eisenhower, among others, had changed his mind), when federal funds were first allocated to what were called "family planning" services to the welfare population within the United States—birth control. Then Moynihan persuaded Nixon to take a bolder step, appointing in 1970 the first (and, so far, only) national commission on population, chaired by John D. Rockefeller II. The commission report, *Population and the American Future* (1972), was based on an admirable and unprecedented research effort to understand the complex issues woven into the question of socially desirable population size and distribution. It concluded: "There is hardly any social problem confronting this nation whose solution would be easier if our population were larger. . . . We have concluded that no substantial benefits would result from continued growth of the nation's population [and urge that] the nation welcome and plan for a stabilized population."

With federal programs extending birth control services to the welfare population and the report of the Rockefeller Commission, the population issue was moving from the latent to the manifest level. But the Nixon who appointed the commission in 1969 was by 1972 worried about his reelection campaign. Several conservative intellectuals, led by writer Patrick Buchanan and *National Review* editor William F. Buckley, had already broken with the president, and Nixon evidently feared that the Population Commission's recommendations that abortion laws be liberalized and abortion publicly funded would draw the ire of the right edge of his party and the Roman Catholic hierarchy. When the population report was ready for presentation, Nixon refused to receive or endorse it, then at a press conference denounced the two abortion recommendations. Congressional efforts to adopt by Joint Resolution the commission's principal goal of a stabilized population size fell short of enactment without Nixon's active support.

The Abortion Issue

Abortion of pregnancies was an ancient practice, and in postwar America it was widespread, terminating perhaps a fourth of all pregnancies. The practice was not of concern to governments until the late nineteenth century, when reform laws were passed in every state abolishing abortion unless the life of the mother were threatened, leading by 1900 to a complete "medicalization of the abortion decision," in historian Kristin Luker's phrase—physicians officially making the decision on abortion, not women alone (illegal abortions of course continued, with the aid of physicians, quacks, or abortifacients).

These laws came under attack in the 1960s, and on the eve of a Supreme Court testing of a Texas law, seventeen states had liberalized their statutes to allow abortion almost if not quite "on demand"—whenever a physician would certify that the mental or physical health of the woman was jeopardized. Then came the 1973 Supreme Court decision in *Roe v. Wade,* invalidating the many contradictory state laws and establishing a national standard. Abortions were not to be regulated in the first trimester of pregnancy; in the second the state's interest in the fetus was recognized and regulation was introduced; while in the third trimester abortion was made very difficult for women to buy or physicians to sell. The ground of the decision was the Fourteenth Amendment, in which the word "liberty" was presumed to include a "right to privacy" held by women. It was dubious constitutional construction, but the decision established a new system in which legal abortions increased. Prior to *Roe* it was estimated that 600,000 legal abortions were performed annually (1972); by 1980 the estimate was 1.55 million (the Allan Guttmacher Institute estimated that another 200,000 to 1 million abortions went unrecorded). At the end of the 1970s, abortion was ending one in four pregnancies before live birth; in Washington, D.C., the estimate was at least half.

NIXON AND THE U.S. ECONOMY

The American economy in the 1970s entered a time of troubles not understood, and not welcomed, by contemporaries. Looking back, we can see that the 1969–1970 recession marked the end of the strong expansionary era which stretched from World War II through the buoyant 1960s. There would be growth in the 1970s, but it would be slower, and three times interrupted by recession. More ominous than falling rates of growth in overall GNP was the steady decline in measured productivity growth rates, a fundamental source of any nation's wealth and competitiveness. Contrary to conventional economic theory, there would also be rising inflation. The erosion of American economic strength had complex roots, and it came at a time when improvements in transportation and communication combined with lowered world trade barriers (sponsored by the United States) to fuel a sustained surge in global commerce. Not only did the volume of world trade increase seven times from 1945 to 1970, its composition also changed. Japanese and European industrial economies were rebuilt, and the arts of industrial production spread rapidly in Pacific Rim societies (the two Koreas, Taiwan, Singapore, and Hong Kong). Manufactured goods began to surge in U.S. domestic markets, bringing good news to American consumers as they shifted their tastes to include German and Japanese automobiles, Italian typewriters, Taiwanese textiles and shoes. But foreign import competition was hard news for many older American industries, whose shrinking production and idled workforce were a primary cause of the U.S. economy's slowdown.

This transformation in the world economy was most painfully reflected in the American auto industry, which had never faced serious competition from abroad. The first sign of change came with the arrival in 1955 of the German Volkswagen, a durable, fuel-efficient small car that quickly established a beachhead in American markets. The popular "Beetle" surpassed the Ford Model T in February 1972 as vehicle 15,007,034 rolled off the line, and U.S. sales accounted for part of the record. Japan, however, was to be the most serious rival to the great industry the Americans had invented. Ford and General Motors had set up production facilities in Japan in the 1920s and dominated Japanese markets until World War II, and would not have noticed that Japan made 20,268 autos in 1955, as her industries rebuilt. But the Japanese made 1 million cars in 1967 and surpassed Germany in the U.S. market, with popular models such as the Toyota Corona entering in 1965, the Datsun Z in 1969.

The auto industry experience repeated a pattern already seen in steel, textiles, and consumer electronics. Rising imports reflected improving industrial skills abroad, backed by aggressive marketing and service. In 1971, the United States experienced its first overall trade deficit since 1893, and Japan—her economy growing by an astonishing 10 percent a year (1955–1970)—was responsible for a rising proportion of it.

As Nixon began his presidency neither he and his advisors, nor the American public generally, were aware that the economic lead of the United States over the rest of the world was narrowing so quickly. The most visible problem in 1969–1970 was the inflationary pressures left behind by Lyndon Johnson's wartime expenditures, and Nixon in 1970 tried the standard remedy: cut federal spending, encourage monetary tightening. This harsh medicine should in theory have brought relief from inflation at the price of somewhat higher unemployment, but somehow the rules had changed. The economy exhibited continued inflation along with higher unemployment, was stagnant yet still inflationary—afflicted with "stagflation," a new term. Inflation rose from 3.5 to 6 percent by late 1970, but joblessness was uncomfortably high at 5.9 percent, and critics were vocal: "Nixonomics means that all the things that should go up—the stock market, corporate profits, real spendable income, productivity—go down," said the chairman of the Democratic National Committee, "and all the things that should go down—unemployment, prices, interest rates—go up."

A debate surged around the president, the traditionalists urging Nixon to "hang tough" and let the textbook remedies slowly wring inflation out of the economy, while Treasury Secretary John Connally spoke for those who thought wage and price controls preferable to drifting into the election season. "Controls! O my God, no," Nixon had said in 1969 when the heresy of price controls was first mentioned: "I was a lawyer for the OPA during the war and I know all about controls. They mean rationing, black markets, inequitable administration. We'll never go for controls."

This history lesson restrained him for some time, but with the 1972 election approaching, Nixon became again the experimental pragmatist with a liking for bold, historic moves. On August 15, 1971, he announced that he was freezing wages, prices, and rents for 90 days to break the psychology of inflation, the freeze to give way to a complicated series of phases during which controls would diminish. And in a move of historic proportions which was not well understood at the time, Nixon ended the convertibility of the dollar to gold and "floated" U.S. currency to seek its own level on world exchanges. This move resulted neither in disaster nor in improvement in the trade balance, though both had been forecast. Nixon himself had predicted inequities under the controls, and indeed they bore more heavily on labor than on corporations or salaried professionals. The business community chafed at the interference, yet the inflationary spiral seemed checked; prices increased only 4.3 percent in 1971, then 3.3 percent in 1972. Nixon had not found the right combination of remedies, however, for the easing of controls in January 1973 triggered a new surge of inflation, requiring another freeze and a new round of controls in an atmosphere of confusion and uncertainty. But this was all after the election. With the recession over, inflation briefly under control, and unemployment holding at around 5 percent, Nixon neutralized the economic issue just in time for the presidential campaign of 1972. His other social policies presented no clear target for Democratic critics. This left only foreign policy, where presidents have more room to maneuver, and here Richard Nixon took the political offensive.

"WINDING DOWN THE WAR"

The most pressing matter abroad was the Vietnam War, which had toppled Nixon's predecessor and divided the country. He claimed in the 1968 campaign to have "a plan" to end the war, but Nixon no more than Johnson knew how to extricate the United States without suffering political damage. Nixon charted a middle course, at least as he read public opinion and aides' advice, announcing in June 1969 a gradual withdrawal of American troops (25,000 would be the first contingent of the total force of 540,000 to leave Vietnam), which he hoped would satisfy the doves without arousing hawks who bristled at any sign of defeat. But peace groups wanted a prompt and complete withdrawal. They launched massive demonstrations in hundreds of communities in October, and in mid-November they gathered in Washington in a crowd estimated at a quarter of a million. Nixon, and more vociferously Vice President Spiro Agnew, responded by criticizing protestors as "bums" (Nixon) and "an effete corps of impudent snobs" (Agnew). Despite tension, gradual troop withdrawals continued through the winter.

Could the South Vietnamese army carry the burden of the war with a reduced American force? Not if the North Vietnamese were allowed their sanctuary in Cambodia, responded the American military command. So Nixon on April 29, 1970, ordered a ground invasion of that country. This stunning enlargement of the war, combined with Nixon's aggressive rhetoric in a televised address ("We will not be humiliated. We will not be defeated.") sparked demonstrations on 400 college campuses. Four students were killed at Kent State University in Ohio when guardsmen opened fire on a rock-throwing crowd, and two black students were killed and eleven wounded when highway patrolmen fired on a dormitory at Jackson State College in Mississippi. It was, as Columbia University President William J. McGill said, "the most disastrous month of May in the history of American higher education." Yet by June the campuses had emptied, the Cambodia incursion was ended, and the troop withdrawals continued. Nixon ordered the sustained bombing of North Vietnam, attempting to increase pressure for some sort of face-saving settlement that would not look like American defeat. Antiwar protests continued through 1971, but the president held support from citizens he liked to call "the silent majority," who much preferred the costs of a war against armed communists to what they thought would be the humiliation of simply "getting out."

Nixon entered the election of 1972 having prolonged the war for four years with the loss of 15,000 American and many more Vietnamese lives. Yet he had also cut U.S. troop strengths to below 100,000 and, through National Security Advisor Henry Kissinger, was engaged in secret negotiations in Paris with the Vietnamese. "Peace is at hand," Kissinger announced twelve days before voting. But Nixon backed away from a peace agreement which Kissinger arranged with the North Vietnamese. Polls showed that he could win the election without giving Kissinger credit for the peace. The election had priority; to win it, let the war go on. Nixon had navigated a political passage where Lyndon Johnson had run his presidency aground.

DETENTE

For Nixon and Kissinger, the handling of the Vietnam War was a diversion from their hopes for larger moves. Time had brought an opportunity for dramatic rearrangements in world politics which might be favorable to the United States, and the two men perceived the opening. Soviet leadership, burdened with their portion of the $130 billion spent annually for armaments by the two superpowers, and increasingly fearful of armed conflict with Red China, announced in March 1971 a desire to improve U.S.–Soviet relations. The same signals came from the Chinese, and for much the same reasons. The Chinese leadership had concluded that war with Russia was more probable than with the United States, and the administration moved quickly to exploit both openings. At a summit meeting in Moscow in May 1972, Nixon and Premier Leonid Brezhnev signed two nuclear arms pacts and opened up new cultural and economic exchanges. The more dramatic realignment had come the previous February, when astonished Americans who remembered his anticommunist past watched Richard Nixon on television as he toured the Great Wall of China and met cordially with Mao Tse-tung and Chou En-lai, perhaps the world's leading revolutionaries. The trip to China, carefully planned by Kissinger, normalized relations between the two nations, initiated limited political and cultural contacts, and ended the twenty-year ostracism of Peking by Washington.

"Detente," as the new relationship was called, meant a lessening of tensions, enlarged contacts, and talks which might lead to further arms reduction. To hawkish Americans who had been taught by Nixon for years that one should maintain unflinching hostility to all our communist enemies, detente was cast as a national security measure: the United States, by its willingness to talk, had split the communist monolith and thus could play rivals off against each other. Some Americans, delighted at the opening glimpse into two fascinating civilizations at the repudiation of the weary cliches of the Cold War, expected too much from Nixon's rearrangement of global politics. Others did not understand how their anticommunist president could have been lured into such cordial relations with sworn enemies, but they, too, had overreacted. The truth about detente was more modest, and lay somewhere in between. It did not end international rivalry, or the arms race, and it did not signify that former enemies now trusted each other. Yet it did momentarily break the deadly momentum of animosity, and it opened up a window for negotiated curbs on expensive and destabilizing nuclear competition. Richard Nixon signed eight arms control agreements with the Soviets, chief among them the Strategic Arms Limitation Treaty (SALT I).

THE ELECTION OF 1972

Historically, the odds were against unseating any incumbent president at the end of one term, especially one who had just completed a spectacular round of diplomacy with major adversaries. The Democratic convention delegates, chosen under party reforms undertaken after the tumultuous 1968 convention, seated far more activists, women, and racial minorities, and far fewer traditional political stalwarts, than in the past. It was thus a convention whose sentiments were well to the left of the electorate (as it turned out), and proved to be in the same mood in 1972 as the Republicans had been in 1964: Let us have a choice, not an echo, a clear liberal challenge to the Nixon government rather than a candidate who would crowd toward the moderate center (Hubert Humphrey, Edmund Muskie) or even toward the right (Henry Jackson or George Wallace). And so the Democrats on the first ballot nominated South Dakota Senator George McGovern, a former historian and minister who had been a long-time opponent of the Vietnam War.

McGovern was a plain-spoken man of great moral earnestness. Robert Kennedy had said of him, "George is the most decent man in the Senate. As a matter of fact, he's the only one." He was also a social reformer who thought that the times called for change. Commenting openly that "I am not a centrist candidate," McGovern advocated an immediate withdrawal from the war, a cut of some $30 billion in the defense budget (the money to be used for urban and environmental programs), a generous minimum-income plan for welfare recipients, and progressive tax reform. These themes brought McGovern the ardent support of campus and antiwar activists and those who had always detested "Tricky Dick" Nixon. But McGovern's ideas did not sit well with what Nixon liked to call "Middle America," or with parts of the New Deal coalition— organized labor, southerners.

The Nixon camp was delighted when the Democrats offered this sharp alternative to the Nixon–Agnew ticket. Indeed, Nixon operatives had sabotaged Senator Muskie's presidential hopes during the primaries, an early harbinger of what became the Watergate scandal. This fact was not made public at the time, however, and Nixon was able to campaign against McGovern as a leader above the political battle, the man who was ending the war, the middle-of-the-road candidate. He asked his speech writers "how it would play in Peoria," his metaphor for small-town America, where he sensed that McGovern was viewed as too radical. The outcome of the balloting was the first decisive evidence that Lyndon Johnson had been right to fear that the Democrats' liberal policies on race (and he might have added welfare and the war) would prove politically costly for many years, at least in presidential elections. Surrendering to the impulse to seek victory by posing sharp alternatives had brought disaster to the Republicans in 1964; it had the same effect on the Democrats in 1972. Nixon polled 61 percent of the vote to McGovern's 38 percent—45.9 million votes to 28.4 million, 521 electoral votes to 17. McGovern carried only Massachusetts and the District of Columbia. Nixon claimed an historic mandate for himself and his policies.

The election, however, had conferred no mandate. Only 54 percent of eligible voters had turned out to vote, the lowest total since 1948. McGovern had been judged unreliable and "too radical," but Richard Nixon was not a popular figure. Middle-aged liberals could not forget or forgive his opportunistic exploitation of the McCarthy fever in the political battles of the 1950s, and few people responded warmly to the president's wooden, restrained manner and elusive personality. The appearance of a historic political breakthrough which the 1972 landslide created was further undercut by the voters' tendency toward ticket-splitting. The Republicans held the White House, but Democrats were again given control of both houses of Congress, actually gaining two seats in the Senate. Postwar politics, it seemed, were still gridlocked on dead center, with neither major party able to hold a working majority for long.

CHAPTER 8

The 1970s: A Decade of Short Presidencies and "Malaise"

OUT OF THE QUAGMIRE

After the election of 1972, the Nixon administration faced unfinished business abroad. Finding too much American humiliation in the peace terms offered by the North Vietnamese in Paris that autumn, Nixon ordered an intense two-week bombing north of the 38th Parallel. Perhaps this bombing, costly both to the Vietnamese and to the American B-52 fleet, made the enemy more accommodating. In any event a cease-fire was signed on January 23, 1973, with terms that did not sound exactly like an American defeat. The United States would withdraw the last contingent of its troops (27,000 men) and would exchange prisoners of war. The shooting would end on both sides; the withdrawal would be orderly. Nixon claimed "peace with honor," since our leaving would be deliberate and the South Vietnamese government of President Nguyen Van Thieu was expected to be able to defend itself successfully against aggression, with American financial assistance. It seemed a face-saving solution to a costly and divisive entanglement halfway around the world.

THE 1973–1974 ENERGY CRISIS

As entanglements in Asia loosened, the United States discovered how the nation's future had become tied to events in the Middle East. Harry Truman's commitment to Israel in 1948, confirmed by all subsequent administrations as they registered the power of the Jewish lobby within American politics, made the United States through the postwar era the guarantor of the survival of a new, immigrant-built Jewish state which inevitably displaced Palestinian Arabs. The nation-building Israelis owned the American heart, but Arabs (defined as people who speak Arabic) owned desert kingdoms sitting atop fabulous oil reserves. Thus the conflict between Israel and the Arab world would always involve the United States, patron to one and lucrative customer to the other.

A sudden war in the Middle East caught the United States by surprise. Humiliated by Israeli success in the "Six Day War" of 1967, Syrian and Egyptian forces, rearmed by the Soviets, attacked Israel by surprise during the Yom Kippur holiday in October 1973. After desperate fighting, the Israelis drove the Syrians back toward Damascus and broke across the Suez Canal to encircle the battered Egyptian army. A massive American airlift helped resupply the Israelis, confirming Arab images of the United States as partner to Zionism. Tireless "shuttle diplomacy" by Henry Kissinger, now Secretary of State, secured an uneasy peace by the spring.

U.S. support for Israel in the Yom Kippur War pushed the Arab states to the only form of retaliation available to them, an embargo on oil shipments to the West. The embargo was lifted in March 1974, since oil sellers need oil buyers, but a new element had entered the world energy picture. The Organization of Petroleum Exporting Countries (OPEC), an international oil cartel composed of thirteen Arab and non-Arab states, was ready to test its strength. Prices charged to foreign oil companies were increased fourfold. This translated at once into a 25 percent increase in gas prices at the pump (other costs, such as refining, administration, and taxes remained constant, moderating the increase) and dramatized the high degree of dependence on foreign oil into which the American economy had gradually slipped. Foreign oil cost $3.39 a barrel in 1972, but was $28 per barrel in 1980 and $38 by mid-1981. The OPEC cartel was taxing each American family of four some $3300 yearly over the market price of pre-OPEC days.

The oil crisis of 1973 resulted in long lines and very high prices at the gasoline pumps, and fostered an awareness of U.S. dependency on foreign oil.
(UPI/Bettmann)

The discovery that the nation's economy and life-style were so easily manipulated from abroad was a shock to a public that was woefully ignorant of the facts about the American energy system and the degree to which the economy was dependent upon fossil fuels. The news about energy vulnerability was carried by inflation, and shortages. Heating oil was chronically short during the harsh winter, and long lines reminiscent of World War II gasoline rationing appeared at service stations across the nation. "The oil crisis of 1973–74," wrote the authors of a Harvard Business School report on energy, "constituted a turning point in postwar history," the crossing of a divide into a new era of limits.

The Nixon government's response to the "oil shock" of 1973–1974 was blustery, superficially conceived, and ineffective. The era of cheap energy was coming to a close, and the central components of federal policy should have been candor and education. Yet the White House, judging (probably correctly) that the public was not ready to be told to alter life-styles toward conservation in order to buy time for even more difficult alterations in the energy base of the society, announced Project Independence, promising "energy independence (from foreign oil supplies) by 1980." A package of measures was offered to increase domestic oil drilling, promote coal use, and stimulate nuclear power— a source the president declared capable of providing 30 to 40 percent of U.S. electricity by the end of the 1980s.

"Energy independence" was both an impossible and an unwise goal, since the period of transition to a nonpetroleum economy would be long and difficult, and some foreign oil would be needed to supplement domestic oil and gas as the bridging fuel in that interim. The chief potential source of "new" energy was not production, but conservation, which was not tapped by the Nixon proposals.

The superficiality of the administration's response to foreign oil shortages was in some ways predictable. Polls showed that only 36 percent of the public thought the crisis was "real," most believing it to be contrived by the oil companies to boost profits. The public still thought oil cheap and abundant, and wished their government not to call for stringency but to break up the OPEC cartel. On such a vital matter the Nixon government was not inclined to step out in advance of public understanding. More useful than anything done by the government were the rising prices themselves, which hastened the adoption of conservation measures by citizens acting as consumers.

The sudden disruption of energy supplies and higher petroleum prices came at a time when the Nixon economic program was losing its grip on the forces of inflation. The jump in energy costs was joined by an inflationary surge as the wage and price controls of 1972 and 1974 were phased out, and as a worldwide drop in wheat production and the fish catch pushed up the prices of basic foods. Inflation reached double-digit figures in 1974, the Consumer Price Index reaching an annual rate of almost 15 percent by summer as a recession cut the real earnings of Americans below that of the preceding year. The times were unsettling. Americans were not accustomed to slipping backward materially as the calendar turned over, and they were not sure whether the principal blame should be placed on their government, on oil companies, on foreigners, or—more ominously—on some tide in the affairs of humanity too inexorable for blame or remedy.

WATERGATE

Even before Nixon's landslide returned him to office, a series of events was underway that would drive him to an unprecedented resignation in 1974. On June 17, 1972, a security guard in the Watergate apartment complex in Washington, D.C., surprised and arrested five intruders in the offices of the Democratic National Committee. They were found to be employees of the White House-based Committee to Re-elect the President ("CREEP"). Relentless investigation, initially spurred by two *Washington Post* reporters, disclosed that the break-in was part of a broad campaign of political sabotage and "dirty tricks" directed against "enemies" of the administration, financed by secret contributions extracted from corporations and totaling $55 million. Each time the story seemed about to end, a new revelation expanded its damaging significance. While the administration denied that any official was involved in wrongdoing, investigation revealed an ascending linkage of conspiracies, payoffs, and cover-ups leading from the Watergate burglars up through a series of White House officials to the Attorney General and the president's highest-ranking staff. Critical testimony implicating Chief of Staff Robert Haldeman and Domestic Counselor John Ehrlichman in obstructing justice came from the president's lawyer, John Dean, and these men resigned under fire on April 30, 1973. If aides so close to the president had known of the scheme without cooperating with the authorities, they were obstructing justice. And how could the president have been entirely outside these events? "What did the president know and when did he know it?" became the central question framed by Republican Senator (Tenn.) Howard H. Baker.

The administration staggered under revelations of perjury and cover-up in high places. A Senate investigating committee held televised hearings revealing evidence of a "Plumbers Unit" housed in the White House basement and carrying out illegal break-ins and sabotage, and an "enemies list" of people Nixon disliked, sent to the Internal Revenue Service as candidates for harassing audits. The sense of corruption was deepened when Vice President Agnew resigned to avoid indictment for tax evasion on income from bribes accepted in his White House office from a Maryland contractor, and Nixon was charged $450,000 plus penalties for back taxes. Then came a discovery that a tape-recording system had preserved conversations in the Oval Office. Nixon refused to turn over the tapes to the special prosecutor, Archibald Cox of Harvard Law School, but an edited version of the tapes was released in April, 1974, with critical conversations erased. A Supreme Court order forced Nixon to release all tapes in late July; they revealed Nixon actively involved in directing the cover-up, and the House Judiciary Committee voted three articles of impeachment.

bombing raids, artillery, destruction of villages and North Vietnamese urban infrastructure, and the poisonous effect of over 1 million pounds of air-dropped defoliants upon Vietnamese plant and animal (including human) life. In the face of such costs, Americans began to search for at least some saving benefits to place on the scales, beginning a debate over the "lessons of Vietnam" which continues to the present.

Assessing Gerald Ford

Beyond fashioning an uneventful and taint-free administration, Ford offered little leadership. In part this stemmed from his personal qualities, in part from his long background as a minority-party legislator whose main concern was resistance to change. No major domestic program or cancellation of a program came from the Ford White House, and probably no major changes could have been enacted even if proposed. All saw his reign as an interlude. Ford used the veto frequently, opposing legislation to expand public works, education and conservation spending. His brief administration was fiscally cautious. Inflation slipped down to 6 percent by 1976, joblessness climbing close to 10 percent at the end of his two-and-one-half years in office. Economic stagnation was blamed on Ford, but had of course deeper causes. "I am a Ford, not a Lincoln," he remarked, following essentially Nixonian social policies but with an engaging lack of pretense. Ford entered the 1976 election an underdog, his capacities for leadership much in doubt.

THE ELECTION OF 1976

Judging by the intense competition for both major party nominations, aspiring presidents still thought it was a good time to be in charge of the country. Ford narrowly survived a challenge from the Republican right wing led by California ex-Governor Ronald Reagan. On the Democratic side, a series of primary victories gave an insurmountable delegate majority to a well-organized but virtually unknown "Jimmy" (James Earl) Carter, former governor of Georgia. Carter, a peanut farmer and ex-Navy submarine commander, promised an active presidency blending liberal and yet "frugal" impulses. He was for full employment but also a balanced budget. His central theme was a promise of a shake-up in the stodgy, smug capital. Carter the Outsider, the born-again Christian Southerner from the grassroots, ran "against the government" much as George Wallace, Reagan, and others were doing as the 1970s advanced. He capitalized on the same cultural resentment of "Eastern elitism" that Nixon had harnessed. But Carter appeared to offer more than merely relief from the Eastern establishment, whatever that was. His TV debates with Ford confirmed his high intelligence and grasp of detail. His victory in November was narrow but solid; he compiled 40.8 million votes to Ford's 39.1, with an electoral edge of 297 to 241. Voter participation continued its gradual decline, with only 54 percent of those eligible

In the wake of Watergate, Southerner Jimmy Carter, an openly religious man, seemed to many Americans to embody the honesty and integrity that the presidency had lost with the disgrace of Richard Nixon. To further establish his "man of the people" image, Carter and wife Rosalynn chose to walk the inaugural parade, foregoing the usual limousine ride.
(*AP/Wide World Photos*)

bothering to vote. Yet there was some appearance of change, for Democrats took control of both houses of Congress. The nation's third century began in 1977 with eight years of "divided government" at an end, one party in command of the executive and legislative branches, and a confident engineer with populist leanings in the White House.

THE CARTER PRESIDENCY

Carter's election came in the year of the nation's bicentennial, and the imagery of "America's third century" suggested, at least to Carter and hopeful Democrats, a sharp break with the troubled recent past. America was a nation rent by many differences—of race, geographic region, social class, cultural values. Carter appeared in many respects favored with the qualities of leadership which might indeed make headway against stubborn social problems and the general sense of aimlessness. He was an intelligent engineer, an outsider with no debts to past policies, a man with ties to rural America, the military, conservation, evangelical Christianity. His moderate-liberal civil rights record brought him 91 percent of the black vote. Four years later, with Carter repudiated, the optimists of 1976 wondered if they had overestimated Carter or underestimated the tidal forces that buffeted America's political and economic systems. In 1977, however, Carter and his allies saw themselves not in the seventh year of a decade of troubles, but in the first year of a new, third American century.

Carter understood well that the events of 1965–1974, from Vietnam through Watergate, had dangerously eroded public confidence in its governing institutions and those who managed them. Determined to reverse the trend toward an imperial presidency, he wore a business suit to his inauguration, walked with his wife from the ceremony to the White House, and set a pattern of wearing cardigan sweaters on television or while visiting in the homes of working-class citizens. This was symbolism; behind it, Carter had more substantial plans. In his first year he sent to Congress proposals for sweeping reforms of the welfare system and the tax code, declaring the former a mess and the latter a disgrace. These were familiar problems which other Presidents had unsuccessfully attacked, as was executive branch reorganization, another Carter priority. Three large reforms was much to attempt, but the president, buoyed by his high ranking in public opinion polls (these are traditional for new presidents in their first year, but each president thinks them an enduring mark of public esteem), launched in the spring of 1977 an even bolder effort. In a major speech on the energy crisis, Jimmy Carter badly misjudged what the American people were willing to hear: "Tonight I want to have an unpleasant talk with you about a problem that is unprecedented in our history," he began. But Carter found it difficult to present the problem in a compelling and simple fashion. Americans were dependent on foreign energy sources that were in the long run nonrenewable, a problem "for our children and our grandchildren," Carter told voters who were interested mostly in themselves, and certainly not in "unpleasant talks." Fundamental change in Americans energy uses should become "the moral equivalent of war," the president said, borrowing a 1906 phrase from philosopher William James.

Energy Policy

Carter's "National Energy Plan" was a break with the past in several respects. Nixon and Ford, the first two post-OPEC presidents, had promised "energy independence" (from the Arabs or any other foreign suppliers) through technological solutions. They had not asked Americans for sacrifice or changes in life-style, and had not admitted to the public that the era of cheap energy was over. Carter decided to convince the nation that basic change lay ahead. Explaining that the era of hydrocarbons was soon to end, he offered a complex set of policies to move the nation toward new sources of energy. This would require a transitional use of coal and nuclear energy; allowing oil and gas prices to rise to OPEC-inflated world market levels in order to encourage conservation; taxes to recapture for the public some of the resultant oil company profits; accelerated research and development in solar energy and synthetic fuels from oil shale or biomass. Carter took the risk of suggesting major changes in the American life-style, concentrating mostly on the need to end the era of the heavy "gas guzzler" auto of which the American public was so fond. He said nothing about stabilizing population growth, a vital part of any cap on the growth of energy demand.

His energy speech was long and complicated, his plan even more so. The president's grasp of technical detail was remarkable even for a former nuclear engineer, but the speech was not praised by any segment of opinion. Carter vastly underestimated the American people's dislike for being asked to make do with less.

Congress entered a long and drawn-out debate, from which no consensus emerged. Energy politics in the Carter years proved once again that large policy decisions rarely come unless there is some pressing crisis. Lobbyists for oil companies, coal interests, regions with or without energy supplies, environmentalists, public utilities, and industry swarmed the halls of Congress and threatened reprisals if major changes were forced upon them. The public at large found the energy issue tedious and unpleasant, and signaled to Congress its doubt that there actually was "an energy crisis" by buying more large cars in 1977 than it had in 1976.

When it did not confuse, the energy issue seemed to divide. Conservation could come only with higher prices, but these hurt the poor and those on fixed incomes, and set energy-supplier and Sun Belt states against energy-consumer and Snow Belt states. The immensely complex energy plan had been drafted largely in secret, and Carter could not manage to produce goals and methods simple enough to submerge objections in a general consensus. Reorienting energy use was not so simple a goal as winning a war or going to the Moon. A popular joke asked if the public was ignorant or apathetic on the energy issue, to which the answer was: "I don't know and I don't give a damn!" A new Department of Energy was set up in 1978 to facilitate public investment in synthetic fuels and in conservation, but the National Energy Act which Carter signed in November 1978 contained at best one third of what he had asked. Higher gas taxes were rejected, along with taxes on oil company windfall profits. Rising energy prices were slowly forcing a public shift toward conservation, but the shift was slow, and Carter was unable to reorient federal policy to make the shift more rapid. Gasoline prices broke through the dollar-a-gallon barrier in the summer of 1979, but low taxes on fuel allowed much of that wealth to go abroad. Imported oil siphoned off a hardly noticed $8.4 billion from American consumers in 1973 prior to the OPEC action, but by 1978 the sum was $45 billion, a staggering transfer of assets. Polls, however, showed that a majority of the public did not even know that half their oil came from abroad.

New Directions in Foreign Relations: "Human Rights"

While Jimmy Carter was having little luck in moving his domestic proposals, he hoped for more room to maneuver in setting a course for U.S. foreign policy. The administration's guiding idea was to support "human rights" abroad, a theme which Carter pursued with enthusiasm. It seemed more positive than merely denouncing communism, and Carter was by nature an activist. "No member of the United Nations," he asserted in January 1977, "can claim that mistreatment of its citizens is solely its own business. Equally, no member can avoid its responsibilities to review and to speak when torture or unwarranted deprivation occurs in any part of the world." Interpreting human rights as chiefly political rather than economic or social, the administration attempted to bring more pressure to bear upon the Soviet Union by meetings and correspondence with Soviet dissidents such as scientist-historian Andrei Sakharov and writer Alexander Solzhenitsyn. Yet Carter tried to be even-handed, condemning also the brutal dictator of Uganda, Idi Amin, and curtailing aid to the anticommunist rightist regimes in Uruguay and Argentina.

This new policy broke sharply from the *realpolitik* of the Nixon-Kissinger era, which had studiously ignored the internal affairs of other states in order to strike bargains on matters of economic or strategic importance. Carter was proposing to move from the rigid and often unthinking anticommunism so dominant in Washington from 1947 through the 1960s. Some called it a welcome shift from a negative opposition to anything that was called communism. Defense of human rights appealed to the American yearning to stand for something in the world other than Coca-Cola or Hollywood movies, and there was evidence that authoritarian regimes were in fact moderating the use of torture and the repression of political opponents. Critics countered that the administration was inconsistent, overlooking the police-state methods of the governments of South Korea and the Philippines, whose friendship was strategically important. More fundamental was the charge that the human rights campaign was moralism run amuck, injecting into international relations a disruptive fixation on morality, when states should deal only with the hard realities of power.

All administrations have critics of their basic assumptions (if they have basic assumptions), and Carter's government at the halfway point, in 1978, had made an impressive beginning in foreign policy. The human rights thrust gave American international efforts a coherent rationale which escaped the narrow anticommunism that had confined earlier administrations. A politically difficult fight to ratify a new treaty with Panama was won by Carter in 1978, allowing the Canal Zone to revert to Panamanian control by the year 2000. More difficult and impressive was the president's successful brokerage of the Camp David Accords, an agreement between former enemies Egypt and Israel which returned the Sinai Peninsula to Egypt, normalized relations, and established a framework for a possible settlement of West Bank disputes. Flushed with success and justifiably proud of his own persistence in bringing about the agreement and the embrace of Arab and Israeli heads of state, Carter and most of the media claimed that the Camp David meetings had solved more of the tortuous Middle Eastern tangle than events would confirm. But no American president had addressed these complex problems with more resolve or better immediate effect.

At Home—Growth Management and Full Employment

At home as well, 1978 was a reasonably good year for Jimmy Carter—as it turned out, it was the apex of his popularity and effectiveness. With an engineer's receptivity to planning and systems approaches, Carter announced in 1978 that a National Urban Policy would replace the government's myriad and inconsistent policies affecting cities. The plan was a conceptual innovation among urbanists, but it generated more political opposition than support—a pattern oft repeated in Jimmy Carter's initiatives. Labor and minority interests were officially delighted when the president accepted the Humphrey-Hawkins full employment law of 1978, though they privately grumbled that he had insisted on changes placing inflation control on a par with lower unemployment, leaving the measure mostly a catalog of good intentions. In urban and economic matters Carter was holding the traditional Democratic constituencies in 1978, even if they were restless with his caution on spending. Environmentalists generally found Carter the most responsive chief executive since FDR, praising his appointments to the Council on Environmental Quality and EPA, his support for the Alaska Lands Act, his willingness to object to dubious water projects.

If a general election had been scheduled for 1978, Jimmy Carter would probably have been returned as president. Even at that time, however, there were signs in the polls and elsewhere that his presidency was being pulled apart by a complex swarm of problems, a public irritated and deeply uneasy about the basic direction of American life, and by Carter's own shortcomings. A group of political scientists, meeting in New York at the end of 1978, gave Carter mixed reviews: "He has identified the major problems facing the country . . . has not ducked them the way his predecessors tended to do," commented James Sundquist of Brookings; yet there was "a scattering of energies," thought Lester Seligman of the University of Illinois, "no clear picture of the administration's direction. . . . What is needed is a focus." Said another scholar: "He [Carter] seems to have no sense of differentiation between large and small issues. One has grave difficulties determining his priorities."

Contemporaries, in assessing the state of the nation, tended to expect much of presidential leadership, as they had been taught by presidents themselves. If the economy, social values, or America's world image were in an unsatisfactory state, it must be Carter's fault. His was a risky job to hold, as Eisenhower's four successors had all learned. The nation was passing through changes in the world economy which weakened America's industrial preeminence, and through what would surely be a long and painful transition from her resource-rich frontier past to a future hedged with limits on the growth which had so long served as our national purpose.

SOCIAL MOVEMENTS AFTER THE 1960s

What became of the social protest and reform movements of the 1960s in the years that followed?

One, at least, was terminated by events—some would say, by success. The anti-Vietnam War movement lost its rationale in 1973, with the January signing of a peace agreement between the Americans, North and South Vietnamese, and Vietcong, providing for U.S. troop withdrawals and a vague sketch of continued political cooperation. The South Vietnamese regime lasted only until communist armies entered Saigon in April 1975. A frantic airlift removed the remaining Americans and some Vietnamese allies, and America's longest war was over.

The 1950s movement in opposition to nuclear weapons had been to some extent swept up in the anti-Vietnam War passions, but seemed exhausted by it. The nuclear arms race of course continued, indeed escalated through the 1970s and beyond. But the grass-roots anti-Bomb energies that organizations like SANE had mobilized in the 1950s and that justly claimed much credit for the test ban treaty of 1963 seemed depleted. A grass-roots Nuclear Freeze Movement formed in the early 1980s in response to President Reagan's rapid arms buildup and spurred by Jonathan Schell's 1982 book, *The Fate of the Earth,* but the Peace Movement would not regain the street-filling power of the 1960s.

Civil Rights: Diffusion and Uncertainty

The term "civil rights" arrived in the 1960s as virtually synonymous with the effort to end the inferior legal status of African-Americans. The achievements of the social movement mobilized behind this idea were stunning—the termination of Jim Crow, after domination of the domestic agenda by innovative tactics displayed on "the moral high ground." Leaders of the handful of organizations working to mobilize other nonwhite "minority groups"—Native Americans, Hispanics—insisted that they, too, had faced discrimination, were a part of the civil rights movement, and intended that their turn would come next. If black Americans could mobilize against discrimination and compel the government to fashion remedies, why not other minorities?

Red Power

The small pan-Indian movement launched by Native American veterans of World War II was the foundation for the establishment of the American Indian

Militant members of the American Indian Movement (AIM) staged a 71-day protest at Wounded Knee, South Dakota, to demand basic reforms in federal Indian policy, especially increased autonomy in tribal governance.
(UPI/Bettmann)

Movement (AIM) in 1968, which was much influenced by the tactics of direct action to catch public attention through the media. Activists from AIM, under the slogan "Red Power," occupied Alcatraz Island in San Francisco Bay in 1969, a Bureau of Indian Affairs office in Washington, D.C., in 1972, and—in conflict with leaders of the local tribal community—a trading post at the site of the 1890 Battle of Wounded Knee in 1973. The mass media gave these episodes wide and generally sympathetic coverage, marking a growing tendency to see Native Americans as the original victims of the westward expansion of Europeans. But the Native American activists who saw themselves as expanding the civil rights movement had profoundly different goals than Martin Luther King, Jr. He aimed at integration, but to Native American activists this meant a despised "assimilation" when their goal was tribal and cultural self-assertion, an argument powerfully made in Vine Deloria, Jr.'s *Custer Died for Your Sins* (1969). Federal courts began to reopen Indian claims cases and Congress initiated several transfers to millions of acres from federal agencies to Indian tribes—restored to legal status in the Indian Self-Determination Act of 1974, surprisingly sponsored by Richard Nixon. Underlying economic conditions for the nation's three-quarter-of-a-million indigenous descendants remained stubbornly dismal, another reminder that social movements producing federal policy reforms do not quickly transform social reality.

Brown Power

If demands for "black power" and "red power" caught national attention, why not "brown power"? In the 1960s the gradualist and assimilationist strategies of the long-established League of United Latin American Citizens (LULAC) seemed to younger Mexican-American activists as outdated as NAACP lawsuits before the Supreme Court. Where could direct action in community or workplace settings bring about for Hispanics what the black marches in Alabama and Georgia had done for blacks? The answer came in California's fertile interior valleys, where large-scale agriculture depended on a labor force essentially derived from Mexico. Cesar Chavez, a California farm worker and unionist, saw in 1964 that the end of the federal government's "Bracero" program (1942–1964), bringing Mexican nationals to work temporarily in southwestern agriculture, offered the first real chance for unionizing the resident workforce. With annual waves of Mexican migratory labor no longer brought into California by the Bracero program, Chavez saw an opportunity to unionize the American workers who had come earlier from Mexico, and in a controlled labor market could organize and bargain for decent wages, working conditions, and housing.

Chavez and his United Farm Workers (UFW) mounted a broad strike in the grape vineyards around Delano, California, in 1965, attracting sympathetic visits from Senator Robert Kennedy and United Auto Workers chief Walter Reuther. A nationwide consumer boycott of California grapes helped break growers' resistance to unionization, and the UFW was recognized as a collective bargaining unit. Chavez made no effort to translate his success into a political career, but remained a revered and gentle farm labor unionist until his death in 1993, his cause made more difficult by continuing flows of mostly illegal migrants across the U.S.–Mexican border, available as workers to replace and depress the wages of Chavez's unionists.

Chavez was through the 1970s and 1980s the most visible leader and strategist of a Hispanic social movement that was uncertain of its future direction and inherently fragmented, since the term "Hispanic" might mean people tracing their lineage to Puerto Rico, the Philippines, Cuba, Central and South America, or Mexico. But Chavez was a rural union organizer, a limited model for an increasingly urban population. The focus of protest shifted to a series of small, urban, usually university-based movements. In Colorado, Rudolfo "Corky" Gonzales launched a Crusade for Justice that did not last, but more durable organizations followed. The Ford Foundation sponsored the Mexican-American Legal Defense Foundation (MALDEF), launched in 1968 in San Antonio and modeled after a similar legal arm attached to the NAACP. Southwest Texas in 1970 saw the beginnings of a group with a name ("La Raza Unida") that if white groups had used it would have been deemed racist, but which spread to other

United Farm Workers president Cesar Chavez organized many protests in order to unionize farm workers, especially the migrant farm workers of the west. Here Chavez leads demonstrators in a picket line outside a Los Angeles supermarket selling boycotted (non–union-picked) grapes.
(UPI/Bettmann)

regions. In California, a "Chicano" movement with strong separatist overtones mobilized mostly college and university Mexican-Americans to repeat black protest movement tactics by claiming similar "minority" status and demanding ethnic studies departments with community research and organizing missions. These efforts at cultural preservation and social mobilization fell far short of the goal of creating a brown version of the legendary black crusade of the 1950s and 1960s, and were frustrated in large part by the assimilationist aspirations and moderate political views of the majority of Hispanics in America.

The Civil Rights Crusade as Government Project

The movement for civil rights never recovered from King's death, which removed the only leader with the ability, many thought, to chart new directions now that Jim Crow was buried. But to a considerable extent the initiative for devising new tactics in the struggle to improve the lives of black Americans had shifted away from the streets, and from established black leaders, toward federal patrons. Two governmental instruments were fashioned in the 1970s, both of them unpopular with the public and slow to produce tangible results. Federal judges used school busing as a tool to achieve greater racial balance in metropolitan schools where residential patterns and existing school district lines would otherwise produce segregation. "Forced busing," as unhappy parents (some of them black, though most were white) termed it, was for years the courts' chief tool to produce integrated schooling. But it also produced "white flight" to private schools or family relocation to other communities.

A second governmental policy, affirmative action, was taking root in government agencies, private corporations, and nonprofit institutions, altering established practices in hiring, higher-education admission and financial aid decisions, and federal, state, and local contracting. Affirmative action had been launched in 1965 by President Johnson in Executive Order 11246. Despite language in the order indicating that federal policy would remain color blind ("employees are [to be] treated during employment without regard to their race, creed, color or national origin"), the intent of affirmative action was to take special steps to ensure that equal opportunity to compete with whites for jobs and other desired positions would translate into roughly proportional success. The logic behind race-based preferences was the recognition that centuries of slavery had handicapped African-Americans in ways that would be hard to eradicate, requiring a period of special assistance of unspecified duration. The shaping of affirmative action fell to the bureaucracy and the courts. The Department of Labor's Office of Federal Contract Compliance in 1970 took a step that other governmental and private organizations would follow: defining the groups eligible for affirmative action as not only African-Americans but Hispanics, Asians, and Native Americans. Women were subsequently added. Congress in these years did not debate affirmative action, and the extension of its benefits to groups other than blacks was never explained or justified. Beyond the definition of eligible groups, there arose the question of "quotas." The Nixon administration in 1969 quietly began the practice of establishing numerical goals for affirmative-action hiring. Goals soon began to look like quotas.

To many people, affirmative action was an innovative policy which could move society more rapidly toward a goal of equal results than simple nondiscrimination. But affirmative action was snarled in problems from the first. Beyond the broadened definition of favored groups, affirmative action aroused deep philosophical objections. There was something alien to the American sense of fairness about government-imposed preferment of one race, ethnic group, or sex over another, especially when qualifications appeared to be unequal and those passed over for jobs or other valued openings were innocent of any connection with slavery or documented discrimination. Affirmative action pushed aside the traditional (and not always honored in practice) reliance on individual merit, replacing it with preferment by group status. Even its supporters were uneasy with the possibility that this expedient might become permanent. Some blacks objected that it stigmatized those who were preferred, tainting their advance with the odor of favoritism.

Inevitably, affirmative action wound up in the courts, where the argument was not much clarified. The Supreme Court decided by a 5–4 vote in the case of *Bakke v. Regents of the University of California* to limit but not end the policy. Allan Bakke, a white medical school applicant rejected by the University of California, Davis, Medical School in 1973 in favor of minority applicants with weaker qualifications (as measured in the usual ways), had sued for admission. Because Bakke had not been allowed to compete for 16 (of 100) openings Davis set aside exclusively for minorities, the divided Court agreed that he had been wronged. Affirmative action was unconstitutional when rigid quotas led to the ignoring of individual qualifications. With these admonitions, however, the Court in *Bakke* agreed that race could be taken into account on the positive side of the ledger in matters of distributing society's opportunities. This indecisive result meant that affirmative action would continue to guide federal policy and all the institutions it affected, but would return to the Court in other areas. Busing and affirmative action both acted as lightening rods collecting and focusing antigovernmental resentments, a political cost paid mostly by Democrats.

Environmentalism

While antiwar protests ended in the 1970s and the crusade for racial equality lost its guiding strategy, the environmental movement grew larger and more influential than ever. Apparently construing Earth Day's impressive turnout in April 1970 as a mandate for action, Congress enacted a burst of federal legislation during two Republican presidencies: the Clean Air Act of 1970; six major laws in 1972, including the Coastal Zone Management Act, the Water Pollution Control Act, and measures on ocean dumping, pesticides, marine mammal protection, and noise pollution; an endangered species act in 1973; and the Toxic Substance Control Act in 1976. A new regulatory framework had been hurriedly thrown into the path of pollution. Only with time would Congress and the public realize that the laws were constructed on a slight scientific base and overly optimistic assumptions. Assuming "the environmental problem" to be mostly one of point-source (sewer pipes, smokestacks) air and water pollution, a lawyer-dominated Congress mandated immediate results without sufficient attention to the inadequacies of the scientific base in both public health and soil–air–water chemistry, and largely ignored economic costs. Unrealistic goals were set, as when the Clean Air Act proclaimed that ambient air standards thrown together in 90 days would be attained by American cities in five years, or the water act of 1972 declared it "to be national policy that . . . the discharge of pollutants into navigable waters be eliminated by 1985."

Critics complained loudly that the costs of controls would be passed on in the form of inflation and industrial shutdown. Supporters of federal environmental regulation gave two answers. The costs of environmental cleanup would indeed be substantial, they argued, since the nation had built its basic production processes and life-style on what turned out to be the temporary availability of free dumping grounds for wastes, so that current prices were not "normal" and did not reflect the full environmental costs of production. "History is finally presenting America with its bill" for an unsustainable way of life, wrote David Calleo in *The Imperious Economy* (1982). Second, if the public did not pay the higher costs of goods produced and disposed of in environmentally sound ways, they would pay it in health costs resulting from pollution. When the Brookings Institution estimated that the bill for "clean air" by 1985 would reach $375 billion, it was argued that health savings from lung cancer, emphysema, and other pollution-related maladies would likely exceed that sum in the same period.

Even those who thought the costs of environmental protection might be lower than the costs imposed upon the environment and public by business as usual, environmentalists' methods and mentality were challenged by land developers, industrialists, farmers, and opponents of regulation in general. Environmentalists, said their critics, were against all growth and change, were not average citizens but comfortable elitists defending their suburban neighborhoods and their access to distant national parks. They were disguised religious fanatics, antitechnology and antiscience, hostile to "progress." They were responsible for an irrationally strict new regulatory structure typified by the Endangered Species Act, whose provisions allowed environmental activists to block for a time the construction in 1978 of the TVA's $100 million Tellico Dam because a tiny fish called the snail darter might lose that one creek of its habitat, or stop a Maine water project because a snapdragon called the furbish lousewort seemed endangered. Environmentalists, it was said, cared for bald eagles, grizzly bears, even coyotes and snakes, but not for people whose jobs were threatened by expensive regulations of the use and disposal of resources.

Efforts to caricature and discredit the environmentalist impulse were partially successful. "I'd prefer not to be known as an environmentalist," said a New Hampshire man. "That means a do-gooder, a do-nothing, always in somebody's hair." His wife responded: "They're interested in birds and bees, flowers and fauna and all that." But the couple offering these views were environmentalists, activists in a New Hampshire campaign against hazardous waste dumps.

The environmental movement was a vast, nationwide, and diverse coalition with no center and many different faces. The larger organizations—Sierra Club, Audubon Society, Wilderness Society—maintained skilled Washington lobbies, shaped the initial regulatory laws, and worked for their improvement. A growing number of young lawyers formed new public-interest environmental law firms such as the Natural Resources Defense Council (NRDC), the Sierra Club Legal Defense Fund, and the Environmental Defense Fund, suing federal development agencies, state and local utilities, and industry to block the Storm King power plant on the Hudson River near West Point, a Walt Disney ski resort in Mineral King Valley in the Sierras. The couple in New Hampshire were not lawyers utilizing the courts, but, like thousands of other activists hearing of proposals to "develop" a waterway or forest or mountain crest, install a waste dump or build a nuclear power plant, became overnight activists to block the proposed development through political pressure.

Historian Samuel P. Hays has observed that, contrary to the description of the environmental movement as romantic opponents of technology and progress, characteristics which might fit a few, the movement as a whole as it grew through the 1970s displayed a positive outlook for the future and was optimistic about a better tomorrow if the public could only be awakened. Environmentalist values overlapped with the rising interest in personal health, increasingly seen as achieved through active attention to "wellness" rather than sought in a doctor's office when illness came. Judging from extensive reading of environmentalist magazines and newspapers, journals such as *Mother Earth News, Co-Evolution Quarterly, New Age, Organic Gardening,* or *The Whole Earth Catalogue,* and the fugitive little newspapers and newsletters of activist groups found especially on the Pacific Coast, New England and Florida, Hays found environmentalism tied closely to a commitment to active physical fitness through exercise and vegetarian and organic-food diet, an interest in solar power systems, and an inclination to seek spiritual deepening through contact with nature. Were environmentalists the heirs of the Counterculture? Hays thought not, for the latter had stressed personal expression as well as social rebellion through dress, drugs, and sexual experience, whereas the environmentalists revealed in the "underground press" of the 1970s valued independence and self-reliance, and "stressed self-discipline and the development of personal skills in order to organize life effectively."

Like the New Left of the 1960s, American environmentalism was not founded upon one great book, idea, or ideology. Expressed mostly in action, environmentalism was anchored in few formal ideas. An impressive intellectual foundation stretched back to the writings of Thoreau, Marsh, Muir, and Leopold, but activists in the 1970s spent little time clarifying their creed or disputing its internal contradictions. Increasingly they called themselves "ecologists," a label borrowed from a holistic approach to biology which had emerged in the 1920s and which in the 1970s meant someone who knew that "everything is connected to everything else" and that humanity must stop thinking of itself as apart from the living systems within which people existed. A few philosophers wrote about "Deep Ecology," a radical critique of the Western idea that humanity is the measure and master of all things. Most environmentalists gave this radical idea little systematic thought, and found more useful the appreciation of alternative or "appropriate technology" on a smaller, human scale as described with considerable technological expertise as well as grace in E. F. Schumacher's *Small Is Beautiful* (1973) or Amory Lovins' *Soft Energy Paths* (1977).

Two broad groupings could be discerned in the mosaic of environmentalist expression. A moderate wing sought a middle ground with industrialists, land developers, and the labor movement, accepting compromise with existing economic interests and a gradualist path toward the attainable goal of adjusting industrial life to nature's requirements. They believed that such accommodation could come through the social regulation of individual and corporate pollution, relying on science, technology, education, and democratic political processes to guide a growing America toward tolerable levels of pollution and resource depletion. They favored recycling of household waste, bicycle trips to work whenever possible, small families, and when in the mountains were adept at packing out all their litter.

There were also more impatient sorts of environmentalists, given to a more radical challenge to American society. They were not inclined to negotiate compromises with developers or dam builders, and felt that behind these enemies was a larger foe. "The American life-style is the culprit," said Robert L. Sansom in *The American Dream Machine* (1976). What must be confronted was a consumption–throwaway life-style, and the basic growth-oriented, human-centered, and nature-exploiting values which lay beneath it. To them, time was alarmingly short in which to repudiate the goal of population and economic expansion, to stabilize both population and overall output while altering the composition of what was produced toward environmentally benign products, to shift life-styles from mass consumption to "lives of voluntary simplicity" producing minimal ecological disturbance. They aspired to what economist Herman Daly called "a Steady State economy" or a sustainable society, where the challenges of growth were sought in the inner spaces, the realm of the spirit where harmony with nature displaced materialism and self-aggrandizement. They hailed Ernest Callenbach's bestseller *Ecotopia* (1975), a novel in which environmentalists secede from the United States and establish a regional rural utopia north of San Francisco, one run by women in recognition that the materialist, power-centered values of men had lost their usefulness. The urge to take direct action against nature's exploiters drew inspiration from southwestern novelist Edward Abbey's *The Monkey Wrench Gang* (1975), in which a small group of desert lovers swept out of the canyons to sabotage developers' bulldozers and police helicopters, and plotted to "free the wild rivers" by dynamiting dams, starting with the Glen Canyon Dam on the Colorado. New organizations began to develop the tactics of direct, often illegal disruption of economic extractive industries thought to be especially threatening to nonhuman life—Greenpeace (1969–) and the Sea Shepherd Conservation Society (1979–), groups interested in sea mammal protection, and Earth First! (1980–), whose founder Dave Foreman said in *Ecodefense: A Field Guide to Monkey-Wrenching* that "it is time to act heroically and admittedly illegally in defense of the wild. We will take pure, hard-line, pro-Earth positions. No nukes, no strip mining, no pollution, no more development of our wilderness. We are concerned about people but it's Earth first." This was a call to environmental civil disobedience, clearly influenced by the civil rights movement.

Feminism

Another social critique and reform impulse of the 1960s which retained force and influence during the succeeding decade was feminism. The women's movement, like civil rights, continued less as a movement one could follow on TV screens or in headlines and more as millions of private efforts to define and test new opportunities and roles. Unlike civil rights, where the 1964 and 1965 laws had achieved at least the large goal of ending Jim Crow, feminists in the 1970s had unfinished governmental business. They still pursued one great policy objective, the Equal Rights Amendment (ERA) to the Constitution.

The brevity of the ERA belies the proposed amendment's capacity to stir emotion, both for and against. It reads:

Section I: Equal rights under law shall not be denied or abridged by the United States or by any state on account of sex.

Section II: The Congress shall have the power to enforce, by appropriate legislation, the provisions of this article.

Section III: This amendment shall take effect two years after the date of ratification.

First drafted in 1923 by Alice Paul's National Woman's Party, the amendment endured decades of internment by committees. The ERA drive was revived when Paul, by then 82, persuaded the National Organization for Women to support it in 1967. ERA, gaining momentum from the civil rights movement, promised to codify the national commitment to equality and erase the remaining legal discriminations against (also, those in favor of) women. By 1970 active lobbying by NOW and the Women's Equity Action League had neutralized earlier opposition from labor unions and women's groups hesitant to lose protective legislation, and a wide range of organizations from the Girl Scouts to the American Bar Association had endorsed the amendment. ERA passed the House in October 1971, by a lopsided (354–23) vote, the Senate early in 1972 by a vote of 84–8, and went to the states. One year later thirty states had ratified it, and thirty-five had done so by 1977. To liberal feminists it was a matter of the utmost national importance; to most citizens it seemed a desirable expression of a national consensus that gender must not carry legal handicaps in America.

But 1977 was ERA's peak year, as it turned out, one benchmark of the broad conservative reaction which altered the tone and agenda of American public life. The drive for ERA brought counterorganization by antifeminists. Phyllis Schlafly launched STOP ERA in 1972, with allies such as the Rev. Jerry Falwell of the Moral Majority, the Mormon Church, and (according to NOW) business groups fearful that women's wages would have to be raised if ERA passed. Five states retracted their endorsement of the amendment in 1973, and the drive for ERA stalled under charges that it would legalize homosexual marriages and unisex toilets, and force women into combat duty. The polls showed majority support for ERA throughout the 1970s, with 58 percent supporting it at decade's end. Despite such support, ERA was beaten.

Gay Rights

As the civil rights movement had moved feminists toward activism in the 1960s and 1970s, it also spurred both homosexual males and lesbian females into a movement for "gay rights." Americans with a sexual preference for their own sex had an unbroken history of social and legal stigma. In postwar America, they were cited as security risks in the rhetoric of McCarthyism, faced ousters from military and other federal employment if discovered, and were routinely harassed by police raids on homosexual bars or assignation sites such as bus stations and parks. Their tiny organizations—the Mattachine Society, established by homosexual males in Los Angeles in 1951, the Daughters of Billitis, formed in 1955 in San Francisco by lesbians—had no visibility or national influence.

The climate established by the civil rights movement opened channels for a "gay rights" effort at many levels. The estimated fifteen gay and lesbian groups in 1966 had expanded to fifty by 1969, magazines such as *Ain't I a Woman?* and *Furies* addressed lesbian concerns, and a new spirit of resistance was seen in the flurry of rocks and rioting that followed a police attempt to arrest suspected homosexuals at the Stonewall Bar in Greenwich Village, New York, in June 1969. Asserting that gay life-styles were not a form of illness, gay and lesbian groups successfully pressed the American Psychological Association in 1973 to remove homosexuality from its diagnostic manual of mental health disorders, and spurred several states—led by Illinois in 1961—to decriminalize same-sex relations between consenting adults in private. Demanding their own "liberation" from an inferior position in society in language recalling the civil rights demands for "freedom now," gay men and women formed organizations for mutual support and political lobbying, and, much as blacks had done, struggled, in historian John D'Emilio's phrase, "to discard the self-hatred they have internalized."

The New Conservatism

Those involved in the social movements of the 1960s saw themselves as "progressives" on the left, and it was not long before they were answered by a resurgence of conservative sentiment and political activism—meaning by "conservative" an affection for traditional institutions of the patriarchal family, the local church, free-enterprise pursuit of wealth, and traditional moral values. Barry Goldwater's lopsided defeat in the 1964 presidential campaign created the false impression that this "conservatism" was a marginal force in American public life, and Nixon's 1968 election with 43 percent of the vote hardly disturbed this conclusion. But the pendulum of politics was in fact swinging hard to the right. Liberalism, hoping to be judged by its admirable ends of social justice and equality, had become associated with the unpopular means it adopted to achieve those ends: a bureaucratic structure of social regulation, a welfare state with an expanding clientele, affirmative action, school busing. Many yearned to abandon these policy pathways, and address other pressing issues, such as crime, which by government figures had increased (crimes of violence) three times from 1960 to 1980. Chief Justice Warren Burger reflected this concern when he told the American Bar Association that "crime and fear of crime have permeated the fabric of American life. Like it or not we are approaching the status of an important society whose capability of maintaining elementary security . . . is in doubt."

Beneath these secular concerns moved religious tides which have periodically altered American politics. Evangelical protestantism found the 1970s a boom era for converts, energy, money, and influence. Both *Time* and *Newsweek* declared 1976 to be the year of "The Evangelical," noting the large membership gains among churches offering a religion of born-again fundamentalism. Former Black Panther Eldridge Cleaver announced his born-again conversion, convicted Watergate felon Charles Colson published *Born Again* and enjoyed best-seller status, while Billy Graham's *Decision* sold 24 million copies. On college campuses, revivals and crusades for Christ gathered large followings, and private schools run by evangelical sects experienced strong growth—Bob Jones University in South Carolina, Pepperdine University in California, Wheaton College in Illinois. While mainstream churches such as the Methodists, Episcopalians, and Presbyterians were static or slightly declining in membership, the Southern Baptist convention grew above the 13 million mark, and the Assemblies of God grew 30 percent during the 1970s.

The energies of the fundamentalist religious revival flowed into politics, reinforcing the political right. The anti-ERA campaign was a leading example, but deeper emotional currents were tapped by the abortion issue, a primary stimulus to conservative activism. The Supreme Court's *Roe v. Wade* decision provoked a groundswell of antiabortion protest by people whose moral universe made no sense if human life was not absolutely and always inviolate. "Pro-life" or "right to life" organizations burgeoned into political activity, pressing for a reversal of the *Roe* decision, for laws to force minors to obtain parental consent for abortions, for elimination of all federal funding for family planning services here and overseas. "Pro-choice" groups resisted, defending abortion not as a good idea in itself but as an inalienable right of women. The public was divided, a majority apparently favoring some right to abortion, certainly when the mother's health was endangered.

The abortion issue siphoned large political energies into conservative political activism in the 1970s, aided by objections to the radical feminist challenge to female domesticity, the widening demand for tolerance of homosexuality, the civil libertarian defense of pornography. Many streams came together to form a New Right in the 1970s: evangelical Christians, antifeminists, conservative businessmen from the Sunbelt, southern opponents of racial integration. And taxpayers in June 1978, by a landslide vote, passed Proposition 13 in California, a measure designed to reduce property taxes by 57 percent and force the politicians to live within reduced means.

What was sometimes called the New Right in 1978 was a loose coalition of groups and collected grievances, with no acknowledged leader, in view of Barry Goldwater's defeat in 1964 and California actor and former Governor Ronald Reagan's age (67). Called a "conservative" social movement, it was essentially populist in its anger at eastern centers of power and at modernism in culture. It proclaimed a mission of radical change: more government for moral regulation and fighting the Cold War, less government in the marketplace. These sentiments found simplistic and hyperbolic expression in the sermons of evangelical preacher Jerry Falwell and the "direct mail" solicitations of Richard Viguerie. They found more reasoned and factual exposition from "neo-conservative" intellectuals, writing in journals such as *The Public Interest, National Review,* and *Policy Review,* or convening in "think tanks" such as the American Enterprise Institute or the Heritage Foundation.

Jimmy Carter had come to office in 1977 in part because of these conservative-populist currents. He was an outsider, a born-again Baptist, a Sunbelter. Yet he was also a Democrat tied to the New Deal coalition and heritage, and found it increasingly difficult to navigate between the older liberals on one side of him and the aroused New Right on the other. It was not good news for his presidency that California voters in 1978 confirmed Proposition 13, signaling that the pendulum was moving farther to the right.

BIBLIOGRAPHY FOR PART FOUR

ABERNATHY, M. GLENN, et al., eds. *The Carter Years: The President and Policymaking.* New York: Viking, 1984.

ADAM, BARRY D. *The Rise of a Gay and Lesbian Movement.* Boston: Twayne Publishers, 1987.

AMBROSE, STEPHEN. *Nixon: The Triumph of a Politician, 1962–1972,* Vol. II. New York: Simon & Schuster, 1989.

———. *Nixon: Ruin and Recovery, 1973–1990,* Vol. III. New York: Simon & Schuster, 1991.

ANSON, ROBERT S. *McGovern: A Biography.* New York: Holt, Rinehart and Winston, 1972.

BARNEY, GERALD O., ed. *The Unfinished Agenda: The Citizen's Policy Guide to Environmental Issues, A Task Force Report Sponsored by the Rockefeller Brothers Fund.* New York: Crowell, 1977.

BERNSTEIN, CARL, and BOB WOODWARD. *All the President's Men.* New York: Simon & Schuster, 1974.

BOWDEN, CHARLES. *Killing the Hidden Waters.* Austin: University of Texas Press, 1977.

BRODER, DAVID S. *The Party's Over: The Failure of Politics in America.* New York: Harper & Row, 1972.

CARTER, JIMMY. *Why Not the Best?* Nashville, TN: Broadman Press, 1977.

COLE, H. S. D., ed. *Models of Doom: A Critique of the Limits to Growth.* New York: Universe Books, 1973.

COMMONER, BARRY. *The Closing Circle: Nature, Man, and Technology.* New York: Knopf, 1971.

CRAWFORD, ALAN. *Thunder on the Right: The "New Right" and the Politics of Resentment.* New York: Pantheon, 1980.

DAVIES, CLARENCE J., AND BARBARA S. DAVIES. *The Politics of Pollution.* Indianapolis, IN: Pegasus, 1975.

D'EMILIO, JOHN. *Sexual Politics, Sexual Communities: The Making of a Homosexual Minority in the U.S., 1940–1970.* Chicago: University of Chicago Press, 1983.

EVANS, ROWLAND, AND ROBERT NOVAK. *Nixon in the White House: The Frustration of Power.* New York: Random House, 1971.

FLETCHER, W. WENDELL, AND CHARLES E. LITTLE. *The American Cropland Crisis.* Bethesda, MD: American Land Forum, 1982.

FLINK, JAMES J. *The Automobile Age.* Cambridge, MA: MIT Press, 1988.

FRASER, T. G. *The USA and the Middle East since World War II.* New York: St. Martin's, 1989.

FREEMAN, JO. *The Politics of Women's Liberation: A Case Study of an Emerging Social Movement and Its Relation to the Policy Process.* New York: McKay, 1975.

GARROW, DAVID J. *Liberty & Sexuality: Right to Privacy and the Making of Roe v. Wade.* New York: Macmillan, 1993.

GRAHAM, HUGH DAVIS. *The Civil Rights Era: Origins and Development of National Policy, 1960–1972.* New York: Oxford University Press, 1990.

GRAHAM, OTIS L., JR. *Toward a Planned Society: From Roosevelt to Nixon.* New York: Oxford University Press, 1976.

GREEN, DONALD. *Land of the Underground Rain: Irrigation on the Texas High Plains, 1910–1970.* Austin: University of Texas Press, 1973.

HALDEMAN, H. R. *The Haldeman Diaries: Inside the White House.* New York: Putnam, 1994.

HEALY, ROBERT. *Land Use and the States.* Baltimore: The Johns Hopkins University Press, 1976.

HEILBRONER, ROBERT L. *An Inquiry into the Human Prospect.* New York: Norton, 1974.

HERSH, SEYMOUR M. *The Price of Power: Kissinger in the Nixon White House.* New York: Summit Books, 1983.

HOFF, JOAN. *Nixon Reconsidered.* New York: Basic Books, 1994.

HOLDREN, JOHN, AND PHILIP HERRERA. *Energy: A Crisis in Power.* San Francisco: Sierra Club, 1971.

JONES, CHARLES. *Clean Air: The Policies and Politics of Pollution Control.* Pittsburgh: University of Pittsburgh Press, 1975.

JORDAN, HAMILTON. *Crisis: The Last Year of the Carter Presidency.* New York: Putnam, 1982.

KAUFMAN, BURTON I. *The Presidency of James Earl Carter, Jr.* Lawrence: University of Kansas Press, 1993.

KELLY, KATIE. *Garbage: The History and Future of Garbage in America.* New York: Saturday Review Press, 1973.

KESSLER-HARRIS, ALICE. *Out to Work: A History of Wage-Earning Women in the United States.* New York: Oxford University Press, 1983.

KUTLER, STANLEY. *The Wars of Watergate: The Last Crisis of Richard Nixon.* New York: Knopf, 1990.

LAWSON, STEVEN F. *Running for Freedom: Civil Rights and Black Politics since 1941.* Philadelphia: Temple University Press, 1991.

LOVINS, AMORY. *Soft Energy Paths: Toward a Durable Peace.* New York: Penguin, 1977.

LUKER, KRISTIN. *Abortion and the Politics of Motherhood.* Berkeley: University of California Press, 1984.

MAGRUDER, JEB STUART. *An American Life: One Man's Road to Watergate.* New York: Atheneum, 1974.

CARTER'S SECOND HALF

Neither modesty of goals nor recognition of limits on presidentially initiated change were part of Jimmy Carter's outlook. This was especially true in foreign policy, where his goals were ambitious and idealistic—to safeguard human rights, settle the Arab–Israeli quarrel, return the Canal Zone to Panama, and end the arms race. The latter was a goal that had eluded every president since Warren Harding. Carter's intentions were announced at the very outset of his presidency, when in his inaugural address he made the astonishing pledge to seek the elimination of all nuclear weapons. Within weeks he had challenged the Soviets to a mutual slash in missile numbers, and moved to negotiations toward a second SALT (Strategic Arms Limitations) Treaty to extend the controls agreed to in 1972 under SALT I. Though nuclear weaponry was awesomely complex, Carter's basic position seemed clear enough: The limits imposed by SALT I still allowed each superpower sufficient ability to destroy the other several times over (the U.S.S.R. was permitted 2600 missiles, the United States 1700, but with about equivalent destructive power), so further reductions could safely be made. The military on both sides were suspicious of any reductions, but so great were the financial burdens of the nuclear arms race that both governments persisted in negotiations, and Carter was able to sign the SALT II treaty with Brezhnev in May 1979.

Even as the arms negotiators had worked toward that ceremony, changes had taken place which would make it an empty exercise. Spurred by the humiliation felt by their military and political leadership during the facedown with the United States during the Cuban Missile Crisis, the Soviets in the early 1960s had begun an intense effort to strengthen what they, too, called "defensive capabilities." By the late 1970s, U.S. intelligence reported great advances in Soviet missile accuracy, deployment of multiple warheads on single missiles, medium-range weapons along the Ural Mountains aimed at NATO forces, as well as modernized conventional forces and a large civil defense program. No one in the West, of course, could be sure what these developments meant. Some analysts saw this as merely a Soviet drive for equality with their dual adversaries, the West and China. In this view the Soviets still dreaded war and desired peace, and their achievement of rough nuclear parity with combined opposing forces set the stage for a mutually acceptable cap on the arms race that so strained both sides. But conservative politicians, publicists, and most high-ranking military officers trumpeted a different and deeply alarming interpretation: The Soviet government, a malevolent clique quite capable of launching a surprise attack to demolish the West, was within reach of nuclear superiority, or at least a first-strike capability (the two claims were often confused). In this view the time for arms limitation agreements had passed, and the United States required its own rapid arms buildup, both to demonstrate "will" (an important word to hawks in the United States, and presumably also in the U.S.S.R.) and to ensure against falling behind.

As the nuclear strategy debate surged through the media and the halls of

Congress—where most members claimed very little technical grasp of the issues—it was reported that Cuban armed forces were operating along with Soviet advisors in Angola and Ethiopia. Then, in the last week of 1979, Soviet troops invaded Afghanistan to suppress a simmering rebellion. A great outcry occurred, as some Americans, forgetting that our military and paramilitary interventions in places such as Vietnam and Guatemala might once have been seen in the same light, declared that the Soviets were enlarging the Cold War. With the public alarmed and anti-Russian feeling running high, the critics of SALT II held the upper hand. Republicans questioned Carter's "toughness with the Russians," even though the president condemned the Afghanistan invasion as "the most serious threat to world peace since World War II," ordered a boy-cott of the 1980 Olympic Games, and launched an arms buildup centered around an expensive and implausible mobile-basing racetrack for the new MX missile. Aware that the Senate would not ratify even the modest SALT II treaty in this climate, the administration left it in limbo—signed by heads of state but unratified, a symbol of dashed hopes.

This outcome underlined a larger pattern in the Carter administration's record in both domestic and foreign affairs. Carter's resolute idealism was car-rying him beyond where the Congress, presumably reflecting the public's anx-ieties and new truculence toward communists, was willing to go. The president had repeatedly taken what he thought was the high moral ground in interna-tional matters, striving for arms reduction and working for human rights. He appointed an articulate black Congressman from Georgia, Andrew Young, as ambassador to the United Nations, and Young used that platform to express ringing sympathy with oppressed racial minorities in South Africa and else-where. Carter asked the Senate to ratify two treaties with Panama in the spring of 1978, returning control of the canal to that nation by stages. In both cases, the administration maneuvered to set a new course for American diplomacy, aimed not at the "communist threat" which had so transfixed much postwar diplo-macy, but at grievances felt by masses of people abroad. Yet there seemed more criticism of Young's sympathy with black Africa and of the Panama Canal "giveaway" (narrowly approved by the Senate, with only two votes to spare) than there was public support.

Anticommunism, one might have concluded, still played best in American foreign policy.

A Presidency in Difficulty

Despite use of the presidency's many means of influencing public opinion, Jimmy Carter slipped steadily downward in the polls throughout 1979. By year's end his "approval rating" matched Harry Truman's low ranking when he left office in 1952. While such polls may be questioned, and every president begins with high approval and slips in office, the administration was not given high marks on Capitol Hill or in the nation's editorial pages.

White House aides conceded that activist presidents like Carter must expect to stir criticism, but they were privately baffled, for there was much that was praiseworthy in the Georgian's record. His cabinet appointments were highly regarded for ability, and blacks and women found the administration more open than any in history. Carter named two women to his cabinet, one of them black, placed black ambassadors in six capitals abroad and at the United Nations, appointed blacks as secretary of the army and solicitor general. His environmental record may have been the strongest of any president, and included an unprecedented challenge to the pork-barrel, environmentally careless system of selecting water projects, support for a tough strip-mining control bill that became law, and appointment of a commission to project environmental trends and recommend appropriate corrections (the Global 2000 Committee). He backed and enthusiastically signed the Alaska Land Act, doubling the size of the national parks, wilderness areas, and game refuges in one stroke. Responding to the fiscal and social crisis gripping many of the nation's older cities, the administration announced a concerted urban policy in 1978, the first positive response of any president to a 1970 congressional request for a rationalization of federal policies affecting urban growth. Carter also attempted to lead Congress toward new solutions of several notoriously difficult problems that legislators prefer to evade: the tax system, welfare, immigration policy.

And Carter's announcement in September 1978 that President Anwar Sadat of Egypt and Prime Minister Menachem Begin of Israel had signed "A Framework for Peace in the Middle East" was a triumph of personal diplomacy. Though they were only a first step toward ending thirty years of violence between Israel and Arab states, the Camp David Accords were the most positive development in that region since the series of wars that began in 1967. They were possible only because of Carter's painstaking mediation between the two leaders during an intense two-week conference at the presidents's retreat in the Catoctin Mountains west of Washington.

Beyond this part of the Carter record, supporters would correctly point out that his vice president, Walter Mondale, was actively involved in decision making, a decided improvement over the traditional role for vice presidents. Carter's wife, Rosalyn, was articulate, attractive, and conceded to be a strong asset. And Jimmy Carter himself, who demonstrated a formidable grasp of detail in his frequent press conferences, was fond of homework and long hours in the office.

Yet the Carter administration had achieved no major legislative successes, no large rearrangements of any of the ailing systems which it addressed— whether they be energy policy, the complex welfare system, urban decline, or taxation. The president's approval rating stabilized below 30 percent in 1979, and critics compiled a portrait of inadequate presidential leadership: Carter's administration lacked a compelling theme; he was swamped in detail and offered no clear sense of priorities; he was a poor educator; he could not work with Congress. He was "a sensible President," editorialized *The New York Times*, "but not yet a leader or teacher, even for a quiet time."

Carter's mounting difficulties ran deeper, however, than what he did or failed to do. The public mood in the 1970s had slipped into a pessimism and frustration that would deepen as the century moved toward a close. America had lost a war, expelled a president who unconvincingly denied that he was "a crook," and then entered a decade of economic difficulties in which the standard of living stagnated. Political turmoil in Iran in 1978 produced an oil-led inflationary surge, the inflation rate jumping from 7 percent to 11.3 percent in a year, and interest rates surging toward a high of 18 percent, which they would reach in 1980. The public was resentful of the oil companies and the rich in general, three fourths of those polled in 1977 agreeing that "the rich get richer and the poor get poorer." But the main target was government, as taxpayer backlash rippled across the latter part of the decade. Proposition 13 in California in 1978 passed by a two-to-one majority, pushing property taxes back to preinflationary levels and limiting the ability of governments to fund social programs. Ineffective government seemed especially evident in surging crime rates. In large cities the rate of violent crime—homicides, rapes, and robberies—tripled from the 1960s to the end of the 1970s.

The public distrust of government thus ran deep, and Carter was exposed at the pinnacle. Then bad luck arrived in the form of the Iranian revolution. In the spring of 1979, a second Arab oil embargo was launched by the new and virulently anti-American revolutionary Islamic government that had overthrown the U.S.-backed Iranian government of Shah Mohammed Pahlavi in February. Again there were long lines at the gas pumps. Then, in November, an Iranian student mob stormed the American embassy in Teheran and took fifty-two American hostages. Carter could not keep "the hostage crisis" out of the headlines, and a frustrated public felt further humiliation when, in April 1980, an American helicopter force launched toward Teheran from a carrier in the Persian Gulf was turned back by dust storms and equipment failure.

Eventually the signs of political deterioration jolted the White House into dramatic efforts to reverse perceptions of weakness or drift. Receiving a candid and alarming memo from top aide Stuart Eisenstat, which reviewed the political weakness of the administration and detected a "malaise of the spirit" in the nation, Carter suddenly canceled a scheduled July 5 speech on energy policy, secluded himself at the Camp David retreat, and summoned over 100 citizens and officials to give him their complaints and advice. He reported his findings and conclusions in a dramatic television appearance on July 15, speaking of a "crisis of confidence" permeating the national atmosphere while admitting that legitimate criticisms had been made of his own leadership. Carter clearly wished to reverse the perception of himself and his government, pled for a sense of urgency about what he saw as the nation's chief problem—the energy crisis—and announced a sweeping reorganization of his cabinet and White House staff.

These bold maneuvers did not reassure the media or, apparently, the public. Carter appeared so vulnerable in early 1980 that several leading Democrats decided to challenge the president for renomination, chief among them Senator Ted Kennedy of Massachusetts and Governor Jerry Brown of California. With all the advantages of incumbency, Carter was barely able to stave off the strongest opponent, Kennedy, and was renominated in July by a divided and disgruntled Democratic convention.

THE ELECTION OF 1980: ANOTHER INTERRUPTED PRESIDENCY

With the Carter administration in trouble, the Republican nomination became more than usually attractive. The field of aspirants was full, but the nomination could not be denied the persistent former governor of California and former movie actor (he acted in fifty-three films), Ronald W. Reagan.

Reagan had been mentioned as a presidential contender in every campaign since 1968, and he tirelessly traveled the lecture circuit to bolster the spirits of hard-line conservatives with "the Speech"—an unvarying and skillfully delivered recitation of the evils of government and of the liberals who assigned it so much to do. Reagan was a former liberal himself, by his own admission "a very emotional New Dealer," who had voted for Franklin Roosevelt four times. But he had moved quickly and far to the right during the 1950s as he appeared as spokesman for the General Electric company, and switched his affiliation to Republican in 1962. Now he was an uncompromising opponent of the entire welfare-regulatory state, as well as an aggressive proponent of large appropriations for the military and a clear commitment to victory in the Cold War. These ideas put him to the right edge of his own party where Goldwater had originated, but Reagan was a master of television and platform, a genial man of simple but obviously sincere views. His backers were well financed and intensely loyal, and Reagan swept through the primaries to nomination.

Democrats began by underestimating Reagan's strengths. His age (sixty-nine) appeared to be a considerable handicap, but this was offset by his robust health and relaxed self-assurance. President Carter hoped to depict Reagan as an extremist in both domestic and international matters, but the Californian phrased his conservative convictions with an air of reasonableness and geniality. He promised a return of prosperity by "getting the government off the backs" of businessmen and consumers, an appealingly simple idea which still had a nice ring to Americans. The public appeared to respond to the antigovernment theme, or at least were not alarmed by Reagan's affable version of it. Ironically, this had been the theme that Jimmy Carter rode to the White House in 1976.

Carter was burdened not only by his personification of "the government," but also by the state of the economy. Inflation reached 11.3 percent in 1979 and 13.5 percent in 1980, with interest rates in that year reaching 18 percent; unemployment at the end of 1980 stood at 7.1 percent, or 7.4 million people; the federal deficit jumped to $59 billion in 1980 ($130 billion over Carter's four years). He was also the victim of intense public indignation at the government's continuing failure to free the fifty-two American hostages held in Iran. His early lead over Reagan in the polls eroded as the campaign went on, the public apparently concluding that Reagan was after all an acceptable choice to replace an ineffective regime. The Republican presidential campaign was also lavishly financed, the GOP outspending the Democrats by $152 million to $98 million, thus purchasing more of the slick television spots which an increasingly skillful public relations profession eagerly sold to both parties. The Californian closed his last TV debate with Carter by turning earnestly to the camera with the request that Americans "ask yourself, are you better off than you were four years ago?" This seemed to simplify the choice. Voters dismissed Carter in favor of a man whose vocabulary apparently did not include the word "sacrifice." Reagan's margin of victory was sizable, the Californian carrying forty-four states to Carter's six, the popular vote reaching 43.9 million to 36.4 million (with 5.7 million going for independent John B. Anderson, whose votes appeared to come largely from disaffected Carter voters from 1976). The Democrats lost twelve seats in the Senate, and yielded control of the House.

Reagan and his party claimed a mandate for whatever it was they now wished to do, but to the exultant Republicans there might well have been sobering after-thoughts. The election of 1980 produced a weak turnout of a shade less than 54 percent of the eligible voters, the lowest since 1948. While this decline in voter participation had been underway for decades, many voters had expressed to pollsters and reporters that they despaired at the low quality of both candidates. It was a choice, quipped political scientist Gerald Pomper, between "the evil of two lessers." Carter's pollster Patrick Cadell saw the election not as an endorsement of the winner but as a repudiation of both the administration and the party in power. It was "a mass protest vote against the in-party," he summed it up; "There's been a lot of frustration and anger out there." Unless one believed that Carter's defeat was the result entirely of his own mistakes, the recent pattern of one-term presidents hinted at structural problems within American political and economic systems which would surely plague Ronald Reagan in his turn.

ASSESSING JIMMY CARTER

Given the American media's preoccupation with the personal virtues and flaws of public figures, the first efforts to account for the resumption of a rightward turn in our politics marked by the 1980 election was to stress Jimmy Carter's defects as a political leader. Though normally seen smiling in public, Carter did not easily project personal warmth, and failed to establish a strong bond either with congressional Democrats or the public. A former engineer and farmer, a self-avowed populist and born-again Christian, his own image was diffuse, as was the direction in which he wished to lead the nation. At times he delivered speeches laced with inspirational language, but he seemed a technocrat rather than a visionary. The kindest assessment came from Carter's attorney general, Griffin Bell, in his memoirs: "Jimmy was about as good a President as an engineer can be." Historian Eric Goldman was more blunt: "Carterism does not march and it does not sing. It is cautious, muted, grayish, at times even crabbed." Or as a former aide stated as he resigned his White House position, "Carter does not lift off."

While such assessments provide part of the answer to the repudiation of Carter's leadership, his troubles revealed deeper problems within American government and society. Enormous expectations are laid upon any president in the United States, but the chief executive's powers are quite circumscribed. The federal bureaucracy, or "permanent government," is often resistant to his directions. Congress is a fragmented assemblage of independent policy entrepreneurs left even more undisciplined each decade as the political parties continue to decline in importance.

A group of forty-nine scholars, polled in 1981, listed Jimmy Carter among America's ten worst presidents. With time and perspective, it is very likely that Carter will receive much better marks than when he was voted out of office. He attempted much, and proposed thoughtful solutions to many major national problems. With the passage of time, his defeat seems less a reflection of his qualities and performance than of the continuing erosion of his party's electoral base, and the public's longing for the sort of easy path back to the "good old days" promised by the former movie actor from California.

THE "REAGAN REVOLUTION"—FIRST PHASE

Some of the new administration's policy proposals had been worked out in advance, much of the spadework being done by a conservative think tank, the Heritage Foundation. The basic political strategy was sketched by a team headed by Congressman Jack Kemp and Reagan's designated head of the Office of Management and Budget, David Stockman. In a December 1980 memo to the president-elect, Kemp and Stockman urged him to strike quickly on the model of FDR's famous "hundred days." Economic recovery could only come, they reasoned, if bold policy changes were forced through Congress in the early honeymoon period. The changes they recommended were a triad of tax cuts, budget reduction, and deregulation of business. If done slowly and hesitantly, these measures together would merely run up huge deficits, and recovery might not come. If done dramatically and quickly, with flair and confidence, they should produce the altered public and investor psychology which would "turn the economy around."

The theory behind these proposals was "supply-side economics," meant to replace the Democrats' postwar fascination with priming the "demand side" of the economic equation through federal spending. To the Reaganites, the troubled performance of American capitalism was simply explained: The government (the federal government—inexplicably, they did not include state or local governments in this charge) stifled enterprise with burdensome taxes and regulation. Reagan's advisers broke sharply with GOP tradition in their willingness to accept federal deficits for a time, since they knew that a Democrat-dominated Congress would not cut spending as fast as the administration cut taxes. In the end, however, economic growth produced by Reagan's policies would ensure rising revenues even from a smaller tax base. The underlying theory was the old Coolidge-Mellon "trickle-down" theory in modern dress, the notion that if the rich are relieved of taxes they will have unimpaired incentives

Ronald and Nancy Reagan greet the inaugural day crowd.
(*UPI/Bettmann Newsphotos*)

to invest and will make the economy hum with jobs and growth. "It's kind of hard to sell 'trickle-down,' " Reagan's budget director admitted to a journalist, "so we invented 'supply-side.' "

Armed with this mix of old and new-sounding ideas, Ronald Reagan took the oath of office, criticized his liberal predecessors and the meddling government he was about to head, and plunged into the task of reform. The administration moved on two fronts. Cabinet and other senior appointments went to conservatives who shared Reagan's ideology—make the government smaller in regulation and welfare, make it larger in defense and secret intelligence institutions. When Caspar Weinberger went to head the Defense Department, James Watt to Interior, William French Smith to Justice, and Anne Burford to the Environmental Protection Agency, they took with them like-minded aides who would begin at once to change policy through administrative rule making. "Don't just stand there," was the motto attributed to Reagan's chairman of the Council of Economic Advisors: "Undo something!"

But reform on the scale Reagan and his movement wanted would also require legislation. Reagan went to Congress in the spring of 1981 with requests for sharp budget reductions in some forms of domestic spending: welfare benefits to the poor (food stamps, aid to families with dependent children, public housing), education, regulatory agencies. Only $30 billion could be wrung from such areas, and Reagan was afraid to cut into the large portions of the domestic budget—the middle-class entitlement programs, such as social security, Medicare, and farm programs. "Waste" and "fat" were said by campaigning Republicans to offer targets for enormous savings, but once in charge of the government they discovered that very little could be saved there. Still, Reagan in 1981 led the way toward a historic capping of the growth of the welfare and regulatory state.

The "Reagan revolution," as journalists in search of exciting copy began to call the administration's 1981 program, required legislation in two other areas. Tax cutting was seen as a central reform, and the cuts should come mostly in the rates of the wealthy and corporations.

Most Democrats complained at the Reagan budget-cutting proposals and did not like the tax reform program any better. But Reagan had seized the momentum in that "honeymoon" period when presidents are most popular and are thought to deserve a try for their theories, however implausible they may seem. Reagan's reform plans were also given a boost by the popular reaction to the president's courage and composure when he was shot by a would-be assassin on the afternoon of March 30, 1981, while leaving the Washington Hilton Hotel. Mentally unbalanced James W. Hinkley, Jr., disappointed in love and with personal fame rather than politics as his motivation, fired six shots at close range from a cheap revolver. Four men were hit, the president receiving a ricochet bullet off the side of his limousine which entered under his left armpit, struck the seventh rib, and lodged in Reagan's lung. The president recovered quickly after surgery and a period of hospitalization, benefiting in the polls from his display of calm, stamina, and lack of anger at his assailant, who was captured at the scene.

That spring, no one in either congressional party had a set of ideas in which they believed as strongly as the administration believed in its economic package. Most Democrats decided to give the new and now wounded president the benefit of the doubt. The Economic Recovery Tax Act of 1981 thus became law, though it became more sweeping than the White House intended. Sensing a general tax cut, special-interest groups rushed to add their own tax breaks to the list. "The hogs were really feeding," admitted startled budget director David Stockman as he watched the summertime gutting of the tax code in 1981.

On the defense side of the budget, Reagan went in the opposite direction. A buildup of conventional and nuclear defense forces was perhaps Reagan's central commitment, and the president proposed a $181 billion increase in defense spending over five years, a sum three times as large as the increase required for the Vietnam fighting from 1965 to 1970. "They got a blank check," said Reagan's budget director of the military-industrial complex in 1981.

The year 1982 proved a hard one for Ronald Reagan and his allies. Supply-side theory was not working, or at least not immediately. Reagan's policies led to historically huge budget deficits—$58 billion in 1981, an astonishing $111 billion in 1982. And the deficits did not at once spur economic growth—quite the reverse, as the deepest recession of the postwar era gripped the economy in 1981–1982. The unemployment rate at the end of 1982 reached 10.8 percent, the highest since 1940, with mounting business and bank failures. The only good economic news was the falling inflation rate, down from 13 percent in 1980 to 4 percent in 1982. The "Reagan recession" sharply ended the president's honeymoon, Democrats condemning not only the faltering economy but pointing out that the budget cuts had been unfairly aimed at the poor while the tax cuts aided mostly those in upper-income brackets.

REAGAN AND THE LARGER WORLD

Ronald Reagan approached the conduct of foreign relations with simplistic but deeply held views. He liked to recall a story (no one knew if it was true) that President John F. Kennedy was told by Clare Booth Luce that the only question to be asked of any president was whether he "stopped the Communists" on his watch, or not. Reagan agreed, and he meant to oppose communists everywhere—in skirmishes in our hemisphere, but most especially in the long-term struggle against the Soviets' "evil empire." His early budgetary choices favored more government spending only in the arms buildup, where he accelerated trends begun under Carter. Beyond this, the administration seemed to have no clear strategy for persistent problems in the Middle East, Latin America, or Africa.

Sensing American irresolution, the Begin government in Israel aggressively expanded Israeli settlements in the West Bank, an ominous move which was in clear violation of the Camp David Accords. Israel invaded Lebanon in June 1982 to eliminate the Palestinian Liberation Organization bastion there, and soon Lebanon was split between Israel and Syrian armies, with Lebanese factions

chose foreign-made products, U.S. industries declined. Once-dominant heavy industries lost shares of domestic and world markets. The United States produced 39 percent of the world's steel in 1955 but 15 percent in 1981, 68 percent of the world's cars in 1955 but 21 percent in 1981. Displaced workers found jobs in the Reagan-era expansion that began in 1983, but often these were lower-paying jobs—cooking MacDonald's hamburgers instead of assembly-line work in steel mills or automobile plants. These trends meant lower standards of living, but through the 1970s and 1980s this outcome was postponed by importing more than we exported, consuming more than we produced. This in turn meant huge trade deficits, the first one coming in 1971 after seventy-six years (1894–1971) of consecutive trade surpluses. Americans had reinvested their foreign earnings and become the world's #1 creditor nation, enjoying a stream of wealth from abroad. Then a small trade deficit of $–2.3 billion in 1971 signaled a weakening new trend. The trade deficit was $–33.9 billion by 1978, then surged to huge numbers under Reagan: $–41.5 billion in 1983, jumping to $–123.3 billion in the election year. Leading Democrats challenged the president's optimism in the face of such numbers, but the public seemed not to understand that such trade and budgetary deficits meant that the current prosperity was being borrowed, the debt to be repaid and the lower standard of living finally borne by the next generation of Americans. And voters in 1984 could not know that in 1985 Treasury officials would reluctantly announce that the overseas surplus had been erased by 1982 and by mid-decade the United States was the world's #1 *debtor* nation.

The Democrats struggled to find a way to make these signs of U.S. economic weakness Reagan's legacy, but made little headway with talk of ominous long-term trends in federal budget and trade deficits. What, indeed, did they propose to do differently than the deficit-spending, smiling Reagan? Among Democrats there was much interest in the idea of an "industrial policy" as the Democrats' answer to Reaganomics. This took various forms, but was essentially a proposal that the United States create a coherent strategy for international competition and fashion its plans through the sort of government-industry cooperation evident in Japan and elsewhere in the capitalist world. Ultimately, the "industrial policy" idea was shunned by the party's nominee, Walter Mondale, and it made no appearance in the campaign.

When Democrats raised "the fairness issue"—that Reagan's tax reforms had favored the rich, and his budgetary choices burdened the poor—they had impressive academic support and hoped for an attentive public. An Urban Institute report by Isabel Sawhill and John Palmer concluded in 1984:

> from 1980 to 1984, the typical middle-class family's income rose . . . about 1%. The average income of the poorest one-fifth of all families declined . . . by nearly 8%, whereas the average income of the most affluent one-fifth increased . . . by nearly 9%. These changes have caused the distribution of income to become more unequal. . . . The federal tax burden on business has declined dramatically.

Democrats hoped that such reports would help mobilize opposition to Reagan. Another natural constituency for an anti-Republican vote seemed to be the black community, whose leadership proclaimed that the Democrats' program of generous welfare, affirmative action, and school integration efforts were far better than Reagan's "neglect" of black America. Indeed, the Reagan administration's position on "civil rights," (which to most Americans meant race relations) was not neglect but a noticeable tilt in another direction. Reagan appointees to the U.S. Civil Rights Commission, the Justice Department, and the federal branch tended to be people who had doubts about the idea of affirmative action when it implied quotas based on race, were uneasy with busing for school integration, and argued that blacks would make faster social progress if they abandoned reliance upon the welfare state and turned to individual effort in the marketplace. Some black intellectuals were taking such positions—economist Thomas Sowell, journalist Walter E. Williams, EEOC Chairman Clarence Thomas—but Democrats hoped that millions of African-Americans would see Reagan's civil rights policies as the problem rather than the solution.

To this potential anti-Reagan vote might be added women in the "gender gap," where public opinion polls showed that women were 7 to 10 percent less likely to support the president at the end of his first term than men. Reagan had been passive on women's issues, except for opposing ERA and expressing steady opposition to the idea that abortions might sometimes be legally permitted. He had also offended the entire environmentalist community by appointing James Watt as Secretary of the Interior and Ann Gorsuch (Burford, after her 1983 marriage) as Director of the Environmental Protection Agency, signals that the administration intended not to enforce but to internally weaken the environmental regulations put on the books during the 1960s and 1970s.

Watt and Burford, both former Colorado lobbyists for business groups opposing environmental controls, took decisive command of their agencies and sharply altered the government's course without any change in the underlying statues. Watt ended the acquisition of new parkland and wetlands, launched a campaign to sell off "surplus" federal properties desired for development, virtually ended work on extending the Wild and Scenic River program, opened wilderness lands to oil and mineral exploration and development, and sped up the leasing of public lands to energy corporations at what a Congressional Budget Office study showed to be below-market prices. At the EPA, Burford and her aides first purged lower administrators and scientific consultants suspected of environmentalist leanings ("clean air extremist," read an EPA internal "hit list" leaked to Senator Gary Hart in 1983; "an environmental extreme environmentalist, should go," "get him out fast, extreme anti-nuclear type," or "all snail-darter types"), completed quick and generous settlements with companies charged with improper discharge of toxic wastes, and presided over a 40 percent reduction in the EPA's budget from 1981 to 1983. "The administration has broken faith with the American people on environmental protection," began a 1982 report of ten environmental groups, citing lax enforcement of existing air, water, toxic substance, and strip-mining laws, and giveaway sales of mineral, water, and range resources on public lands to private developers.

Burford and Watt were both eventually driven from office for careless statements and administrative irregularities, but it was not clear that Ronald Reagan's critics among environmentalists, African-Americans, and feminists gave the Democrats the upper hand. Would the public respond with anger to what some called the "sleeze factor," noting that top administrative officials (William Casey, head of the CIA; Edwin Meese, domestic counselor and attorney general) led a substantial list of those forced from office by charges of benefiting from their positions?

And what of Reagan's own reputation for ignorance and factual carelessness? Mark Green and Gail MacColl wrote a 1983 book (*There He Goes Again*) of 300 specific errors made by Reagan in response to press questions, and the president was widely known to be careless with facts. He was also careless of tongue, jokingly remarking on a microphone prior to an August 1983 interview that "I am pleased to tell you I have signed legislation to outlaw Russia forever. We begin bombing in five minutes." Reagan's biographer Lou Cannon wrote in the fall of 1984:

> Small wonder that Reagan . . . is kept away from the news media lining the ropes . . . and sequestered at other times with no excuse at all. Reagan's handlers understand far better than his critics how uninformed he is on many of the day's major issues. It is not accidental that they have made him the most isolated president of modern times.

Would Reagan falter under such criticisms, as had a series of presidents from Johnson through Carter? Or had America finally discovered a "Teflon" president, in the words of Congresswoman Pat Schroeder of Colorado—someone who remained unmarked by the mistakes that would damage anyone else? Renominated with Vice President George Bush at a euphoric Republican convention in August, Ronald Reagan entered the presidential campaign as a polarizing figure.

THE ELECTION OF 1984

The Democrats nominated Jimmy Carter's likable Vice President and former Senator Walter F. Mondale, who guaranteed at least a mark in the record books by selecting a woman, Representative Geraldine Ferraro of New York, as his running mate. Early polls ranked Mondale and the energetic, intelligent Ferraro even with the president, but their campaign was hampered by mishaps, and Reagan proved adroit at fashioning simple quips that called attention to the Democrats' liabilities as the party of high social spending and high taxes: " Democrats see an America where everyday is April 15th, Tax Day, we see an America where everyday is the Fourth of July." Reagan's television and movie background proved especially effective at projecting and rallying a sense of national pride, claiming not only that the economic recovery that had begun in 1983 was a sign of the return of America's former

Presidential candidate Walter Mondale and his running-mate, Congresswoman
Geraldine Ferraro, wave to their supporters at the 1984 Democratic Convention in
San Francisco. Ferraro was the first woman nominated by a major party to the
national ticket.
(UPI/Bettmann Newsphotos)

"Number One-ness" but that his military buildup and the end of the "Vietnam syndrome" of national self-doubt (Reagan had ordered U.S. troops into
two theaters in the fall of 1983, Beirut, Lebanon, and the Caribbean island of
Grenada) had restored the military side of America's dominance. "Just about
every place you look," Reagan claimed, "things are looking up. Life is better—
America is back—and people have a sense of pride they never thought they'd
feel again."

While Reagan did not perform well in the two TV debates, the outcome
was decisive. On election day, Reagan carried forty-nine states and 59 percent of the vote, amassing majorities among both the elderly and the young,
and pulling away from the Democrats a majority of Catholic voters, a large
number of Jews, and many blue-collar workers. The south and the Sunbelt
were now solidly Republican, and the nation clearly had a new majority
party—at least for presidential races. Democrats retained a majority in the
House and gained two seats in the Senate. Divided government would
continue.

REAGAN'S SECOND TERM

It is said that presidents have only three years for real achievement, since years 1 and 2 are spent learning the ropes, the fourth is preoccupied with reelection, and in years 7 and 8 the executive is weakened by the anticipation of retirement. For Ronald Reagan, however, the fifth and sixth years were a time not of fulfillment but of stumbling. A reorganized White House staff did not function well, top aides were associated with influence peddling, and stories multiplied that Reagan dozed at meetings and paid little attention to details. And by late 1986 the details of the "Iran-Contra affair" filled the news media, revealing an administration mired in confusion, bad judgment, and possible illegality.

Iran-Contra

By 1985 the White House-based scheme to raise money in the Middle East for Nicaraguan rebels was ready for action. To get around congressional restrictions, the administration, or parts of it (the State and Defense Department heads opposed the scheme, and stood clear), would secretly sell arms to Iran, which was then locked in a long, costly war with Iraq. Iran would then use its influence to release American hostages held in Lebanon. The cash from arms sales would be funneled to the Contras, along with other funds that "Ollie" North had secretly been raising from wealthy businessmen, foreign governments especially dependent on the United States or—like the sultan of Brunei—especially rich. Foreign policy, at least in Central America, would be untethered from any requirement to consult with Congress or seek funds from that branch.

The sales took place from 1985 through the middle of 1986, but only three Americans were released, and others were taken hostage in the interim. The illegal scheme was not working smoothly, and in November a Lebanese magazine broke the story. The Reagan administration had made five secret "arms for hostages" sales to Iran—a terrorist state that had recently been holding its own batch of American hostages—and diverted public money to the Contras. Reagan denied impropriety while Oliver North and his secretary shredded incriminating documents in the White House. As the story unfolded in the media, the president's public approval rating dipped below 50 percent for the first time. To contain the scandal, Reagan phoned Oliver North, called him "a national hero," and fired him and Poindexter. A review board headed by former Senator John Tower reported in February that there was no hard proof that Reagan was aware of the specific transfer of funds to the Contras, but to excuse the president from wrongdoing the commission had to portray him as often confused, disengaged, and unaware of the activities of aides he saw each day and who insisted they were carrying out his policies. Reagan's "management style," said the report, was badly flawed, and "chaos had descended on the White House." Television hearings through much of 1987 left the telegenic Colonel North a cult hero on the right, but Ronald Reagan's Teflon coating had slipped away, replaced by an image of befuddlement and a disordered government. Nixon was assumed to be in charge and was thus held

In 1981 Sandra Day O'Connor, appointed to the Supreme Court by Ronald Reagan,
became the first woman appointed to the nation's highest court.
(*UPI/Bettmann Newsphotos*)

responsible for Watergate; the elderly Reagan evaded indictment over "Irangate"
amid a wave of denials that he even understood what was going on.

The Reagan Revolution Falters

The administration held to the same domestic agenda through these setbacks. If
Reagan could not command Congress to give him his way in Central America,

environmental regulation, and other matters, he could appoint judges who shared his views. Reagan named 400 judges to the bench during his two terms, selecting those who seemed to share his views on civil rights, civil liberties, school prayer, and abortion. He named William Rehnquist Chief Justice of the Supreme Court and named three other conservative Justices, including the first woman on the Court, Sandra Day O'Connor. In the second term, the ebbing energies of the Reagan revolution moved from legislative to administrative and judicial activism.

Continuity: The Arms Buildup

The arms buildup that had been the very core of Reagan's approach to world affairs moved relentlessly ahead during his second term. The Pentagon asked for and received a 600-ship navy, and placed on line or into development expensive high-technology weaponry—100 MX intercontinental missiles, the B-1 intercontinental bomber (at $200 million apiece), a range of new tactical missiles including the Pershing II missiles deployed in Europe and pointed eastward. Presumably these would work as planned, but that could not be said of Reagan's most fantastic and expensive military gadget, the Strategic Defense Initiative (SDI), quickly dubbed "Star Wars."

SDI was the brainchild of nuclear physicist Edward Teller, who easily persuaded the president that a space-based "X-ray laser" could be orbited around the earth on platforms and direct energy beams powerful enough to destroy Soviet missiles in space before they descended toward American targets. The gullible president embraced the idea, and launched the plan for his "space shield" in a speech delivered in March 1983. Critics charged that the technology was dubious and the project fantastically expensive, but Congress appropriated $17 billion in R&D funds to Star Wars by the end of Reagan's first term in office. The project mystified and unnerved the Soviets, but American scientists found by 1987 that the laser-beam technology would not work as claimed. Star Wars research continued in another fantastic direction, this time on a plan for millions of cheap interceptors—"brilliant pebbles"—that would collide with Soviet missiles.

The "Evil Empire" Softens

Years later Reagan would claim that his arms buildup and staunch moral denunciation of the U.S.S.R. were responsible for the startling change in superpower relations that began in the 1980s, but neither he nor American experts in Soviet affairs foresaw the dramatic changes in Soviet leadership and the transformations to follow. Leonid Brezhnev had been General Secretary of the Communist Party since 1964, and after his death in 1982 Soviet leadership slipped aimlessly from one elderly bureaucrat to another. Then, in 1985, energetic, fifty-four-year-old Mikhail Gorbachev gained the leadership post, and not only the Soviet Union but the world would never be the same.

Gorbachev proved at once a critic of his own country's basic political and economic arrangements and an agent of internal reform. The Soviet Union, Gor-

Soviet leader Mikhail Gorbachev meets with President Ronald Reagan at one of their several historic "summit" meetings, where the two ideological opponents forged cordial personal ties.
(Reuters/Bettmann)

bachev admitted publicly, had for years been falling behind the West in technological innovation and basic economic progress. Stagnation ran deep into the society, and the answer was basic reform—*perestroika,* or restructuring of the Soviet economy by introducing modified market incentives, and *glasnost,* a new tolerance of dissent and an invitation to open discussion within the U.S.S.R., both coupled with a more cooperative relationship with the West. Britain's Prime Minister Margaret Thatcher commended Gorbachev to Reagan as "charming." After a stiff first meeting in Geneva late in 1985, Reagan and Gorbachev nine months later in Iceland struck up a friendly personal relationship that grew more cordial as the year went on. At Reykjavik Gorbachev surprised the United States by proposing eventual elimination of long-range missiles, and Reagan astonished his staff by suggesting the elimination of all missiles within ten years. The meeting was a fiasco, but a new spirit of "builddown" seemed to be replacing buildup. Both Ronald and Nancy Reagan were beginning to reveal an end-of-presidency desire to make a large mark in the quest for world peace, and Gorbachev's serious interest in arms reductions rested firmly on a growing economic crisis in the Soviet Union.

The only tangible progress made in this direction during Reagan's presidency was the 1987 U.S.–U.S.S.R. treaty removing intermediate-range missiles from Europe, accompanied by the astonishing Soviet agreement to permit mutual on-site inspection. Gorbachev visited Washington late in 1988, mixing with crowds and American celebrities in a public-relations coup, and began the withdrawal of Soviet troops from Afghanistan in 1988. There was talk of the "end of the Cold War," even whimsical suggestions that Gorbachev run for president of the United States in 1988. Reagan's presidency, on the single large issue of relations with the "evil empire" ("They've changed," Reagan said in 1987, and stopped using the phrase), was closing on a positive and even epoch-making note.

CHAPTER 10

It Was Not Morning in America: Reagan and Reality, 1984–1988

STORM CLOUDS: A TROUBLED ECONOMY

At home, economic trends made the Reagan legacy look increasingly dubious. The economy expanded steadily from the trough of late 1982 through the rest of Reagan's tenure, seventy-three months of consecutive growth with negligible inflation, and the president's economic report claimed much credit for "the Great American Job Machine," which created nearly 19 million new jobs during his two terms. It felt like prosperity, though certain regions (especially the energy-producing areas of the southwest) and sectors (agriculture) still did not find the 1980s to be good times. Beyond the unevenness of the prosperity, financial and structural trends were ominous.

Carter left office in a year in which the government ran up a $74 billion debt, which Reagan had of course denounced. But cutting taxes while launching a 40 percent increase in military spending produced staggering budget deficits: $208 billion in red ink in 1982, $220 billion in 1984—by the end of his presidency, cumulative debts of $1.338 trillion. Reagan blamed Congress, though he had never submitted a balanced budget and his advisors would later reveal that they had become converts to the Democrats' belief that deficits were useful things. How harmful were the deficits? In the short-term view of politicians of both parties, deficits were a way to satisfy the public's demand for more services without tax increases, and the Reagan era seemed to prove that they also drove the economy ahead. People who took a longer view were invariably alarmed. The deficits were an intergenerational crime, some pointed out, a "mortgage on the future" that would require our children to pay for us to live beyond our means. Worse, foreigners who had earned dollars trading with the United States purchased a large portion of each year's Treasury notes, which meant that a growing amount of the interest payments on the public debt was paid overseas to noncitizens.

(*Christian Science Monitor*)

The flow of foreign capital into the United States to acquire assets—Treasury and private securities, real estate, voting stock in American corporations—derived from huge annual trade imbalances, which left more dollars in foreign hands after American imports had been paid for. Jimmy Carter's last year saw a trade deficit of $25.5 billion, but the deficits registered in the Reagan years were staggering: $152.6 billion in 1986, $153 billion in 1987, $137 billion in 1988. In 1985 it was reported that the United States had, in the space of five years, erased a seventy-year accumulation of foreign assets and become not only a debtor nation, but the world's leading debtor. Behind the figures was a national pattern through the 1980s of spending $3 and earning $2: American exports rose from $19.7 billion in 1960 to $214 billion by the mid-1980s, a tenfold increase, but imports multiplied 25 times, rising from $14 billion to $338 billion over the same period. America was on a consuming binge, but its production was falling behind. The 1980s were filled with anxiety that the standard of living in the Reagan years was unsustainable, purchased by debt and putting off the *Day of Reckoning*, the title of a popular 1987 book by Harvard economist William Friedman. To many observers, it was clear that the economic troubles of the 1970s had not been remedied in the Reagan years, but only camouflaged with a debt-purchased prosperity. "The nation had chosen subsidized consumption now," wrote journalist James Fallows, "in return for a lower standard of living in the future."

The Competitiveness Issue: A Declining America?

Annual trade deficits apparently posed no serious immediate problem for the economy or the administration in office, but they were clearly a sign of economic weakness persisting beneath the Reagan reforms. American consumers were voting daily with their purchases, signaling that goods produced at home were often inferior in quality and price compared to those offered by foreigners—in textiles, steel, automobiles, consumer electronics, semiconductors, optical equipment. American manufacturing had moved out of the sheltered period after the World War II destruction of the manufacturing capabilities of our major trade partners and now faced a world in which German, Japanese, and a host of other Asian, Latin American, and European nations were producers of quality goods in both the older and the new, high-technology industries. Increasingly, Japan, with by far the largest part of the U.S. trade deficit, seemed to have found the secret to global economic power that the United States carried into the twentieth century and somehow lost in the 1970s. *Japan as Number One*, a best-selling book by Ezra Vogel published in 1979, was also a bestseller in an increasingly confident Japan. And whether the foreign goods beating American competitors were Japanese, Brazilian or Italian, "for the first time in American history we can neither dominate the world nor escape from it," in Henry Kissinger's words.

Such concerns buffeted the Reagan administration in its last years. To meet the criticism of Democrats that he was doing nothing on "the competitiveness problem," Reagan appointed a Commission on Industrial Competitiveness, but their December 1985 report was not what he had hoped. Instead of reporting that Reagan's reforms had eased such problems, the commission found that "the U.S. is losing its ability to compete in the world's markets. . . . While it is still the world's strongest economy . . . a close look at the U.S. performance during the past two decades reveals a declining ability to compete" with foreign-made products. It recommended "a strategy" to address declining competitiveness, a stronger governmental role within a business–government partnership. Reagan declined even to respond to the report, and the administration held through the second term the basic position taken in the first: Be optimistic; the problems of the U.S. economy would be cured by American business without government help or interference. "I believe that the most constructive thing government usually can do is simply get out of the way," the old actor wrote in his final (1988) economic report.

A Good Time to Be Rich

In reality, the basic Reaganite philosophy had two thrusts: getting government out of the way of Americans trying to make money, and getting government more in the way of communism abroad (thus a larger military and CIA) and in the way of abortion and pornography at home (thus aggressive courts and police enforcement). There had been considerable success on the first part of the agenda: A smaller governmental role through deregulation had been achieved in environmental oversight, transportation, and the banking and savings and loan industries. Taxes had been reduced for all taxpayers, most especially for corporations and the top income brackets. But with what results?

The administration claimed that the principal result was a long season of economic growth. Critics, however, credited the growth to massive deficit spending with an assist from tough monetary restraint on inflation by the Federal Reserve, which the administration did not control. There was, however, wide agreement that Reagan had made a difference. The core principle of Reaganism—that the central purpose of American life is to produce and consume wealth, and that the government's role is to bless and never impede this pursuit—encouraged a climate of materialism and speculation that prompted comparison between the 1980s and the 1920s.

With apparent envy rather than indignation, the media reported and the public absorbed the news of multimillion-dollar salaries for professional athletes, and compensation rates for corporate executives that seemed unbelievable. The chief executive of Walt Disney was paid $40 million in 1987, Reebok's head earned $11 million and United Airlines' chief $6 million, while the average annual compensation of the chief executives of America's top 330 corporations rose 62 percent between 1986 and 1988 to average $2 million. As the 1920s had seen binges of speculation in Florida real estate and Wall Street stocks, so the 1980s featured binges in real estate and corporate mergers. The public was regaled with stories of the sudden rise to wealth of real estate tycoon Donald Trump, computer services empire builder H. Ross Perot, chain store magnate Sam Walton. More significant to the nation's economy, the prospect of an ardently pro-capitalist, pro-wealth government helped send a "merger mania" through the financial community, the nation's largest corporations buying up rivals or being themselves taken over by purchasers who raised cash by issuing high-risk, high-yield "junk bonds." The justification for the sudden passion to buy and merge corporations was that many were undervalued on the stock market and needed new management. The immediate result of the merger wave of the 1980s was a greatly increased corporate debt burden and much-enriched lawyers, accountants, and brokers. Top Wall Street lawyers involved in such deals were making $50 to $100 million a year, and the fantastic profits earned by "raiders" such as Michael Milken, Ivan Boesky, Carl Icahn, and T. Boone Pickens spread the news of quick wealth and attracted many young lawyers and MBAs to careers pursuing Wall Street's soaring legal and brokerage fees.

Wealth was not only uncritically celebrated in the 1980s, it was being rearranged. While the United States had always held the dubious honor of being the industrialized nation with the sharpest cleavage between the rich and the poor, "by the middle of Reagan's second term . . . America's broadly defined 'rich'—the top half of 1% of the U.S. population—had never been richer," concluded journalist Kevin Phillips after a study of official statistics (*The Politics of Rich and Poor*, 1990). As Reagan's presidency closed, the poorest fifth of American families received 5 percent of national income, while the richest fifth took more than 50 percent. And trends were making for an evermore uneven distribution. From 1979 to 1987, the income of the poorest 10 percent of American

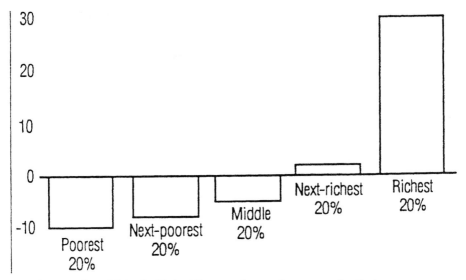

Distribution of wealth in the United States—change in average family income, 1977–1992. 1991–1992 represent CBO projections.
(Congressional Budget Office [CBO])

families fell 6 percent, after inflation, while families in the 90th percentile gained 14 percent, and the top 1 percent enlarged their share of national income from 8 to 15 percent, the number of millionaires growing at a rate fifteen times as fast as the general population. The American pyramid of income and wealth distribution became steeper across the 1980s.

Part of the explanation for such trends lay in Reagan's tax changes. The Congressional Budget Office calculated that the richest 1 percent of American families paid 30 percent less in federal taxes by the 1990s than they would have if the tax system of 1977 had remained in place. A 1978 capital gains tax cut, but especially Reagan's 1981 tax act, had decisively shifted the burden of taxation away from the rich. Indeed, some wealthy Americans found enough loopholes and evasions to make taxation an unimportant part of their lives: "We don't pay taxes. The little people pay taxes," New York hotel owner Leona Helmsley told her maid in the 1980s, just before she had the unusual experience of being indicted and convicted for tax evasion.

But there were other factors at work behind the shifting shares of income. American capitalism was caught up in a dynamic worldwide restructuring, and the industrialization of Asian and Latin American countries created an abundant labor supply to compete with America's blue-collar workforce. As the American economy churned out new wealth, the returns to labor, skilled or unskilled, went essentially flat, while the returns to capital—those who earn income on rents, dividends, capital gains, and interest—ran strongly ahead. The winners in the 1980s were the "paper entrepreneurs" (in Harvard professor Robert Reich's term) who arranged the fabulous corporate deals, investors, corporate executives, the professional classes generally and especially two-income professional families, and the elderly, whose social security payments were pushed ahead of GNP growth. The losers, apart from those losing jobs in factory and business closings, were blue-collar workers with a high-school diploma or less, female-headed households, the regions of the country most dependent on oil and mineral extraction, and small-scale farming. The ranks of those in poverty increased only slightly during the 1980s, but here, too, a dramatic restructuring was underway. Whereas the poor had for most of the twentieth century tended to be elderly and disabled, Great Society reforms had improved their lot while failing to anticipate a trend toward the "feminization of poverty" driven by an expansion in the numbers of unwed mothers. By the end of the decade one of every four births in the United States was to an unwed mother, with the highest rates occurring among blacks and Hispanics. These children, with their mothers, were now a large part of the nation's povertied class. They shared low income and bleak prospects with another mainly urban group, the growing ranks of the homeless—the chronically mentally ill, alcohol and drug addicts, women in flight from abusive spouses.

POPULATION/RESOURCES/ENVIRONMENT IN THE REAGAN ERA

The administration did not believe that there was a growing set of population-driven environmental problems either abroad or at home, and denied that the U.S. government had any business involving itself in such matters in any case. (Abortion, of course, was another matter; it was not seen as a population policy but as a matter of individual lives, and the administration very much wanted the government involved in preventing women from aborting their pregnancies.) Since preceding administrations and Congress had enacted environmental regulations and offered some support for family planning both at home and overseas, the Reagan administration moved energetically to reduce the federal government's involvement in them to a minimum. Thus Ronald Reagan ironically put birth control as well as environmental protection into the spotlight by attempting to roll back the federal government's role. Despite his popularity and some limited early successes, the Reagan revolution could not prevent the issues of the expansion of human numbers and their pressure on the natural habitat from continuing to move from the edges of public concern toward the center.

Global Population Trends

Globally, by the mid-1980s there were 15,000 human births an hour, 359,000 a day, producing after deaths were subtracted an increase of 82 million people a year. This was an unprecedented human expansion, most of them destined for lives of economic hardship in underdeveloped societies. The annual rate of population growth globally had declined to 1.8 percent from the 1960s high of 2.2 percent, good news which was seized upon by a few (most notably Herman Kahn and Julian Simon in *The Resourceful Earth,* 1982) to prove that the population problem was over. Economist Simon was a member of the Reagan administration's delegation to the 1984 World Population Conference in Mexico City. That delegation angered the American environmental community by taking the official position that population increase often stimulated economic growth, making everyone better off, and that where environmental problems arose the real culprit was too much government economic planning.

A clearer perspective came from the World Bank's *World Development Report* (1984), which pointed out that the twelve countries that had achieved zero population growth accounted for only 5 percent of the world's population; and if China with her Draconian birth control efforts were removed from Third World data, the population growth rate in underdeveloped nations had not declined appreciably in a decade. The World Bank asserted that population growth was indeed a threat to economic progress, and urged governmental support for birth control, which the U.S. delegation dismissed as unnecessary. "The population explosion continues on schedule," wrote the Population Reference Bureau, noting that the earth's population would double to 10 billion by 2050 and might reach a total of 14 billion. Some global areas seemed beyond the hope of any early decline in growth rates; the African continent, which could not currently feed its 500 million people, had a total fertility rate (TFR) of 6.4 and would reach perhaps 1.5 billion before leveling off, depending on how quickly governments and individuals altered procreative patterns. "The historical trend scenario is almost a nightmare," wrote the United Nations Economic Commission for Africa. "Short of thermonuclear war itself," said World Bank President (and Kennedy-Johnson Secretary of Defense) Robert McNamara, "population growth is the gravest issue the world faces over the decades immediately ahead."

U.S. Population in the 1980s: Growth without Letup

America's population in the 1980s grew by 23 million, in contrast to thirteen European nations that had essentially stabilized their growth. The United States had the fastest-growing population of any industrialized society in the world, and demographers noted that the explanation was not to be found in sharply higher birth rates. The U.S. TFR at the end of the 1980s had drifted slightly upward to 1.9, above Denmark's 1.5 and West Germany's 1.4, but was still well below replacement level (2.1). Low U.S. birth rates, like similar rates in other industrialized societies, reflected the choices of females, with their spouses or partners, to forego childbearing or limit family size. Contraception was widespread, and the Federal Center for Disease Control reported that abortions numbered 1.3 million as the 1980s began, a rate of about 350 abortions per 1000 live births.

The reason the United States experienced substantial population growth despite low fertility was simple, though not much discussed: immigration. As the 1980s arrived, U.S. policy was annually allowing 800,000 legal immigrants to take up residence in the country (a number far larger than admitted by any other nation in the world) and permitted an untold number of illegal immigrants (estimated from 200,000 to 1 million annually) to enter across our thinly defended borders. Alarmed at illegal entry especially, Jimmy Carter had appointed the Select Commission on Immigration and Refugees in 1979 (the Hesburgh commission, named after its chairman, Father Edward Hesburgh, President of Notre Dame University). The commission recommended that illegal immigration be curbed by enactment of penalties on employers hiring illegals, paired with an amnesty for those who had established roots here. A tortu-

This chart represents actual U.S. population growth from 1970 to 1993, with projections from the Census Bureau's "medium projection" to the year 2050. This projection assumes that fertility, mortality, and immigration rates remain at the 1993 level.
(*Roy Beck,* Re-charting America's Future *[Petoskey, Michigan: The Social Contract Press, 1994]*)

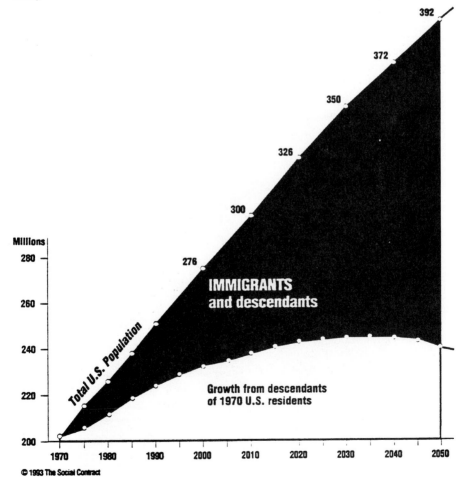

ous legislative path led the Immigration Reform and Control Act (IRCA) to eventual passage in 1986. The law's employer sanctions provision rested on a weak, easily evaded system of worker verification, and future immigration was actually encouraged by a new agricultural-worker program and an amnesty for what would prove to be over 3 million illegals who could prove lengthy residence. The Reagan administration, divided on the issue, exerted no leadership, leaving the legislation to the bipartisan sponsorship of Senator Alan Simpson (Rep., Wyo.) and Representative Ron Mazolli (Dem., Ky.).

Arrests of illegals at the southern border initially dropped with the passage of the employer sanctions bill, but by the end of the decade it was clear that illegal immigration still ranged between varying estimates of 300,000 and 1 million annually, undeterred by IRCA's porous system of worker verification. Legal immigration, fed by large refugee flows from Central America and (late in the decade) the Soviet Union, surged close to the million mark annually. Immigration in the 1980s thus added 7.3 million plus 3 million more through the amnesty, and when illegal immigration was added the total was estimated at 40 to 50 percent of U.S. popu-

Hundreds of undocumented aliens gather at a place known as the "soccer field," just north of Tijuana, Mexico, waiting for dark and a chance to sneak through the porous U.S.–Mexico border into San Diego.
(UPI-Bettmann Newsphotos)

lation growth, with the proportion rising steadily. Without immigration after 1980, the nation's population would level off at approximately 265 million by the middle of the twenty-first century. With immigration, demographer Leon Bouvier estimated that 400 to 500 million Americans would inhabit national space by that time, with the number still growing. Immigration policy had emerged as the nation's population policy, an expansive one not voted upon by the public, which repeatedly told pollsters that immigration should be reduced.

A study of immigration's impact on California, the destination of one third of incoming immigrants, revealed the power of this quiet demographic force. During the 1980s, Bouvier wrote in *Fifty Million Californians?* (1991), immigration helped drive the Golden State's population up by 25 percent, in part by addition of new residents and in part by elevating fertility rates from 1.95 in 1982 to 2.48 in 1989, an astonishing increase of one quarter in seven years. Immigration to California was also radically altering the state's ethnic and racial makeup. At the end of the 1980s, it was clear that the "Anglo" majority was not replacing itself (TFR of 1.7), and the higher fertility rates of Latinos (3.9), blacks (2.5), and Asians (2.5) meant that the Anglo proportion of the state's population would steadily fall until there would be no "majority" ethnic or racial group in California by 2005–2010—if not sooner.

This demographic revolution received little public discussion in the 1980s, but public opinion polls reported strong opposition to current levels of immigration, and a small immigration reform movement pointed to immigration's link with environmental damage, labor market competition with U.S. workers, and rising social welfare costs. Massive immigration did have its defenders, who welcomed the entrepreneurial spirit of the Asians moving into West Coast communities, insisted that the nation's identity should remain forever tied to the concept of a refuge haven, and saw the heavy flows of Latin American and Asian immigrants as equipping the United States for leadership in the new global economy rather than as a threat to social cohesion. With the public favoring restricted immigration but apparently more concerned about other matters, immigration policy continued to be expansionist, both enlarging the U.S. population and altering its racial and ethnic makeup.

Resources

That resources could indeed be depleted had been perhaps the most unsettling discovery of the 1970s. The resource which brought this home was the dark liquid, petroleum (with its smelly sibling, natural gas), around which Americans had built their habitations and economy. The first "oil shock" of 1973–1974 started a price rise that would end the era of cheap energy, but did not fully convince the public that shortage was a permanent part of their lives as consumers of oil or anything else. Between 1972 and 1978 oil imports almost doubled, from 29 to 47 percent of all oil consumed in the United States; the cost was $40 to $50 billion annually, money sent to foreigners. President Carter's repeated efforts to realign energy policy were rebuffed by an irritated Congress, which was aware that the public disliked the topic.

Then the Shah of Iran was overthrown in 1979, Iranian oil was cut off, and the world price went from $13 to $30 a barrel. Americans responded to higher prices where they had ignored presidential lectures. They purchased smaller, lighter cars (often Japanese-built), put on sweaters and turned down thermostats, shopped for appliances with better energy efficiency, weatherproofed homes, rediscovered and expanded the technology of windmills and mini-hydroelectric plants. U.S. oil consumption dropped (for the first time in our history) 8 percent from 1978 to 1981, and though the winter of 1980 was 13 degrees colder on the average than that of 1979, home heating oil consumption decreased by 13 percent.

Americans were conserving, coping with resource shortage not by expanding supply but by curtailing demand. In the energy area there was no immediate choice. Coal was abundant, but conversion from oil to coal was impossible for some uses and slow and expensive for others, as well as entailing environmental risks. Nuclear power had for a time appeared to be the technological cavalry riding in just in time to replace fossil fuels, but the nuclear power industry was plagued by unexpected problems. Construction and maintenance costs of nuclear power plants escalated; equipment and management failures made the public edgy and raised utility costs. In 1975, a thousand nuclear reactors for electrical power production had been predicted by the year 2000, but cancellations in the last years of the decade forced that estimate back to 120. One element was the high cost of placing a nuclear plant on line and keeping it there; another was rising public opposition to the industry, based on objections to the radioactive waste for which there were no safe disposal methods. Then, on March 28, 1979, came the malfunction of a valve at the Three Mile Island power plant near Harrisburg, Pennsylvania, which set off a chain of mechanical and human failures that led to a leak of radioactive steam and a mass evacuation. The entire nation learned of the possibility of "meltdown" of the type fictionalized in the film, *The China Syndrome.*

The accident at Three Mile Island killed no one, but despite utility industry efforts to stress the containment of the problem, it made a large impact upon the public mind and heightened fears of nuclear energy. "In my opinion," said an energy expert after the incident, "we really don't have a nuclear option. The only thing keeping the industry alive is some foreign orders." There were seventy-two operating nuclear plants in the United States in 1980, sixteen cancellations, and seventy delayed orders.

In 1980, polls showed 70 percent of the public "concerned about energy," a sentiment confirmed by data on reduced demand and conservation. At this point the matter of resource shortages, whether in energy or elsewhere, began to recede as a matter of public concern or national priority. Conservation efforts in the industrialized countries had reduced demand below current production, and one read of an "oil glut" on international markets. In 1982 petroleum producers pumped 5 million barrels a day *less* than in 1979, prices declined slightly, and articles appeared such as that in *Harper's Magazine* in November 1981 with the message: "The Energy Crisis Is Over." Polls in 1982 showed only 3 percent of the public concerned about energy, and revealed not only complacency but misconceptions—such as the belief that by the year 2000 solar energy sources would have entirely replaced fossil fuels, an estimate perhaps three decades too short.

Informed people knew that petroleum was finite and shrinking. But the public's conservation efforts had indeed bought some time for the search for acceptable alternatives—which had to mean some mix of coal as a bridging fuel to solar, geothermal, and biomass sources, with nuclear energy a question mark. By the early 1980s the energy crisis was a cancer in remission, the Reagan administration tutoring the nation in the euphoric belief that the energy problem was being met by individual actions and could be ignored by society at large. The euphoria and the oil glut were pleasant, but temporary. America was in transition from the age of cheap fossil energy to a multisource energy era in which that basic resource might never again be cheap.

Other potential resource shortages receded somewhat from public view along with petroleum. The summer of 1983 brought drought to every part of the country, intensifying an already fierce competition for water between thirsty cities and nearby watersheds, between agriculture and suburbs. The 4.2 trillion gallons of rain and snow falling per day on the United States should have been enough for a human population using 450 billion gallons daily, but the resource was not distributed where the people were (or vice versa), and increasingly it was polluted by humanity where it collected. Local government struggled with the issue, not just in Los Angeles, the Great Plains, and the desert southwest, but increasingly in the east and south.

With battles to allocate water supplies came intensifying struggles over land use. The older assumptions that people were free to build on or dig in or litter their land free of public restriction struggled against a cluster of public claims—to regulate the form, rate of growth, and eventual size of communities; to shelter agriculture from sprawl; to protect fragile ecological areas and historic sites. Indeed, there were concerns that even the amount of soil itself was inadequate to future needs. The National Agricultural Lands Study, launched in 1979 and reporting in 1981, confirmed fears that the annual loss of 3 million acres per year of cropland to urban and other uses would virtually eliminate the nation's reserves of prime farmland by the year 2000, leaving only land with low to medium potential for conversion to crops to meet the rising demands of the twenty-first century. The study recommended a federal policy to protect prime agricultural land by directing conversion pressures to nonagricultural soils. Carter, the ex-farmer, was sympathetic to farmland protection, but the idea vanished in the Reagan years.

Carter's *Global 2000* Report: The Environment Ahead

What progress was being made in the environmental protection effort, and what lay ahead? President Carter, in preparing for his 1977 environmental message to Congress, found that the U.S. government could not answer those questions, either for our own national domain or for the planet. He commissioned an intragovernmental study "of the probable changes in the world's population, natural resources, and environment through the end of the century," guided by the Council on Environmental Quality and the Department of State. *Global 2000* took three years to complete and was released in July 1980. The study projected foreseeable trends under the assumption that present policies continued without major change (a defensible way to handle policy uncertainty, but critics would point out that the predictions were thus based on the absence of corrective efforts), and concluded that trouble lay ahead. "If present trends continue," concluded *Global 2000*, "the world in 2000 will be more crowded, more polluted, less stable ecologically, and more vulnerable to disruption than the world we live in now."

Global 2000 was the U.S. government's first effort to survey population/resources/environment trends together. What actions it might have led Carter to take we cannot know, for within months of its publication the Reagan administration repudiated its findings. A private organization based in the United States, Worldwatch Institute, shouldered the task of global environmental monitoring, publishing an annual *State of the World* report. Noting in the 1984 report that "for most of humanity the century's third quarter was a period of unprecedented prosperity," the report pointed out that during that time the world had developed an excessive dependence on oil, moved from farming soils to mining them, and begun to consume the economy's biological support systems. In short, the world economy had moved onto a development path that was unsustainable. Soil, forests, and fisheries were described as under severe pressures of depletion from human activity: "the world is engaging in wholesale biological and agronomic deficit financing," wrote the senior editor, Lester Brown. Three years later, the World Commission on Environment and Development, in its report, *Our Common Future* (1987), concluded that environmental progress was being ominously outpaced by deterioration. Global food production had since the 1960s continued to increase faster than population growth, contrary to some predictions:

> there are more hungry people in the world than ever before, and their numbers are increasing. . . . The gap between rich and poor nations is widening—not shrinking. . . . Each year another 6 million hectares of productive dryland turns into worthless desert . . . more than 11 million hectares of forests are destroyed yearly. Industry and agriculture put toxic substances into the human food chain and into underground water tables beyond reach of cleansing.

These were pioneering efforts to assess the world environmental situation, focusing beyond isolated problems of pollution to call attention to ecosystems at hazard. One threatened ecosystem was the American coastal wetland habitat, 215 million acres when first Europeans arrived, but reduced to 100 million acres as the 1980s arrived. Americans drained and filled coastal wetlands in their desire to live and shop nearer to the coasts, and during the 1980s these estuarial nurturing grounds were being destroyed by developers at a rate of half-a-million acres a year.

An endangered ecosystem of planetary importance were tropic moist forests (TMFs to insiders, rainforests to tourists). Covering 3.5 million square miles or less than 10 percent of the world's land surface, TMFs contained half of the planet's 10 to 100 million species (no one knows for sure, and only 1.4 million have been identified). They were a vital ecosystem for sheltering genetic diversity, absorbing solar energy, producing oxygen. Yet humanity since World War II had set about to destroy them. Timber extraction increased an estimated fifteen times in the forty years after the war, and behind the slash came the burning of stumps to clear tropical forest lands for agriculture. A 1984 estimate by Dr. Norman Myers of the World Wildlife Fund found these forests shrinking by 275 square miles a day, an area the size of Massachusetts every month; the entire biome would be gone in thirty-five years at such rates. A U.N. agency found this estimate conservative.

Given their species richness, the stunning rate of destruction of TMFs was no local problem in a few countries in the tropics, but a global loss of major and permanent proportions. Harvard biologist Edward O. Wilson estimated that at current rates of tropical forest clearing, one fourth of all species would be lost with the destruction of their habitats by the year 2020. When he made that estimate, some 40 percent of all species had already been lost to expanding human settlement. The loss to science would be translated into lost opportunities for improved human life, Wilson predicted, as "still undeveloped medicines, crops, pharmaceuticals, timber, fibers, pulp, soil-restoring vegetation, petroleum substitutes, and other products and amenities will never come to light."

A larger and more diverse ecosystem, the oceans, signaled its strain from postwar human activity when the world fish catch crested and declined in the early 1970s. Repeated oil spills from giant tankers, effluent from human settlements and factories, and the dumping of toxic and radioactive wastes made the ocean an unregulated international sink. And the largest environment at risk from human activity as the twentieth century moved toward its end was the planet itself, enveloped in a gaseous atmosphere that humankind was rapidly transforming as it consumed in a few hundred years the fossil fuel deposits laid down across eons of time.

In the 1970s, concern about the atmospheric effect of fossil-fuel burning had been focused on the problem of acid rain. That issue was muted in the 1980s, as the level of scientific uncertainty was so high that Congress in 1980 established a new research program (the National Acid Precipitation Assessment Program, or NAPAP) with instructions to report ten years (and half a billion dollars) later. The policy question—what, if anything, should be done—was effectively put on hold while the scientists gathered and analyzed data from lake, high forest, and urban settings. The Reagan administration was happy to have the acid rain question sanitized in a research mode, though increasing complaints from Canada over damage to their lakes and forests due to pollutants discharged by the high stacks of midwestern utilities and factories reminded Americans that most environmental problems were now international, trans-border issues.

More Trouble Overhead: Ozone

Ozone is a molecule composed of three oxygen atoms (O_3). In unusually high concentrations near the earth it causes lung and eye irritation, but in the higher atmosphere, approximately 15 miles above the earth's surface, a thin ozone shield forms an indispensable screen protecting humans and other forms of life from solar ultraviolet radiation that is harmful to the human immune system, to some crops, and to microscopic oceanic organisms. Scientists in the 1970s began to theorize that synthetic compounds called chlorofluorocarbons, or CFCs, which were widely used as refrigeration coolants and as propellants in spray cans, were entering the upper atmosphere where they broke down, releasing chlorine atoms which ate away at the ozone shield. The theory took on conviction in 1985 when a team of British researchers in the Antarctic found and measured a springtime "hole" in the ozone shield caused by the unique meteorology of the region. In 1987 another, smaller hole was found over the Arctic circle. The United Nations in 1987 adopted the Montreal Protocol, calling for a phased reduction of the use of CFCs, and by the end of 1988 thirty-four nations had ratified the protocol. But the anticipated 35 to 50 percent cut in the 1 million tons of CFCs manufactured annually, even if it is achieved by the turn of the century, is far short of the 85 percent the EPA estimates to be required to keep atmospheric CFCs at their present level, and ozone-depleting chemicals will continue to do their damage for 100 years. Humanity had upset an ancient, delicate balance high in the skies, launching an irreversible experiment that was now out of control.

Even More Trouble Overhead: Global Greenhouse Warming

The possibility of a "greenhouse effect" from humanity's rapid burning of fossil fuels and wood, releasing heat-trapping carbon dioxide (CO_2) into the atmosphere, had been pointed out by a Swedish Nobel Prize-winning chemist, Svante Arrhenius, in 1895. By the 1980s scientists knew that several "greenhouse gases" had the effect of trapping the sun's energy as it reradiated from the planet's surface and thus causing global warming. CO_2 from burning fossil fuels was responsible for about half of the trapping effect, methane (CH_4) from rice cultivation and animal husbandry for about 20 percent, chlorofluorocarbons (CFCs) and nitrous oxide (N_2O) accounted for most of the rest. That humanity was pumping these gases into the atmosphere at heavy and increasing rates was well known, and as early as 1957 two U.S. scientists pointed out that this amounted to inadvertently conducting "a large-scale geophysical experiment." Were we humans warming the earth, and with what likely results?

Some scientists' models predicted as much as 5 to 8 degrees (Fahrenheit) warming by the middle of the twenty-first Century, with glacier melting, rising sea levels, and widespread climatic disruption. Other models forecast only 1 to 2 degrees warming, and scientists pointed out that currently unknown feedback loops—cloud buildup, ocean absorption of CO_2, even the activity of soil bacteria—might cancel out even that rise in temperature. Agriculture might be curtailed in some areas, they pointed out, but rising levels of CO_2 and warmer climates would probably increase plant productivity in others. The Reagan administration did not like environmental crises, since they suggested governmental intervention and curbs on capitalism, and the President's science advisor scolded the EPA for a 1983 report calling "a global or greenhouse warming . . . neither trivial nor just a long-term problem." Those words, while hardly a call for action, were called "unwarranted and unnecessarily alarmist" by the White House, where it was frequently pointed out that the scientist community was divided on whether a Greenhouse warming was even taking place. The administration welcomed a 1983 report by the National Academy of Sciences which said that while there was "a cause for concern," there was plenty of time to study the global warming problem before precipitate action was needed. However, the parched, hot summers of the 1980s, and news events such as the raging fires that raced through Yellowstone National park in 1988, kept the media interested in the greenhouse effect. And scientists were moving toward a consensus that the problem was real and that the time had come for study to be supplemented by governmental action.

Polluting the American Environment: Hazardous Wastes

The publicity given the Love Canal evacuation in 1978 created widespread public worry about hazardous wastes, reflected in a 1980 poll in which two thirds of the respondents chose "deep concern" as their response. How much of this foul, noxious, dangerous stuff was there beneath American communities, or in the air and water? The 1976 Resource Conservation and Recovery Act (RCRA) had empowered the EPA to track such wastes "from cradle to grave," but the agency made painfully slow progress. Little was known about toxic waste generation or disposal, since the government had shown little interest in either part of this forbidding subject. Since it seemed time both to discover the dimensions of the problem and to begin cleanup procedures, Congress in 1980 enacted the Comprehensive Environmental Response, Compensation and Liability Act (CERCLA or, more popularly, "Superfund"), instructing the EPA to come up with a list of the worst sites (400 were expected) and optimistically allocating a $1.6 billion fund for such remediation that industrial polluters could not be forced to pay for. The EPA and the American people thus began a stupendous journey of discovery that continues to this day, an inventory of America's dumping history and current generation of toxic substances, and a cleanup effort that grew more expensive yearly.

Yesterday's toxic wastes were mostly out of sight, dumped in rivers or the ocean, released into the air from production processes or smokestacks, trucked to remote areas and dumped, buried along with nontoxic trash in one of 75,000 industrial or 15,000 municipal landfills, forced deep into the earth through an (EPA) estimated 400,000 injection wells (5000 new wells were drilled each year, it was guessed), or stored in 170,000 surface impoundments referred to as "pits," "ponds," or "lagoons," which were almost entirely unmonitored and often leaking. Some 75,000 to 100,000 buried fuel tanks beneath service stations were either leaking or corroding.

As for radioactive wastes from the government's nuclear weapons projects, the most deadly of these were stored in four sites around the country in steel tanks while the government debated where to dispose of them "permanently."

Low-level radioactive wastes rested in twenty-two sites in shallow burial or in drums above the ground.

News stories punctuated the 1980s with reports that hazardous wastes were not remaining where they had been put—out of sight and hopefully out of mind. As foul liquids had bubbled to the surface at Love Canal, so toxic wastes were discovered to be migrating out of landfills and ponds, leaking into the air breathed in nearby communities or into the subsurface aquifers that supplied water for 50 percent of the American population. An example was the Stringfellow waste dump above Riverside, California, a stinking pot of acids, heavy metals, organic solvents, and pesticides trucked there for decades by surrounding industries, but found in the early 1980s to be seeping toward the underground water supplies of half a million Californians.

Will "the U.S. . . . one day become," asked *Newsweek* magazine in 1982, "one of those countries where you shouldn't drink the water?" The EPA's first list of the 418 dirtiest toxic waste sites included Stringfellow and was like a roster of many hells, places few Americans had heard of before, such as Tybout's Corner in New Castle County, Delaware, or Price Landfill in (of all places) Pleasantville, New Jersey. Nearby communities demanded cleanup, but the Superfund process was far slower than anticipated, firms charged with responsibility fought vigorous legal battles to spread or avoid the expense, and the EPA lacked a clear standard for what constituted "cleaned up." The 1986 Superfund Amendments and Reauthorization Act (SARA) maintained the basic program despite mounting criticisms from environmental groups that the EPA was mismanaging the Superfund effort. In 1985 the Office of Technology Assessment estimated that the cleanup of 10,000 existing hazardous waste dumps might cost $100 billion and take fifty years. By 1992 there were 32,000 Superfund sites, 75,000 was thought to be the final tally, and the first estimate of costs by a non-government team of scientists pegged the cost as being from $750 billion to $1.7 trillion.

Further, the hazardous waste problem was expanding far beyond the chemical, petroleum, and other industrial producers of toxic materials. The federal government emerged as, in one journalist's phrase, "America's most pervasive and protected polluter," and the EPA's authority over the other parts of the government involved in heavy toxic pollution was in question. The Department of Energy (DOE) was responsible for what turned out to be the most lethal and long-lasting toxic wastes, the radioactive mine tailings, production wastes, and spent fuels from the nation's nuclear weapon and nuclear power industries. In the mid-1980s 9.5 million cubic feet of "radwaste" was stored at four sites, the worst of them Hanford, Washington, where corroding steel tanks, open ponds, and burial sites held 444 billion gallons of radioactive liquid and 700,000 cubic yards of solid wastes. The nearby Columbia River was menaced by pollution of the aquifers beneath the Hanford facility from leaking lagoons and injection wells drilled since the 1940s. The fiscal and technical costs of a cleanup at Hanford were so great that some proposed it be sealed off and declared "a national sacrifice zone," a price to be paid for the weapons the Cold War required.

Of course the spent fuel and other radioactive waste from on-line nuclear power plants had to go somewhere, and the search for a secure depository for wastes that would be lethal to humans for 10,000 to 20,000 years stretched out across the 1980s and beyond. A deep salt mine at Yucca Mountain, New Mexico, at first seemed the most likely choice, but lengthy tests and legal challenges promised to delay a solution to the nuclear waste issue until the next century. Public opposition to the nuclear power industry had long been strengthened by the problems of disposing of radioactive waste, but the additional fear of accidental "meltdown" on site was vastly increased when, on April 25, 1986, a Soviet reactor complex at Chernobyl, 80 miles north of Kiev, exploded, spewing radioactive isotopes in a deadly cloud detected from Sweden eastward to Japan.

It soon became apparent that the federal government's contribution to toxic waste went far beyond the nuclear programs. Every military installation had a history of toxic chemical dumping, and 4000 known military dump sites ranged from the Jefferson Proving Ground in southern Indiana, where 1.4 million of the 23 million artillery rounds fired there were still on site and unexploded, to the notorious Rocky Mountain Arsenal near Denver, Colorado, where wastes from production of nerve gas and ammunition made it what *Atlantic* magazine in 1989 called "the most toxic square mile on earth."

And how much hazardous waste was being generated each year, to add to the accumulated poisons of yesterday? The EPA estimated 91 million tons a year in 1980, raised the estimate to 264 million tons in 1988 (1 ton for every American), but the OTA preferred the figure 360 million tons. Clearly, the government did not know, which meant that nobody did. "Cleanup," whatever that meant, was obviously not going to be enough—as expensive as it was becoming. As efforts to remediate Superfund sites struggled forward, as a search for an underground radwaste depository inched ahead, some progress was made in the most promising direction: source reduction. Waste generation could be reduced by changes in production processes, engineers pointed out. Next in priority was the effort to recycle toxic wastes into usable or inoffensive materials, where much improvement was possible. The science and technology of treatment was also advancing, with reports of fungi that consumed selenium accumulations in irrigated soil, and bacteria that could "eat" petroleum and other residues.

America's industrial corporations held one key to the hope of source reductions on toxic wastes, and some—such as Minnesota Mining and Manufacturing (3M)—voluntarily altered production methods to reduce hazardous waste, altering the corporate culture under the slogan, "Prevention pays." Unwilling to wait for a spread of such examples of good corporate citizenship, a grass-roots toxics protest movement emerged. Lois Gibbs, a Love Canal activist, moved to the suburbs of Washington, D.C., and established the Citizens' Clearinghouse for Hazardous Wastes (CCHW), and Boston activist John O'Connor started the National Toxics Campaign, examples of a rapidly spreading new type of environmentalist organization built around the toxics issue.

Their efforts were given leverage by Title III of the SARA law of 1986, which asserted the "community's right to know" what chemicals were produced, stored, and used in America. Corporations for the first time were required to give the EPA annual data on toxic materials stored and released, and citizens' groups had access to such data on personal computers. When the data arrived from the first national Toxic Release Inventory, they were shocking. Only 320 chemicals, thought to be the most toxic of the 70,000 chemicals manufactured in the United States, were monitored, and only 18,000 facilities reported when the EPA thought that 30,000 would be eligible. Even so, the figures, though understating the problem, were eye-catching: 10.3 billion pounds of toxic wastes were "disposed of" by American companies in 1987: 2.6 billion pounds into the air, 1.5 billion into underground wells, 2.3 billion into landfills, 1.4 billion into sewers or waterways, with the rest shipped off-site to unknown destinations. In addition to reporting such volumes of dangerous by-products of the national life-style, the inventory named and located the facilities of origin—the 500 firms that released 70 percent of the waste, labeled the "Toxic 500"—with the Aluminum Company of America at Point Comfort, Texas, in the lead, followed by the Great Lakes Division of National Steel Corporation, at Wayne, Michigan.

Under pressure from citizens' groups and William K. Reilly, head of the EPA, Monsanto Chemical Company pledged to reduce hazardous waste emissions by 90 percent, and the McDonald hamburger chain promised to spend $16 million to recycle their styrofoam containers. The EPA reported that American large industries released 5.7 billion pounds of toxic chemicals in 1989, 18 percent less than in 1987.

These small signs of progress were heartening, as was the growing recognition that the garbage problem, including the toxic part of it, was much broader than the crimes of a few chemical dumpers. When air pollution in the Los Angeles basin continued to exceed Clean Air Act standards for public health, a new governmental entity, the regional Air Quality Management Board (AQMB), went into action on a broad front. In the latter half of the 1980s the board not only required reductions in toxic emissions from oil refineries and industrial plants, it forced changes in automobile exhaust systems and commuting patterns, made manufacturers of such items as car wax, vinyl cleaners, and household glue curb their use of hydrocarbons, and then banned the sale of lighter fluid used in the customary California barbecue. Thus the search for guilty polluters had led to industrial corporations, then to the government, and finally to the individual consumer in his home or on her patio firing up the charcoal grill. Again Pogo's discovery: "We have met the enemy, and it is us."

THE ELECTION OF 1988

The Reagan years came to an end on mixed signs. Anxiety about environmental woes that seemed mostly over the horizon was not nearly as intense, polls indicated, as the public's worries that the debt-driven economy was fundamentally flawed. A stunning drop in stock market values in October 1987 indicated that Wall Street, at least, had a formidable case of jitters about underlying trends, among them indications that the nation's savings and loan industry, deregulated in 1982 and urged to branch out into riskier and more profitable markets than family housing, was on the edge of bankruptcy. Yet Reagan's last year was the sixth year of economic expansion, and relations with the Soviet Union were in an unprecedented state of cordiality. In August 1988 the Republican party nominated Vice President George Bush (with vice-presidential nominee Indiana Senator Dan Quayle) to succeed Reagan, hoping the half of the electorate that bothered to vote in presidential elections would prefer a team they knew over the little-known governor of Massachusetts nominated by the Democrats in July—Michael B. Dukakis (who outlasted Jesse Jackson and seven other less successful rivals and was matched with Senator Lloyd Bentsen of Texas).

Dukakis led Bush by 17 points in polls taken after the conventions, but the Democrats soon learned that George Bush was a fierce competitor who understood and would take advantage of their vulnerability. The tides of electoral history in presidential contests had long been running against the Democrats. To an electorate that was predominantly white, middle class and increasingly suburban, established in jobs and communities and culturally conservative, the Democratic party in the 1960s seemed to have left the channels cut by Franklin Roosevelt and Truman, and over the next two decades moved leftward in a series of policies having to do, one way or another, with race.

Lyndon Johnson's battle for legal equality and an end to Jim Crow was broadly endorsed by the mostly white electorate. But for fervent liberals eager for equality of results as soon as possible, equality of opportunity began to seem inadequate. The effects of two centuries of slavery and another century of discrimination would not be erased at once merely by ending Jim Crow. Why not take race into account in an affirmative way, granting a temporary preference for those whose ancestors had been so injured by slavery? This reasoning nourished the growth of affirmative action, which quickly spread through the worlds of education, business, and professional life, and blue-collar trades, both in private and public sectors. Initially devised for African-Americans whose handicaps included centuries of slavery, the federal bureaucracy charged with enforcing affirmative action programs soon expanded them to include Hispanics, Asians, Native Americans, and women, since these groups had also been protected from discrimination by the Civil Rights Act of 1964. Preferential treatment for each of these groups rested upon a weaker logic than for blacks, and when Hispanic and Asian immigrants began to qualify for affirmative action it was clear that the program had spread beyond its original conception.

Busing and affirmative action were thus much resented by many Americans, and these programs were associated primarily with the Democrats. Nixon's Watergate debacle, followed by moderate Jimmy Carter's 1976 election, concealed from Democratic liberals the depth of the electorate's distrust of another liberal Democratic presidency. Ronald Reagan's electoral successes sharpened the lesson, for Reagan had mastered the "social" or "wedge" issues that cut the former Democratic presidential majority down to a deeply frustrated minority. Democrats, Reagan insisted, were all liberals, and liberals were the tax-and-spend party, the welfare party, the affirmative action party, the soft-on-crime-and-drugs party—as well as suspect on defense, on their resolve to fight communism wherever necessary.

The 1988 election would turn out to be another event in a long Republican occupancy of the White House by stressing the wedge issues on which the Democrats were vulnerable. Bush soon found the formula. Governor Dukakis had vetoed a Massachusetts law requiring school teachers to lead classes in the Pledge of Allegiance to the flag, and had endorsed a furlough program for prisoners which allowed a black man named Willie Horton to leave prison and rape a Maryland woman. Bush was relentless on the flag and "Willie Horton" issues, and Dukakis could not escape the GOP's negative agenda. "No new taxes," Bush promised, knowing that Dukakis could not politically or credibly embrace such a position. George Bush was elected with 53 percent of the popular vote and carried forty states, 426 electoral votes to 111. The Democrats retained majorities in the House and Senate, suggesting to some that the electorate had decided to install a "mommy party" of Democrats in the Congress, where social benefits would be generous, but in the more important White House gave control to a "daddy party" of Republicans committed to strong national defense and restraints on social spending. Whether the electorate had such a scheme in mind or not, the result was divided government and a deepening sense of policy paralysis.

REAGAN ASSESSED

What difference had Ronald Reagan made? A half century's growth of the size and functions of government had been capped, though not reversed. In 1988, the public sector (federal, state, and local) was about the same as a percentage of GNP and in the number of public employees as when Reagan took office. More important, he led a movement that put the advocates of larger government on the defensive for the first time. The Reagan movement had a limited base in Congress, but eight years in the presidency allowed Reagan to appoint to the judiciary people who shared his basic skepticism of government. These appointments would influence public policy for years to come.

And Reagan was president when the Cold War suddenly dissolved. His improving relationship with Mikhael Gorbachev seemed part of the formula that produced the 1987 treaty to remove all intermediate-range nuclear missiles (INF) from Europe, the first superpower agreement to abolish an entire category of weapons. In 1988 the Soviets withdrew their armed forces from Afghanistan. Was the Cold War coming to an end?

All Americans welcomed these signs of reduced superpower tension, which Reagan graciously presided over even if his role in them was not clear. Whether or not one shared his beliefs about government's role in domestic matters, it must be acknowledged that Reagan had vastly altered the American political agenda and shifted governmental priorities. Even his supporters, however, could not deny that, on his watch, a tremendous deterioration of American economic power was reflected in surging trade and budget deficits. Reagan had avoided the hard choices of budget balancing, and instead invited a willing

CHAPTER 11

End of the Cold War, Beginning of What?

A WOBBLY COMPASS NEEDLE: GEORGE BUSH BEGINS

The political history of the nation since the 1960s had witnessed a floundering of both parties, along with a rising level of public cynicism toward "politicians" and, more ominously, their governing institutions. Could the Republicans at the end of the 1980s somehow build on the viable aspects of Reaganism, and stabilize American politics around a new Republican majority?

"A President is neither prince nor Pope," George Bush said in his January 20, 1989, inaugural address, launching his presidency with a curious and cloudy phrase suggesting that Bush would lack the communication skills and apparent sense of purpose of his predecessor. The new president presented himself as a likable and unpretentious man, no partisan zealot. As for a sense of purpose, Bush wanted "to make kinder the face of the nation and gentler the face of the world," whatever that meant. The public responded to the new president's address with high approval ratings, despite Bush's first major action, proposing a plan on February 6 to close or sell 350 savings and loans, revamp the banking regulatory system (again), and split the cost between taxpayers and the industry. The cost was estimated at a staggering $126 billion, but there was no outcry from either the public or the opposition party.

George Bush was in his "honeymoon" first spring, and the size of the S&L disaster was not yet clear. The federal budget deficit was easier to understand and had been around much longer. Since 1978 the government had been consistently in the red, running spectacular deficits under Ronald Reagan, who presided over a $1.9 trillion runup of the federal debt in eight years. Bush, like the Democratic congressional leadership, had no desire to do more than temporize with this fearsome annual gap between spending and income, and he spent the year in negotiations which led to an October budget that was officially

$110 billion in deficit. The president did not propose significant alterations in spending and taxing patterns, beyond asking for a capital gains tax cut. George Bush was, apparently, not an agent of change. He had promised to be "the education president," but in the face of the massive problems of public education Bush proposed two small incentive programs to raise school standards. While holding few press conferences and without much apparent sense of direction, the president enjoyed high standings in the polls.

Two of the largest events in American domestic life in 1989 had nothing to do with governmental leadership, but were blows exchanged between humanity and nature. Humanity struck first, when on March 24 the oil tanker *Exxon Valdez* ran aground in Prince William Sound, spilling 260,000 barrels of oil that would reach 1100 miles of Alaskan coastline in the largest oil spill in U.S. history (there were at least three other large oil-tanker spills that year). Nature waited until October 17 and then struck back, when a major earthquake rocked the San Francisco Bay area, killing 67, injuring 3700, and demolishing neighborhoods and portions of a freeway. Humanity's crime against nature had been ugly; nature's retaliation hinted at far greater power.

BREAKUP OF THE SOVIET EMPIRE

The central focus of every postwar American administration since 1945 had been to carry on the fight against Soviet military and ideological power, but the Bush government was fated to stand uncertainly and almost passively on the sidelines as the U.S.S.R. broke up due to internal developments. For three years, 1989–1991, the world watched the drama of Mikhail Gorbachev, the leader who had inaugurated the new tolerance of dissent and launched political and economic reforms only to see them inexorably undermine the very communist society and unified empire he had wished merely to reform.

The year 1989 was turbulent with unrest in the Soviet-bloc nations of central and eastern Europe. Czechoslovakia, East Germany, Hungary, and Poland all toppled communist governments, either through elections or by massive public demonstrations; only in Romania was an armed uprising required to end the grip of twenty-four-year communist regime. In November East German crowds surged over the Berlin Wall, and then with the help of West Germans chipped and pounded the wall into souvenirs and rubble. Inside the Soviet Union an unprecedented freedom allowed the revival of religious services and a flourishing free press. Free elections ousted many communists from the Congress of Peoples' Deputies, debate was wide-ranging, and even Gorbachev was heavily criticized. Then, in 1990, came the turn of the non-Russian republics of the U.S.S.R. to demand independence, just as the client Baltic states Lithuania and Latvia were doing. By the end of the year, all fifteen republics had declared their sovereignty, and Americans who had only perhaps heard of the republic of Georgia heard of places such as Moldavia, Uzbek, and Kirghiz. Separatism from the grip of centralized control then moved in a chain reaction inside the

As communist regimes broke up in the late 1980s, the most visible symbol of the Cold War—the Berlin Wall—was destroyed as well. Thousands of demonstrators, such as the man in this photo hammering his way through a portion of the wall, used any tool available to break down the barrier between East and West.
(*Reuters/Bettmann*)

republics, with protests from ethnic groups—Kazakhs, Crimean tartars, Armenians—nursing long grievances against communist authoritarianism and Russian ethnic domination.

What sort of economy and political system would follow communism? Gorbachev seemed to have no clear model in mind, and appeared reluctant to dictate the goals of the social transformations going on throughout and on the edges of the disintegrating Soviet Union. The Bush administration made it clear that the United States would take no advantage of the turmoil and saw Gorbachev as an ally, and the American public expressed strong sympathy for this amiable, eloquent head of our recent enemy, the U.S.S.R. There was talk of Western economic aid as the Soviet economy was crippled by shortages and unemployment in a confused transition to something no one could foresee. Bush met with Gorbachev in 1989 to agree upon mutual reductions in long-range nuclear and conventional weapons, and NATO-Warsaw Pact troop reductions were set in motion. The Soviet Union withdrew from Afghanistan, but elements of the Soviet military and communist political elite concluded that the disintegration of the empire had gone too far. In August 1991, officials of the Army, the Central Committee of the party, and the KGB attempted a coup d'état, confronting Gorbachev in his Crimean retreat with a demand that he yield power. Gorbachev refused, was held in house arrest expecting death, but a remarkable popular uprising across the country revealed a public unwilling to return to the old ways. Russian President Boris Yeltsin rallied crowds around the Russian Parliament building to immobilize the tanks sent into the streets, and the coup collapsed, along with the last vestiges of authority for the Soviet government. In December Yeltsin announced that Russia had assumed the functions of what was increasingly called the "Former Soviet Union" (FSU), and on December 25 Gorbachev announced his resignation from a post no longer attached to a nation. The Soviet hammer-and-sickle banner over the Kremlin was lowered and replaced by the Russian flag, and the Soviet Union was no more.

THE COLLAPSE OF COMMUNISM AND THE END OF THE COLD WAR

The communist world, so menacing and so confident that it owned the future ("Whether you like it or not, history is on our side. We will bury you," Nikita Khrushchev had boasted in 1961), had collapsed with astonishing speed. Red regimes in the countries occupied after World War II had all been overthrown (West and East Germany were reunited in 1990), the Soviet Union was now dismantled into at least fifteen parts, all of them repudiating Marxism and talking of market economies and of democracy. The republics in December 1991 joined together in a loose Commonwealth of Independent States, but the new entity faced an uncertain future. Only China and Cuba remained in the communist camp, both appearing as old regimes hanging on against the clock. In Nicaragua, elections in 1990 replaced Daniel Ortega and the Marxist Sandinista

(Chicago Tribune, Tribune Media Services)

regime with Violeta Barrios de Chamorro at the head of a coalition aligned with the West. These momentous events came about because of broad public repudiation of the old communist regimes, and seemed to be a popular referendum on the principles the Western alliance had been defending since World War II. With a few lapses, Western leaders refrained from bragging. After all, no one knew whether democracy and free economies would actually replace the communist system, and it was sobering to reflect that the best minds in government and university circles had utterly failed to anticipate and forecast the end of the U.S.S.R. and the deflation of communism. The CIA's expansive analytical and spying apparatus had performed especially badly, annually overstating the strength of the Soviet economy and totally surprised by the system's collapse.

The Cold War was over, Presidents Bush and Yeltsin formally announced when they signed a joint statement on February 1, 1992, proclaiming a new era of "friendship and partnership." The communist experiment and Western efforts to cope with it had been a "seventy-year nightmare" to Boris Yeltsin. That era had now passed.

What did it mean? For the peoples of the former Soviet Union there was the relief of the lifting of tyranny, but deep uncertainty about the future. For Americans, the first thought was joy at the prospect of a radical easing of the threat of nuclear war. Russia's Yeltsin in early 1992 proposed a sweeping 80 percent cut in nuclear warheads for both countries, and an agreement not to aim them at each other. After a brief period of negotiation, Bush and Yeltsin signed in January 1993 an agreement (called START II) to destroy two thirds of their respective nuclear arsenals over an eleven-year period, vowing never to attack one another and in fact signing away the nuclear capability for surprise attack. "With this agreement," they announced, "the nuclear nightmare recedes more and more for ourselves, for our children and our grandchildren." This momentous act of sanity and cooperation was clouded somewhat by doubts that the government of Russia was fully in control of the far-flung nuclear arsenal stationed across the former Soviet Union, and complex negotiations began on the question of who would control those portions of the nuclear arsenal that were not within Russia's borders. Early in 1992 Bush halted further production of H-bombs, and later in the year ended the production of nuclear fuels. The administration's proposed 1992 budget contained cuts in defense spending that most Democrats thought fell far short of the "peace dividend" that had been anticipated, but no one denied that the end of the Cold War eventually should mean that resources could be shifted from military to civilian uses.

BENEFITS AND COSTS OF THE COLD WAR

Perspective on the Cold War was in short supply as the conflict ended. Historians would struggle with the question of whether it could have been avoided, whether and how both sides shared blame for its outbreak, and for making it more bitter and protracted than necessary. The general view from the early 1990s, among Americans, was that the half a century of defense spending and struggle had ended as a huge success. The outbreak of fierce ethnic warfare in the former Yugoslavia and elsewhere was a reminder that the superpower standoff of the Cold War era had at least contained conflicts that might otherwise have broken out, and historian John Gaddis proposed that the Cold War be renamed the Long Peace. The first half of the century saw two awful world wars, he pointed out, while the second half avoided the dreaded third and surely nuclear war.

Beyond this, communism had collapsed in its heartland, and was obviously failing in China and Cuba. Soviet-bloc nations returned to the world community and appeared to embrace Western values, which had won the contest by nurturing freer, more economically successful societies. The turn toward Western models could be seen outside the Soviet bloc: in Latin America, where political democracies had replaced every military dictatorship by 1995; and in Asia, where the enviable performance of capitalist economies drew the remaining socialist systems (except North Korea) toward free-market reforms.

If history confirms these apparent results, many will see them as justifying the stupendous costs of the struggle. No authoritative estimate exists of the dollar cost of military spending that the Cold War required, in part because we cannot know what defense spending would have been had the post-World War II world not included a superpower rivalry. But the costs in dollars were huge. A 1995 study by the Brookings Institution estimated the cost of nuclear weapons and their delivery systems alone as costing the U.S. $4 trillion, leaving aside the costs of cleaning up the radioactive wastes that were by-products of making

70,000 nuclear bombs. To this should be added the diversion of national scientific and engineering talent that might have turned to nonmilitary pursuits. The Cold War required, or was the pretext for, the establishment of a vast network of secret intelligence agencies and spending programs, unaccountable to the public through the usual democratic processes. A 1990 study of the Pentagon's "black budget," secret defense-related spending off the books and beyond normal congressional scrutiny, found that it had reached $36 billion a year.

Beyond the creation of secret layers of government, the Cold War energized the production and deployment of nuclear weapons far beyond what could otherwise have been justified. The potential cost of a nuclear accident was never paid, though many near-catastrophes have been reported and more are suspected. The environmental damage caused by the Cold War arms race and shrouded by Cold War secrecy was enormous on both sides, and is only gradually coming to light.

Over the years there had been isolated reports in the United States of environmental and human contamination by the nuclear campaign to defend the nation, chiefly episodes of downwind radioactive fallout from bomb tests in Nevada. In December 1993, Department of Energy Secretary Hazel O'Leary revealed that in the 1940s and 1950s her (predecessor) agency secretly conducted radiation experiments not only on animals but on human "guinea pigs." Doctors irradiated the testicles of prison inmates and injected patients with a variety of radioactive materials. She estimated the number of people exposed in this way at perhaps 800, but admitted that no one knew exactly. O'Leary condemned the "veil of secrecy" concealing these experiments and hinted at reparations. She had "blown the whistle," not only on her own department but on "the entire nuclear establishment," *Newsweek* magazine commented: "It is clear that the U.S. government behaved far more malignly and recklessly than most Americans ever suspected." It would take years of searching recently declassified documents to learn the scale of these wounds inflicted on the public by a government whose defense would be an appeal to history: Federal agencies did not know the extent of danger in exposure to radioactive materials (hence the tests!), such testing was not illegal and conformed to the lax standards of "informed consent" prevailing at that earlier time, and were in any event research as part of an undeclared war against a deadly rival (which was surely doing exactly the same thing).

These Cold War costs to human health were sizable, but the elaborate and secret enterprise of making nuclear bombs and experimental reactors had over four decades piled up immense environmental toxins. The government's far-flung and secret nuclear bomb-making process began with miners digging out uranium ore in Nevada and elsewhere. The product was shipped to Oak Ridge, Tennessee, where uranium was enriched and blended, then to Ohio sites where it was processed into fuel, then to places such as Hanford, Washington, and Rocky Flats, Colorado, where it was converted to plutonium, then to sites in Texas where the bombs were made, with some of them exploded in test sites in Nevada or the far Pacific. At every step along the trail of the seventy-eight nuclear weapons facilities operated by the U.S. government there were waste products to be disposed, with aerial and ground storage leaks of undetermined dimensions. "The government is left with a vast, pulsating landscape of atomic waste dumps," said *Newsweek*. "It's as though you had a party every night for 45 years, and you never cleaned it up," confessed Hazel O'Leary's Assistant Secretary for Environmental Restoration.

The other nuclear superpower, the U.S.S.R., apparently hid four decades of similar environmental damage behind its own tight veil of secrecy. The cost of the Cold War to the people of the former Soviet Union and Soviet-bloc countries is only now coming into view, but it is already clear that the most polluted region of the world is behind the former Iron Curtain, where arrogant communist leaders with no fear of their captive populations scarred their landscape with industrial facilities that emitted poisons into the air and waterways, and more ominously scattered across their vast territory nuclear waste dumps, spills, and radioactive gaseous releases. "Big chunks of the republic are so poisoned they will not be suitable for human settlement for a very long time," admitted Russia's minister for the environment in 1992.

WHO WON THE COLD WAR?

The West, it seemed obvious, had "won the Cold War," a boast sometimes heard in the U.S. media. Presidents Reagan and Bush understood that such bragging would not be helpful to their new friends Gorbachev and Yeltsin, and while they refrained from open declarations of victory, the partisan advantages of such a claim led to language claiming that the Republican party in the 1980s had found the winning formula. Democrats objected that it was the policies put in place by Harry Truman that had led to victory. Wiser heads suggested that "victory" was a silly and mischievous concept, and any back-patting in America ought to be bipartisan. Russia's Boris Yeltsin, in 1992, had a different verdict: "I don't think the U.S. has won the Cold War. I think we all have won it." The comment suggested that unilateral boasting was out of order, and in any event the question was premature. The "seventy-year nightmare" was over, Boris Yeltsin told the U.S. Congress in June 1992, but the future was uncertain and might hold its own nightmares if the transition to open societies did not go smoothly. The republics of the former Soviet Union and the nations of the Soviet bloc moved into the 1990s independent and free to experiment with political democracy and noncommunist economies, but the success of these experiments was very much in doubt. Apart from floundering economies, ethnic and religious tensions flared up where communist regimes had kept them suppressed for seven decades. In 1992 Czechoslovakia split peacefully into two pieces, but in what had been Yugoslavia a bloody war broke out as Serbian armed forces launched an "ethnic cleansing" to drive Croatian and Muslim populations out of Bosnia-Herzogovina. There was something especially ominous about front-page battle stories from Sarajevo, the regional capital where ethnic conflicts had ignited World War I in the summer of 1914.

The 1992 presidential campaign featured a strong challenge from third-party candidate, H. Ross Perot, a Texas billionaire seen here joining President George Bush and Democratic nominee Bill Clinton in one of three televised debates. *(Reuters/Bettmann)*

thus a clearer sense of accountability. The first black woman was elected to the Senate, and the House delegation of women doubled, from twenty-four to forty-eight.

Sixty-two percent of the voters had rejected the incumbent; but fifty-seven percent had voted against Clinton. What did the 1992 election mean? It was clear that Clinton (also Tsongas) had judged correctly that the public was deeply concerned about trends at home, especially now that the Cold War was over. "The economy, stupid!" read a prominent sign in Clinton's Little Rock, Arkansas, campaign headquarters, a reminder not to stray too far from what was thought to be the core concern of the voters. The Clinton/Gore campaign aimed their rhetoric at domestic concerns: the eroding foundations of America's economic strength, dangerous long-term deterioration of the environment, urban vitality and safety, and middle-class values. "One trend got away from us," commented one Bush aide as he reflected not only on the president's losing campaign but on his entire term in office, "and that was the feeling of long-term insecurity Americans have. Bill Clinton and Ross Perot tapped into it better than we did."

The 1992 presidential election was no public endorsement of a Democratic solution to domestic problems, since no clear program was offered. The voters rejected George Bush, choosing leadership that expressed a stronger sense of urgency about trends at home. The election also shifted power to a younger generation. Clinton came into focus late in the campaign, and even more decisively during his ten weeks as president-elect, as a jogging, saxophone-playing veteran not of World War II but of the 1960s, the "first Baby Boomer President" in *Time* magazine's phrase, the "first Rock 'N' Roll President . . . steeped in modern American popular culture," in the words of a Hollywood film executive.

The voters in 1992 had also cast a cold eye on government, giving the establishment-criticizing, deficit-denouncing Ross Perot 19 percent of the vote, and passing term-limitation measures for U.S. Senators and Representatives in all fourteen states in which they were on the ballot. Yet the same voters placed in the White House a government activist, albeit a "new type of Democrat" who offered an activism tempered by respect for market forces and a hard-earned knowledge of the limits of governmental power. Elections convey many and mixed signals, and in 1992 it was still unclear that an electorate again transferring the presidency from Republicans to a centrist Democrat was happy with either party. Clinton struck an appropriately modest note in his acceptance of the Democratic nomination as he pointed to his Arkansas origins: "I come from a town called Hope."

BENEATH POLITICS: CULTURAL UNRAVELING?

The "wedge issues" exploited by George Wallace and Richard Nixon in the late 1960s were potent tools to split off disgruntled Democrats from their party.

Code words and phrases such as "law and order" and "crime," "family values," and "arrogant eastern intellectual elites" offered oblique ways for conservatives to discuss and mobilize resentments about liberal social policies in the areas of criminal justice, welfare, pornography, and affirmative action. Such rhetoric was the equivalent of oil drilling by politicians, in search of the deeper, unfocused, often emotional resentments of voters with the direction of national policy and American life in general. Wedge issues played some role in every election after the 1960s, usually on the Republican side, since the status quo in American social policy had been basically put in place by the Democrats in the 1960s. George Bush in the 1988 election had exploited the issue of urban crime and also race when he ran the "Willie Horton" ads against Michael Dukakis, but in the 1992 election neither Bush nor Clinton clearly sensed or found a way to mobilize for political purposes the underlying anxieties of the electorate, though the polls showed unprecedented levels of generalized dissatisfaction with the direction of national life.

What might be the "wedge issues" of the 1990s? The familiar issues of welfare, crime, and government regulation exploited by Republicans from Nixon to Reagan had lost their novelty and already produced some voter shifts. The abortion issue seemed a stalemate. Untapped potential for mobilizing voters around policy reform perhaps lay in three other areas that had received virtually no public debate at election time: affirmative action, bilingual education, and large-scale immigration, much of it illegally evading the federal government's half-hearted control efforts. These long-standing social policies dated back to the 1960s and had liberal parentage, but through the 1970s and 1980s Republicans had either endorsed or acquiesced in them. Public-opinion polls had for years shown large majorities opposed to all three policies, but no politician in either party had developed a way to turn one or more of them into a wedge issue, probably deterred by the fear of being labeled a "racist" or a "nativist," both very ugly ghosts from the American past. The public-affairs media carried disturbing news about a sudden acceleration of the rate of illegitimate births in the United States, rising from a steady 4 percent level during 1940–1970 to 30 percent nationally by the 1990s and rising. The rate was especially high for blacks: Two out of three African-American children were born out of wedlock and raised without a father, as contrasted with one out of five whites. Yet the rates for all social groups had been rising for a generation, and beneath the numbers were appalling human costs as the children born to unmarried teenage mothers experienced ten times the rates of school dropout, drug use, and criminal involvement compared to children whose parents were married and high school graduates. Memories of the fierce denunciation of the 1965 Moynihan Report that first named black illegitimacy rates as a national problem kept the issue out of public discussion as illegitimacy rates rose steadily over the years.

One other broad, unfocused area of concern seemed to have the potential to enter the political arena of the 1990s—what some took to be signs of the unraveling of the social order itself. Rising crime rates were the foremost sign of a potential crisis in basic social order, and the threat of criminal assault, tied to

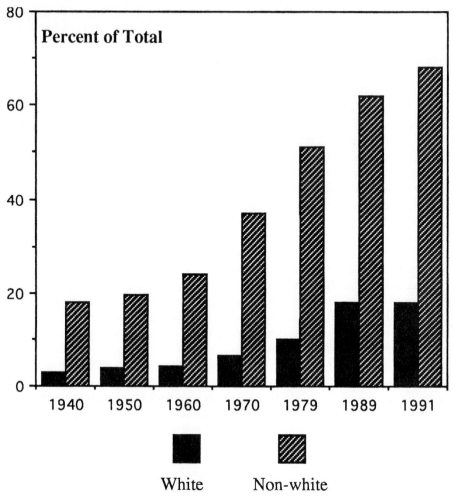

Percent of Total

1940   1950   1960   1970   1979   1989   1991

White   Non-white

Bar graph showing out-of-wedlock births from 1940 to 1991. Only in the 1990s did the high and rising percentage of out-of-wedlock births become a social and political issue, though it was a long-term trend pointed out in the 1960s by Lyndon Johnson aide Daniel Patrick Moynihan.
(*U.S. Bureau of Census*)

drug traffic in the streets, had in the 1980s and 1990s spread outside center cities to suburban malls and schools. Apart from the threat of muggings or random violence, exaggerated daily by the media but real enough, every large metropolis had learned in the 1980s to live with a growing "homeless" population, sleeping in front of stores or in vacant lots by night and begging by day. Most of the homeless—estimated by their advocates at 2 to 3 million, but probably numbering 500,000 on any given night—were mentally ill and/or drug-alcohol addicts who had been freed from institutional confinement by a series of policy decisions, the first made by President Kennedy, followed in the 1970s and 1980s by a series of judicial rulings in response to pressure from civil-libertarian lobbies.

A larger framework for understanding America's underlying dilemma in the 1990s was suggested by events in Europe. The end of the Cold War was followed immediately by an outbreak of ethnic and religious conflicts that dismantled the U.S.S.R. and kept many of its former parts in turmoil. Rising nationalist and separatist emotions troubled other nations: Canada, India, Spain, South Africa, Ethiopia, Burma, Indonesia. Czechoslovakia broke in two, and Yugoslavia in 1989 splintered into a brew of hostile ethnic and religious groups that by 1992 in the Bosnia-Herzegovina remnant were engaged in a full-scale civil war. The phrase "failed states" was applied to the most disastrous of such collapses of civil order, such as in Somalia or Haiti.

With these events as background, historian Arthur M. Schlesinger, Jr., in his *The Disuniting of America: Reflections on a Multicultural Society* (1991), asked if the two centuries of successful assimilation of a multitude of racial and ethnic groups into a unified (except for 1861–1865) nation could continue to be taken for granted. Schlesinger noted the rising tide of ethnic and racial assertiveness in America, a new scorn for assimilation into an English-Western tradition now more associated in memory with genocide for Native Americans and slavery than with the ideals of liberty and democracy, and (to the historian) the especially disturbing drive to rewrite history books and revise the humanities curriculum to deemphasize a common national past in favor of separate histories maintaining racial and ethnic identities and "self-esteem." Had "multiculturalism," once a vague term associated with a receptivity to the positive contributions that foreign cultures had made and might make to the American mixture, evolved into a movement toward the rejection of the Western linguistic and cultural heritage that had served for so long as the core American culture? High levels of immigration, together with vigorous ethnic, religious, and racial group self-assertion, were said to be gaining the upper hand against the assimilative forces exerted by the public schools, common workplaces, and mass media. This concern for social cohesion had not been present in American public life since the turn of the last century, and was intensified by evidence that the Reagan-Bush years had been a time of a widening class gulf. Chief executive officers of America's top corporations earned thirty-four times as much as the typical worker in the same corporations in the mid-1970s; by the end of the 1980s the ratio was 110 times (in Japan, it was still seventeen times), and Reagan-era tax changes had at the same time eased the tax burden on the rich. The gap between rich, middle, and poor seemed to have widened in the 1980s, further weakening the bonds of community.

The potential for "disuniting," in Schlesinger's term, or journalist Kevin Phillips' 1987 forecast of the "Balkanization" of America, was an overarching concern troubling at least some intellectuals, and was nourished by the evident loosening of the bonds holding virtually all nation-states together in the post-Cold War era. If this concern among intellectuals was or came to be shared by average voters, how would some politician successfully turn it into a political issue to add to the agenda?

Thus there were several potential wedge issues for the 1990s, and liberals felt a deep uneasiness that all of them—immigration, affirmative action, bilingual education, social cohesion itself—seemed to them to have an inherent "conservative" coloration; the wedges all moved toward the right. Whether or not this proved to be the case, the 1990s seemed destined to be a time for rethinking the policies and refighting the battles of the 1960s.

CHAPTER 12

A Clouded Future

THE 1990s: THE 60s REVISITED OR REPUDIATED?

What would be the character of the decade that ended not just a century, but a millennium? Writer Andy Aaron published in *The New Republic* a long list of completely contradictory guesses about the defining tone of the 1990s, among them:

> "Welcome to the gay '90s.
> Welcome to the nervous '90s.
> Welcome to the liberated '90s.
> Welcome to the trying '90s.
> Welcome to the social-conscious '90s."

That last prediction conveyed a view frequently heard among liberals, that since the 1950s had been a decade of Republican rule with an emphasis on money-making and the satisfaction of private agendas, follcwed by the social movements of the 1960s, then probably the 1990s would bring another swing of the pendulum toward the social agenda of liberalism.

Bill Clinton's victory in the 1992 election tempted many—almost certainly including him—to conclude that the 1990s would be some new version of the 1960s. Clinton would be Kennedy, there would be revived social movements for progressive reforms and social transformation, and the government in Washington would again be the exciting pivot of action. Clinton in his inaugural address used language that suggested great events ahead. Pledging to "end the era of deadlock and drift," he invited the nation to "celebrate the mystery of American renewal. . . . In the depth of winter, we force the spring. . . ." Historian William Chafe, concluding a history of the postwar era as Clinton entered office, wrote:

It was almost as though the best parts of the 1960s had come together to make a reappearance—feminism, a commitment to fairness, a modern marital relationship, but one framed by devotion to family, an energetic excitement about the ability to use government to make people's lives better.

PRESIDENT CLINTON: TO BE OR NOT TO BE A LIBERAL?

Such expectations of a revival of traditional liberalism in the 1990s were briefly reinforced by the media. Television and print news emphasized the contrast between the new and departing leaderships, which seemed almost as sharp as that between Eisenhower and Kennedy. George Bush was (perhaps) the last of the World War II generation shaped by military service, and was sixty-eight years old at the end of his term. Clinton, forty-four, with a lawyer wife, one school-age daughter (Chelsea)—whose name came from a 1960s ballad—and a talent for playing the saxophone which he displayed at his inaugural celebrations, was "the New Age President," *Newsweek* magazine declared, "part sensitive male, part Southern good ole boy" of the modern sort, postracism. His vice president was another handsome, robust, "modern southerner," suggesting that the Democratic party was renewing itself through leadership from the Sunbelt, where Republicans had made so many gains. The cabinet nominations seemed to be mostly new faces: California lawyer Warren Christopher as Secretary of State, females chosen to head the Departments of Justice, Energy, Health and Human Services, the Council of Economic Advisors, and the EPA, blacks at Agriculture and Commerce as well as U.S. Surgeon General, Hispanics at Transportation and Housing and Urban Development, and a liberal Harvard professor (Robert Reich) at Labor.

Troubles began almost at once, signs that liberalism was not headed for fulfillment, but deep trouble. In his first days in office Clinton chose to fulfil a campaign promise ending the exclusion of gays from military service, thereby generating a fury of controversy that was distracting, inconclusive, and hardly in line with the campaign motto to think first of "the economy, stupid." He decided to delay action on welfare and campaign finance reform to give priority to economic "renewal" and health care reform, and at first this seemed promising. His economic proposals were buffeted by critics within and outside the administration, and emerged as a stew of spending rearrangements and tax increases that aimed at a net deficit reduction over five years of $496 billion. It was a step in the right direction because Reagan/Bush deficits had piled the federal debt to $4.4 trillion

---

Part of President Clinton's and Vice President Gore's endeavors to "reinvent government" included an effort to eliminate waste in federal spending. Here the two leaders pose on the White House lawn in September 1993 to propose the elimination of unnecessary bureaucratic regulations.
(Reuters/Bettmann)

when Clinton arrived, but it was a small one. The budget survived Congress by one vote in the Senate in August 1993, and even with tax increases on the very richest 1 percent of taxpayers and spending cuts on the military and a trimming of federal jobs, there was still a projected annual deficit of $175 billion. Neither Clinton nor Congress were willing to make spending cuts that would affect the sacred cows of the middle class, social security pensions and Medicare, so large deficits continued. Clinton hailed the adopted budget as a "plan" whose enactment demonstrated that "deadlock" was over under his leadership.

If the "economic renewal" side of Clinton's early goals had at least produced a budget agreement and energetic innovations in public–private research "partnerships" in selected high-technology industrial sectors (Clinton and Gore clearly believed in the once-controversial idea of industrial policies, and their efforts, managed by the Commerce and Defense departments, were generally met with cautious approval), health care reform began in a flash of enthusiasm and spiraled slowly toward a defeat that went beyond health care to darken the administration's future.

The Dream and Nightmare of Health Care Reform

Clinton had promised reform of the nation's health care system during the campaign, justifying the issue's importance on two grounds. The costs of health care in the United States had been relentlessly increasing for decades, driven upward by expensive technology in diagnostic tests and treatment, spiraling costs of medical malpractice insurance as patients and lawyers became more litigious, and the stretching out of American lifespans leading to heavy expenses for chronic illnesses at the end of life. In John Kennedy's last year as president the nation spent 6 percent of GNP on health care, but such spending had ballooned to more than 13 percent—$832 billion—when Clinton decided to make the issue central to his administration. If the rise in costs was not contained, one study predicted, 32 percent of the entire economy would be consumed by health care by 2030. And rising costs were only half the problem. Thirty-seven million Americans were not covered by health insurance at all; they wound up with some coverage in hospital emergency rooms (paid for by somebody else), but they had little preventive care, through which long-term savings can be made for both the individual and society. Many other Americans felt deep insecurity about losing their coverage if they changed jobs. The liberal architects of the social security system in the 1930s had wanted to extend medical insurance to all Americans, and Clinton inherited the liberal dream of universal coverage as an entitlement of citizenship.

Hillary Rodham Clinton took command of a task force of over 500 health care specialists, who worked mostly behind closed doors to produce in September 1993 a 239-page plan for reform, which was delivered to Congress. Intense political conflict followed. The plan promised cost containment in the long run through a decentralized system of private insurance through employers who would offer competing plans supervised under federal rules. The insurance would be portable when individuals changed jobs; competition among plans, and government regulation, would contain costs.

The Clintons also had another major goal. Inspired by the memory of the Roosevelts as they crafted the social security system, the Clintons were proposing a vast expansion of the welfare state, extending benefits to include more mental health services and bringing the uninsured into a guarantee of universal entitlement to health care to be paid for out of efficiencies and a tax on tobacco.

Whatever the merits of the plan, a serious political misjudgment had been made. America's health care system was enormously complex, and despite both the Clintons' remarkable grasp of the details and choices, no groundswell developed for a switch from what most Americans had to what the Clintons said all Americans should have. Health care, it turned out, was a public policy swamp. As a *New York Times* reporter said in 1994, "people are fundamentally confused."

The plan met towering resistance and was withdrawn in August 1994. Clinton had lost a major campaign, and in the process allowed the administration to identify itself with the expansion of the welfare state at a time when the political winds blew in the opposite direction. The president was acutely aware of the need to sustain his image as a "new" Democrat who did not turn to government for the solution of all problems, who encouraged individual effort and responsibility. He launched his vice president on a study of how to "reinvent government" through a National Performance Review that would bring modern management ideas to the public sector. But the perception of Clinton's health care reform as "old liberalism" pushed the administration's image left of center. Further distractions came with media attention to allegations that the Clintons in Arkansas had been embroiled in real estate ventures where political favors were exchanged.

Setting a Post-Cold War Foreign Policy

Clinton's two Republican predecessors had been in charge when the United States "won the Cold War." He knew that the nation needed a new set of goals and fresh thinking about its role in world affairs, and that he was expected to take the lead. In matters of international economics Clinton proved to have a strong sense of direction: The United States must not retreat from the bipartisan leadership position on open economies that had guided our trade policy since the Truman era. He inherited the NAFTA trade pact negotiations, and after placating elements in his own party by quickly negotiating largely symbolic supplementary agreements to bar products made under unacceptable (by U.S. standards) labor and environment conditions, steered the treaty through the Senate by the end of 1993. One year later the president was as successful in seeing through to passage another inherited trade negotiation, the Uruguay Round revision of the General Agreement on Trade and Tariffs (GATT), which lowered tariffs and for the first time expanded the rules of the international trading community to sections of agriculture and services. Neither was particularly popular with a public unconvinced that American wages and working conditions could survive expanded competition with Third World goods, but Clinton—and most of the national media, business community, and academic experts—insisted that America could compete successfully and had no choice. He expressed sympathy with the widespread feeling of economic insecurity, and insisted that a highly educated workforce and a readiness to adapt to change would sustain American prosperity.

Early confirmation of this proposition came in 1994, when U.S. exports to Mexico expanded faster than imports. If there was a "sucking sound" (NAFTA critic Ross Perot's term) of jobs or profits crossing the border, it was at least initially from south to north. But a collapse of the Mexican peso in early 1995 brought a severe drop in the standard of living in a country already plagued by unemployment. These signs of fundamental economic weakness and political misjudgment in Mexico—along with news reports of political assassination and corruption at high levels of the Mexican government—suggested that the administration's rush to enmesh the U.S. and Mexican economies (there was talk of extending NAFTA to all of South America) might yet come at a high price.

In other parts of the world the administration displayed little consistent sense of direction. Clinton declined to intervene in the civil wars in Bosnia, while frequently talking as if he were on the verge of it. He agreed with Bush's decision to send troops to end widespread violence in Somalia, increased their numbers, then under congressional pressure pulled them out in the spring of 1994, all without ever defining achievable goals. Neither Clinton nor Secretary of State Christopher clarified U.S. strategy as Boris Yeltsin plunged Russia into a war with one of the breakaway republics. Foreign policy making for Bill Clinton was proving to be an extended improvisation without a larger framework. Clinton read a March 1994 article by Robert Kaplan ("The Coming Anarchy," *The Atlantic Monthly*) addressing the widely discussed problem of "failed states," where social order had collapsed and neighboring states were destabilized by immense flows of refugees. American military intervention in Haiti came later that year, ostensibly to replace military dictators with elected but exiled President Jean-Claude Aristide. Averting another massive armada of Haitian refugees headed for Florida was another reason. Were the brief occupations of Somalia and Haiti models for a new "containment policy" for a world of collapsing states? Such actions brought to mind Teddy Roosevelt's 1904 Corollary to the Monroe Doctrine, in which he declared that in the Western hemisphere, "chronic wrongdoing, or an impotence which results in a general loosening of the ties of civilized society . . . may . . . ultimately require intervention by some civilized nation," or Woodrow Wilson's declaration after sending U.S. troops into Mexico in 1916 that "I will teach them to elect good men." The Clinton administration seemed to need its George Kennan, a theorist of the new world condition and the appropriate American response.

THE CLINTON PRESIDENCY AND THE DIRECTION OF AMERICAN POLITICS

Clinton's approval ratings with the public fell steadily from the early honeymoon months, and in late 1994 reached the lowest numbers recorded by a modern president. As the 1996 election approached there were no more predictions

had been squandered and a window of opportunity had passed. Reagan left Washington with the federal bureaucracy larger, and the deficit much, much larger, than when he came. His hand-picked successor, George Bush, was more interested in foreign affairs than in battling liberals. However, a younger generation of conservatives had been preparing for years to complete the "Reagan revolution."

Their principal leader turned out to be Newt Gingrich, a Georgia history professor with very large ambitions who was elected to the House of Representatives in 1978. Gingrich arrived in Washington uninterested in the usual subcommittee assignments catering to his district's concerns, but focused on a plan to make Republicans a majority party in control of all three branches of the federal government, in order to reverse the wrong turn the nation had taken in the 1960s. Utilizing what came to be called a "Newtworld" of regular meetings with congressional Republicans, a think tank of his own, a televised series of American history lectures, and tireless networking, Gingrich persuaded congressional Republicans to present a coherent message without waiting for a presidential candidate to do it for them. In the autumn of 1994 more than 300 Republican candidates joined in a preelection ten-point "Contract with America," promising sweeping reforms in the "first 100 days" of the next legislative session: tax cuts, a balanced budget amendment, welfare and tort law reform. The details of the contract were probably fuzzy to the electorate, but the general intent of "Gingrich's army" was becoming clearer. He led, some journalists said, a "new populist movement" against, in Gingrich's words, "the counter-cultural, redistributionist, bureaucratic welfare state model."

Other conservative thinkers had prepared the way for this bold assault on the handiwork of 1960s liberalism—Charles Murray's challenge to the welfare state in *Losing Ground*, the emphasis of former Education Secretary William Bennett on the political importance of "a return to American values." But the central link between conservative ideas and legislative power in Congress was Gingrich. In his televised history lectures on "Renewing American Civilization," delivered at Kennesaw State College near Atlanta, Gingrich declared that the 1960s represented for America a decisive cultural break: "Now we've done with that and we have to recover. The counterculture is a momentary aberration in American History." This was a call for a political movement based substantially on cultural objections to the liberal record, though it was also aggressively pro-capitalist. One of Gingrich's most-quoted phrases suggested the targets he had in mind: "It is impossible to maintain civilization with 12-year-olds having babies, 15-year-olds killing each other, 17-year-olds dying of AIDS and 18-year-olds receiving diplomas they cannot read."

The Republican insurgents and their antiestablishment message had important support from a new force in the world of politics, the "talk show" hosts on radio and television who attracted huge audiences with a call-in format in which the grievances of ordinary people appeared to bypass the media managers and reach a national audience directly. The most influential of these was Rush Limbaugh, who daily rained ridicule upon liberalism from his New York TV studios.

And from California in 1994 came a grass-roots revolt against illegal immi-gration in the form of an initiative drawn up in a restaurant in Orange County and placed on the ballot by a signature drive conducted by neighborhood anti-illegal immigration groups across the state. Proposition 187 would prohibit the widespread practice of allowing illegal aliens access to public education and welfare services, turning off one of the "magnets" that drew them across the border. Proponents of Proposition 187 were, as expected, reviled as "racists" by opponents, who outspent them in campaign ads and seemed to include most of the civic leaders in the state except the governor, Republican Pete Wilson. Wil-son, who had earlier filed a lawsuit against the federal government to recover costs of social services to illegals, endorsed Proposition 187 at a time when he was far behind his Democratic opponent in the polls, and both he and the mea-sure swept to a decisive victory. Governor Wilson's successful campaign around an issue most politicians had been avoiding exposed the depth of public hostil-ity to yet another policy—large-scale immigration—mostly defended if not solely authored by Democrats (though Wilson himself, as a senator in the 1980s, had supported a large agricultural guest-worker program).

Republicans across the country, energized by the Gingrich-inspired strat-egy of a frontal assault on liberals as the navigators who took America in the wrong direction in the 1960s and after, swept to power in both houses of Con-gress in the 1994 elections. Gingrich, suddenly, was Speaker of the House, Robert Dole the Majority Leader in the Senate.

Reform was again in the air, but from the conservative side. Gingrich's forces vowed a balanced budget reached in seven years, and since defense was sacrosanct to Republicans and curbs on the ballooning expenses of Social Secu-rity's Medicare and Medicaide programs were a forbidden subject for both par-ties, the GOP majority voted massive cuts in many domestic programs, propos-ing to phase out entire departments and agencies. Only the sweeping cuts in EPA's environmental protection role made moderate Republicans uneasy. Clin-ton uncertainly sought to move to the right to find the new center of American politics, promising to balance the budget in ten years through gentler cuts, and agreed that welfare needed revision. More than 100 bills reforming immigra-tion followed Proposition 187's victory, and when a bipartisan commission chaired by former Representative Barbara Jordan urged Congress to reduce legal immigration by one third and vigorously combat illegal entry, the admin-istration somewhat unenthusiastically agreed. But at times Clinton sensed that public sentiment had not moved as far to the right as the Republicans assumed; he vowed to defend the environment against polluters and extractive industries.

These were familiar battlegrounds, but California, as usual, expanded the agenda. Two white university professors operating out of a tiny office in Berke-ley (of all places) launched another initiative aimed at the 1996 ballot, the Cali-fornia Civil Rights Initiative:

> Neither the state of California nor any of its political subdivisions or agents shall use race, sex, color, ethnicity or national origin as a criterion for either dis-criminating against or granting preferential treatment to, any individual or

group in the operation of the state's system of public employment, public education or public contracting. . . .

This was the high-sounding, antidiscrimination language of the early civil rights movement, but if enacted it would put an end in California (under state law) to the long experiment with "compensatory discrimination" invented by Lyndon Johnson and nurtured by every administration thereafter. In the 1970s polls showed support for the general concept of giving blacks an edge if discrimination were suspected. But as the years went by a growing apparatus of special college admission categories ("quotas," critics said; "targets," said supporters) and "set-aside" provisions in virtually all federal grant and contract programs generated rising objections. Affirmative action, wrote black author Shelby Steele, broke with Martin Luther King's dream of a time when Americans as individuals would all be judged on "the content of their character," and substituted a spoils system of special advantages to groups organized around grievances. At first intended to be temporary, affirmative action showed every sign of permanent entrenchment in a bureaucracy backed by claimant groups. "Affirmative action is like the Vietnam War," said Glynn Custred, one of the college professors who organized the California initiative: "We got into it with the best of intentions. It turned into a quagmire. Now it's time to get out." Before the initiative even reached the ballot it registered 3–2 leads in the polls, and three leading Republican candidates for the presidency, Senators Dole and Phil Gramm (R., Tex.), and California's Governor Pete Wilson, declared that if elected they would end affirmative action nationally. Here Clinton drew his sharpest contrast with the GOP, calling affirmative action "good for America."

DEEPER ANXIETIES: MAYBE IT'S NOT JUST THE ECONOMY, STUPID!

The sharp rebuke to the Democrats in the fall of 1994 ushered in a remarkable scene of liberal confusion and conservative euphoria. But while the Republicans took charge in 1995 with a plan and high energy levels, the political setting was quite unstable. In November 1994 the voters had put Republicans in many formerly Democratic seats, but the number who identified themselves as Republicans was not higher than four years earlier; most voters ranked themselves as "moderates," skeptical that either party could change the national direction. Gingrich had apparently given voice to a broad public consensus on the errors of the past, but the policy reforms in his Contract with America were untested, Republicans still had not faced up to the necessity to direct their reform energies to the real budget-breaking entitlement programs such as social security and Medicare, and many of Gingrich's own notions about electronic democracy had a cloudy quality. The problems the Republican leadership had identified—too much federal (but not too much state and local) government, too much counterculture, too much welfare—were wedge issues that had brought the liberal Democratic tradition to its lowest point since the Great Society. It remained to be seen whether the party of Goldwater, Nixon, Reagan, and Bush could summon a leadership equipped to create an alternative "public philosophy," in the phrase of political scientist Samuel Beers, that could cope as well with social problems as the New Deal public philosophy had done for a considerable time. Gingrich was buoyant at the mid-decade opportunity to try out the ideas of the new, post-Reagan conservatism, and several Republicans were eager to be president. But Bill Clinton had learned just how difficult it was to succeed as head of a government pledged to fix what was broken in a country undergoing baffling cross-currents of change. Actor Paul Newman, a long-time liberal activist, was more honest than most when he confessed in late 1994: "I'm immobilized by the incoherence of it all."

Perhaps the nation's problems were deeper than fiscal irresponsibility, intrusive government regulation, and a growing welfare-dependent class. Aspects of the economic weakness of the 1980s had been reversed, as sectors of American industry regained competitive strength in world trade, and modest industrial productivity gains returned. But the enormous annual deficits meant that the nation was continuing to live beyond its means, a course that could not be sustained indefinitely. An ominous erosion of the international value of the dollar against other currencies had accelerated through 1994 and into 1995, and served notice that limits would eventually be reached and hard realities would have to be faced.

POPULATION

The debate over the eventual size of the human population when global growth finally came into balance with death rates turned in a gloomy direction in the 1990s. Those who predicted a growth of global population to the 12- to 14-billion range were likely to be far more correct than those who optimistically saw stabilization at well below those levels. The United Nations and the World Bank in 1992 projected global population (in a medium scenario) in 2050 at 10 billion, rising to a crest of 11.5 billion in 2150. However, this assumed replacement-level fertility rates very soon; if the TFR remained even a tiny bit higher for a century, at 2.5 children per woman, global population would reach 19 billion by 2100! These grim scenarios ended the complacency nurtured by the apparent standoff in the earlier debate between "doomsters" such as Vogt, Hardin, and Ehrlich, and "cornucopians" such as Simon and Wattenberg. The pessimists were proving right, at least on population numbers. The U.S. National Academy of Sciences joined the Royal Society of London in 1992 in this statement:

> If current predictions of population growth prove accurate and patterns of human activity on the planet remain unchanged, science and technology may not be able to prevent either irreversible degradation of the environment or continued poverty for much of the world.

A press release signed by 1575 leading global scientists, including 100 Nobel Prize winners, warned that population growth pointed toward a planet that was "irretrievably mutilated."

Expressing this emerging consensus, Senator (after 1993, Vice President) Albert Gore, Jr., in his 1991 book, *Earth in the Balance,* noted that "a sudden and startling surge in human population" adding every ten years the equivalent of "one China's worth of people" combined with the modern scientific and technological revolution to produce "an almost unimaginable magnification of our power to affect the world around us." For him and most other informed observers of global trends, the problem of overpopulation should be understood as a combination of large and growing human populations and their increasing power to alter nature through science and technology. Seen in this light, overpopulation was not only a distant source of distress in Bombay and Cairo, but, in Gore's term, a "strategic" concern for Americans, threatening their national security.

Gore was not the first American political leader to link global overpopulation with U.S. national security. Presidents Eisenhower, Kennedy, and Johnson, on separate occasions, and then the Nixon-appointed National Commission on Population Growth and the American Future, had identified population growth in the underdeveloped world as a threat to the goal of rising standards of living, and thus a negative element in the effort to prevent the spread of revolutionary communism. By the 1990s, the national security dimension of global population growth was underscored by U.S. military interventions (in 1994) in two countries where the collapse of civil authority was accelerated by explosive population growth and subsequent environmental degradation.

More "failed states" producing massive refugee flows with rising levels of ethnic strife seemed almost inevitable. A Worldwatch institute study, *Full House,* forecast in 1994 that 3.6 billion people—90 million a year—would be added to the world's population by 2030, although the world's natural support systems were already strained. The rate of increase in world grain output was falling sharply, and the seafood catch had started an absolute decline, with seventeen of the major oceanic fisheries being fished at or beyond capacity. The world environmental conference at Rio de Janeiro in 1992 discussed overpopulation more candidly than any previous U.N. meeting, and a subsequent International Conference on Population and Development in Cairo in September 1994 established a goal of capping global population growth at 7.8 billion by 2050. The goal was nonbinding on any nation, and no one predicted that it would be reached. A gloomier scenario was offered an *Atlantic Monthly* article by Robert Kaplan, "The Coming Anarchy" (March 1994), reportedly read by President Clinton, in which population-induced environmental collapse joined with rising ethnic strife to produce a wave of disintegrating nation-states and massive refugee flows that would inevitably reach and destabilize the West.

Population Inside America

Gore in 1991 erroneously wrote that the United States, while threatened by global overpopulation, was one of those few industrialized societies that had "relatively stable populations." In reality the United States, at over 260 million people and therefore the third most populous country in the world, had the fastest-growing population of any industrialized nation. Gore perhaps relied upon the Census

Bureau's 1989 projection that U.S. population would peak in 2040 at 302 million and then begin to fall. Three years later the bureau decided that it had been quite wrong. The "middle or most likely" scenario in the 1992 report projected a 50 percent increase in the U.S. population by 2050, to 383 million people. Ninety million future Americans had been discovered by the Census Bureau, just three years after the 1989 calculations! Even this estimate was based on fertility and immigration rates that were below the actual levels of 1992. A more likely projection was thus the bureau's high scenario, which assumed fertility and immigration rates as they actually existed in the early 1990s and projected a population totaling 506 million by the middle of the twenty-first century and still growing rapidly.

What had happened? Death rates had not dropped, nor had abortions, which remained at about 1.6 million a year. The key to the population surge was not changes in births or deaths, but instead the passage of the Immigration Act of 1990, which expanded legal admissions by 40 percent. And the census of 1990 revealed that the law of 1986 (IRCA), intended to limit illegal immigration, had failed to stem a growing flow. Thus, legal immigration in excess of 1 million persons a year (1.8 million in 1991), joined with rising illegal entry, drove American population totals up both by adding individuals and by the immigrants' high fertility levels. Global overpopulation was now spilling over into America, its population growing not because of high fertility rates among the native-born but because of immigration.

Also part of the news was the changed ethnic composition of the American population as the stream of immigration continued from Mexico and South America, Asia, and the troubled pieces of the former Soviet Union and its satellites. If current immigrant and fertility trends continue, by approximately 2050— and in some states such as California, much earlier—whites would no longer be a national majority, Latinos would have replaced blacks as the nation's largest minority, and Asians would be 11 percent and a rising proportion of the American population. The growth of the Latino population was especially dramatic. Internally divided by nation of origin—58 percent of American Latinos are Mexican, 12 percent are Puerto Rican, 5 percent are Cuban—the U.S. Hispanic population in 1990 totaled 20 million, a 53 percent increase since the 1980 census.

Despite the nation-changing power of population growth, the political system ignored the issue of upper limits. Few asked: What should the U.S. population be? Two Cornell University agricultural economists estimated the sustainable population to be 40 to 100 million; Paul and Anne Ehrlich of Stanford University arrived at an estimated 75 million. If these scholars were right, the American population in the 1990s was already too large to be sustainable in the long run, and further growth would only aggravate the situation.

RESOURCES

Resource shortages, a vexing and recurrent theme in the human story, had appeared in modern American history to be a problem that usually found a way

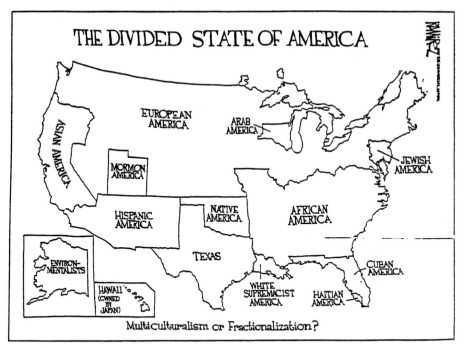

Changing patterns of immigration since 1965 and a new emphasis on separatism and ethnic awareness in the intellectual community sparked increasing worries about the "balkanization" or "fractionalization" of America. Was the "melting pot" now obsolete?
(© 1993, *The Commercial Appeal, Memphis, TN. Used with permission*)

to fix itself. Impending petroleum shortages were predicted in Teddy Roosevelt's day, but discoveries of reserves pushed back the moment of reckoning, along with new power technologies (nuclear). In the 1990s, the natural resource picture was a confusing mixture of looming shortages and optimistic reports of cornucopian abundance.

Energy supplies were critical to future well-being, and here the news in the 1990s seemed encouraging. With gasoline in the early 1990s priced at $1.30 to $1.50 a gallon, depending on the region of the country, the oil shocks of the 1970s and the anxiety about "an era of limits" seemed to be "history," to use George Bush's favorite term for something behind rather than ahead, and therefore irrelevant. In real dollars, automobile fuels and natural gas in the 1990s were at their lowest price levels since World War II, and estimates of world oil reserves actually increased from 615 billion barrels in 1985 to 917 billion in 1990. Thus the energy euphoria of the 1980s stretched on into the 1990s, since there was a glut rather than a shortage of all forms of fossil fuels. Yet the Gulf War was fought in part because of Western dependency on Persian Gulf oil, where 70 percent of the world reserves were located, and the conflict served to remind Americans that their current comfortable energy prospects remained vulnerable.

After the Gulf campaign removed the immediate threat to the energy life-line of Western economies, President Bush attempted to respond to the wide-spread sense that public policy must take the lead in reducing American dependence on foreign petroleum. Bush issued a document called the National Energy Strategy, intended to reduce domestic oil consumption and encourage shifts to renewable resources. Legislation ground forward, and a month before Bush's 1992 electoral defeat he signed the Energy Policy Act of 1992. Intense interest-group lobbying made the complex act a hodgepodge of minor changes, studies, and small R&D programs to elevate alternatives to petroleum. "An overall immobility had taken hold," wrote oil historian Daniel Yergin: "Conservation had run out of steam" and "the effort to develop alternative sources had become even more anemic. . . . Energy crises did seem a thing of the past." America was enjoying the final years of petroleum abundance, ignoring the dilemma Jimmy Carter had thrust into public attention. The inevitable exhaustion of petroleum and natural gas could be foreseen, but was far enough ahead to threaten only nonvoting grandchildren but not voting contemporaries, whose every visit to the gasoline pump told them that supplies were ample and prices showed no sign of any future shortages.

Optimists took comfort from evidence that renewable resources apparently were being renewed even in the face of rising demand. America's forest acreage, whose rates of depletion at the beginning of the twentieth century had inspired the first conservation movement, had been expanding since the 1930s. The total acreage in forests in the early 1990s remained about the same as in the 1920s despite urbanization, and the total number of trees was actually greater. Better fire control, aggressive reforestation, and declining per-capita use of wood products allowed America's stock of timber to increase slightly after the 1920s, though the conversion of much private timberland (which was three fourths of the total) into lumber plantations reduced the forests' ability to serve as an ecosystem nurturing biodiversity.

When forests were seen not as standing storage bins of lumber for future carpenters but as environments that cushion climate change by absorbing CO_2 and as habitats for species that carry much of nature's genetic endowment, the global forest picture was increasingly grim. This was especially true of tropic moist forests (TMFs), where some 90 percent of the globe's species lived. Virtually all of these forests would be destroyed by the middle of the twenty-first century at current rates of clearing, which were accelerating. The U.N. Food and Agriculture Organization (FAO) estimated TMF losses of 11.3 million hectares a year during the 1970s, but the rate jumped 40 percent to 15.4 million hectares during the 1980s and reached 17 million by the early 1990s.

Why worry much about forest clearing that eliminated millions of beetles, fungi, and other life forms? For one thing, many important medicines have been and will be developed from the genetic diversity of these regions. Beyond this, agricultural scientists pointed out that humanity's food supplies were at stake. Modern agriculture was "impressively uniform and impressively vulnerable," in the words of a study by the National Academy of Sciences, *Genetic Vulnerability of Major Crops*. Modern crops are "genetically paralyzed," and quickly rendered vulnerable to a new pest or blight that has evolved beyond their genetic defenses. Biotechnology companies and universities established seed banks where researchers may look for new genetic combinations for modified varieties of corn, wheat, and rice, but the study pointed out that the major source of tough new strains is the "wild relatives" of domesticated plants. The "wild relatives" now live in TMFs, within the national boundaries of governments that are often unable to protect their own forests from destruction by expanding local populations in search of farmland, firewood, or export timber.

Shrinking Resources: Soil, Wildlife

Worries about the loss of topsoil, that fundamental resource whose exhaustion has been linked to the decline of great civilizations, had been voiced repeatedly in the American past, most notably in the "Dust Bowl" emergency of the 1930s. Agricultural land surveys showed that the conservation measures inaugurated under the New Deal had slowed but not halted water and wind erosion of the nation's soils, and conversion of agricultural land to urban uses combined with

The barn owl is one of many animals on the endangered species list. In 1982, only one nest of barn owls was known to exist in Missouri. Because barn owls were once plentiful in Missouri, this prompted an ambitious recovery project. *(UPI-Bettmann)*

erosion to threaten the farming base and imply rising food prices. Rising foreign demand resulting from global population growth intensified pressure on America's agricultural base.

The extinction of wildlife species by human action, another concern of the first conservation movement, continued to threaten the furry and feathered creatures that were most humans' strongest emotional link to nature. The Endangered Species Act of 1973 set up a registry that provided a crude measure of the problem, and the original list of 150 threatened species grew to 530 by the beginning of the 1990s. Vigorous efforts had boosted the national flock of whooping cranes from 13 in 1941 to 200 by 1991, and dramatic increases in the numbers of beaver, white-tailed deer, bison, and wild turkey were recorded from perilously low levels in the early years of this century.

However, the overall wildlife picture was alarming. Migratory bird populations, especially waterfowl, were showing signs of distress and decline as the end of the century approached, due to human intrusions on habitats, especially the draining of wetlands and the fragmentation of forests. Off the nation's coasts, depletion of bluefin tuna and cod in the Atlantic and red snapper in the Gulf of Mexico signaled a fast-building crisis in ocean fisheries under intense pressure from high-technology fishing fleets scouring the waters to feed a global population that was 90 million larger every year. No fish decline was more sudden or upsetting, perhaps, than the disappearance of the salmon from the rivers and coastal waters of the Pacific northwest. Once 16 million strong in the Columbia-Snake River system alone, salmon numbers dropped to 1 million by the early 1990s, with 300 of the 400 stocks either extinct or endangered. A panic set in among residents of the Columbia River region as returning chinook salmon dropped from 21,000 a year to 3116 in 1994, a sign that they were at the end of their biological fight against humanity's dams, hydroelectric turbines, and chemical runoff into river and coastal waters.

THE EMBATTLED ENVIRONMENT

Trashing the Earth

The struggle of humans to bring their own pollution of the natural environment within tolerable limits sometimes seemed like a sports contest. Was the Cleanup Team winning or losing to the Foulup Team? In the United States, after the passage of the environmental control laws of the 1970s and 1980s, there was a growing supply of public data on human-generated wastes entering the environment, and some of it suggested gains for the Cleanup Team. The annual Toxics Release Inventory, first published by the EPA in 1989, had embarrassed U.S. manufacturers, and the 1993 report showed for the first time that American companies had cut their toxic waste releases; chemical manufacturers led, with a 35 percent reduction achieved through internal recycling and altered production processes. Total toxic waste generation held at the awesome level of 33.5 billion pounds a year, "the equivalent of a line of tank trucks that stretches halfway around the world," in the words of EPA Administrator Carol Browner. The good news was that industry was internally recycling about half of it; on the downside, the Toxics Inventory initially required industry self-reporting only on 320 chemicals (increased to 586 in 1995, mostly pesticides), and did not include the mining and oil-exploration sectors. Still, the shift toward recycling represented a measurable success for public policy and the public interest, and American households were moving slowly in the same direction. Each citizen threw away about 4.3 pounds of solid waste a day in the 1990s, 195 million tons of trash—but 17 percent of that was recycled (up from 7 percent in 1960) through municipal programs aimed at extending the life of rapidly filling land-fills.

Optimism about such gains was frequently shattered when wastes escaped the human systems built to isolate and contain them. The oldest problem of all, human fecal matter and urban sewage, asserted itself again repeatedly in the 1990s despite all the effort spent on control. More than 2000 beaches were closed along the U.S. coastline in 1991, as raw sewage from overburdened systems fouled coastal waters. More dangerous were the mounting incidents of spills of poisonous substances shipped daily around America as part of the economy—chlorine to purify the water, pesticides for home and farm use, acids and corrosives for industrial plants. The *Los Angeles Times* surveyed the shipment of hazardous materials after a 1991 spill of a highly toxic weed killer into the Sacramento River, and found that every day in America some 500,000 shipments of 4 to 8 million tons of hazardous materials moved across our landscape (no government agency knew the true figures). In the 1980s some 68,000 hazardous materials spills were reported, with a 37 percent increase during the decade. The most spectacular was the March 1989 dumping of 10.8 million gallons of crude oil when the *Exxon Valdez* tanker ran aground in Prince William Sound, Alaska, causing widespread damage to local populations of shorebirds, fish, and sea otters.

The Skies Overhead

When the huge "ozone hole" over Antarctica was confirmed in 1985 and the 1987 Montreal Protocol bound signatory nations to a phase-out of one of the industrial revolution's most useful inventions—CFCs, the odorless, nontoxic chemicals that cool refrigerators, help make plastics, and propel aerosols—hopes were expressed that the depletion of stratospheric ozone would soon peak and reverse itself. Indeed, a few scientists in the 1980s still disputed both the link between CFCs and ozone depletion and the harm to be expected from a thinning of the ozone layer. Reagan's Secretary of the Interior, Donald Hodel, had proposed that, if there was a problem, it be met by wearing sunglasses and hats in the summer. By the 1990s no one took the matter so lightly. A thin ozone layer allows larger doses of a form of ultraviolet light, UV-B, that is strongly linked not only to skin cancer in humans but to crop losses and damage to ocean microorganisms. Then, in 1992, researchers found that the ozone hole over Antarctica had expanded to 9 million square miles, 25 percent larger than in any previous measurement. A scientific consensus had formed (with a few dissenters, as usual): The cause was principally CFCs, and the depletion would become worse for at least another decade, even if industrializing nations such as China changed their minds and joined the Montreal Protocol. There was an ominous sense than an out-of-control experiment was underway. "For five decades," in the words of a *Newsweek* report:

> industrial societies have pumped potent chemicals into the atmosphere, unintentionally setting in motion the largest, longest and most dangerous chemistry experiment in history. Now there is substantial evidence that the chemicals are destroying the ozone layer that girds the earth, and that loss will be counted in more cancers and agricultural failures. . . . It may be too late to do much more about it than record the coming miseries.

There was at least one area where the struggle to protect the American environment took a promising turn. Throughout the 1980s the Reagan administration had called for the repeal rather than the strengthening of the 1970 Clean Air Act, and successfully fended off demands from environmentalists and the Canadian government that the United States address and remedy the acid rain problem. In 1989, however, President Bush proposed to rewrite the clean air legislation to deal with its inadequacies rather than continue to ignore them. In October 1990 he signed the Clean Air Act of 1990, a formidably complex measure designed to limit the output of toxic industrial pollutants and those that cause acid rain, phase out chemicals that threaten the protective atmospheric ozone layer, and establish schedules for the reduction of urban smog and automobile emissions. No one could estimate the law's success in reaching goals set so far in the future. Business critics cited a $25 to $35 billion price tag when the law took full effect; but an EPA official noted that this amounted to 24 cents a day per American, compared to the 63 cents the average person paid for alcohol and 43 cents for tobacco. One undeniable gain was the air quality treaty President Bush was able to sign with Canada in 1991, now that the United States had finally faced its own acid rain problems.

The depletion of the ozone layer and acid rain were not the most ominous problems that humanity had unwittingly created in the planetary atmosphere. Greenhouse warming promised more wrenching environmental disruptions. The Reagan administration had fended off scientific warnings of global warming by pointing out that there was no consensus in the scientific community. This was George Bush's initial position, but it was increasingly untenable. In 1991 the National Academy of Sciences (NAS) altered its earlier skepticism, and saw a 2- to 9-degree centigrade warming ahead. *Science* magazine in 1992 found that "the consensus is stronger than ever," foreseeing a doubling of carbon dioxide and a warming ranging from a "modest" 1.5 degrees centigrade to a "hefty" 4.5 degrees centigrade. The result would be disruption of agricultural systems, glacier melting, coastal flooding, unpredictable climate change. At current rates of warming, by one estimate, Chicago's summers would be as warm in twenty years as those in New Orleans today. "The world, I am afraid, is not yet ready for this," remarked EPA Administrator William Reilly in 1989.

What might be done? Scientists recommended reducing carbon dioxide emissions in a number of ways—replacing internal combustion engines with electricity-driven vehicles, moving generally toward renewable energy sources, halting deforestation, phasing out CFCs in all nations, reducing methane and nitrous oxide emissions, and stabilizing and perhaps even reducing human populations. When governmental leaders translated these recommendations into costs and life-style changes, they were appalled at the political risks of leadership on the greenhouse problem. The many steps necessary to reduce carbon dioxide emissions would cost $95 billion a year, estimated the Department of Energy. Wealthy nations would have to shift away from the automobile as currently designed, move rapidly out of fossil fuels, and alter many industrial production methods. This was especially hard news for the countries that were most responsible for greenhouse gas emissions: the United States with 21 percent, Europe and the former U.S.S.R. with 14 percent each, China with 7 percent. Underdeveloped societies faced painful readjustments as well, if they were to curb their own contribution to the greenhouse problem. The methane emitted by their cattle herds was seventy times as effective in trapping reradiated energy than CO_2, and planetary deforestation was almost entirely confined to the Third World. Further, the developing world was the home of the high fertility rates driving up population. The greenhouse problem could not be contained unless global population growth ended and then declined, until lower human numbers and altered life-styles allowed sustainable economic activities.

The Bush administration avoided discussion of such hard choices, leaving them to a government whose vice president had written a book insisting that global warming was perhaps the foremost environmental issue. Gore's *Earth in the Balance* was a 1992 bestseller, but more public education probably took place when CBS television presented to a national audience "The Fire Next Time" in April 1993. Described by one critic as "a flawed but powerful drama," this eco-disaster story began in a tiny community on the Louisiana coast and traced its citizens as they were driven northward by stages to New England in a desperate effort to escape the hurricanes and heat waves launched by global warming. It was the first glimpse millions of Americans had of the sort of wrenching dislocations and migrations that global warming might inflict, if and when it arrived.

Facing the Problems: The Environmental Movement and the Global Future

Environmentalism in the 1990s was a century-old movement to confront human damage to and alteration of the environment, to gather and analyze the facts, to bring to bear science, technology, law, and moral-religious ideas to bring about a more harmonious humanity–nature relationship. Would it prove adequate to the task of leading to modifications of human behavior at the required scale and speed? Certainly there was activity across a broad front. Washington, D.C., was the operating base of "the nationals," the ten large environmental organizations including the Audubon Society, the Natural Resources Defense

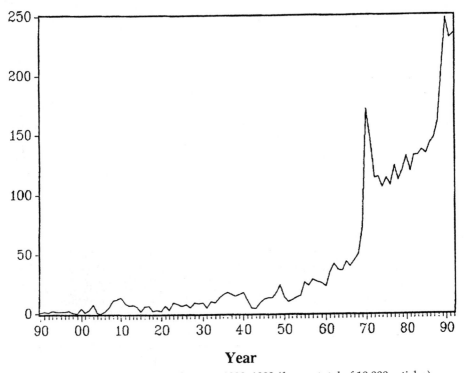

Media coverage of environmental issues, 1890–1992 (from a total of 10,000 articles). *(Reader's Guide to Periodical Literature)*

Council, the Wilderness Society, and the Sierra Club, working within the system as lobbyists and publicists to strengthen the nation's environmental policy structure.

Behind them and their sizable memberships was a larger concerned public cycling to work, choosing "natural foods" that had not been treated with pesticides, recycling bottles, cans, and paper. The scale of public cooperation with municipal recycling efforts also testified to the depth of the conservation impulse. Further evidence of the grass-roots foundations of environmentalism was the spontaneous formation of citizens groups to resist community-level threats to the environment. The NIMBY ("not in my back yard") phenomenon brought bursts of local protest against a new (or a leaking old) toxic waste dump, a garbage incinerator, a new pipeline, a shopping mall planned for a wetland, a refinery, a shipment of nuclear waste. A glimpse of the size and fervor of the broader environmentalist public came on the second Earth Day, April 22, 1990, a worldwide event that mobilized perhaps 20 million people for tree plantings, rallies, and speeches on how to "live lives of voluntary simplicity" and "eat lower on the food chain" (i.e., vegetables and grains, not beef). This growing citizen involvement in one part or another of the effort

Environmental demonstrators march in Afton, North Carolina, to protest the building
of a toxic waste dump in their area. Using strategies successful in the civil rights
movement, black and white environmentalists argued that toxic waste dumps were
too frequently located in poor, black areas of the United States.
(UPI-Bettmann)

to achieve environmentalists' ends by law and persuasion had a radical
fringe—the "monkeywrenchers" associated with Earth First, the interruptions
of commercial fishing by Greenpeace, the "animal rights" groups breaking
into corporate and university labs where animals were caged for medical
research.

Despite all this activity, environmentalists took little optimism from the
trends of the 1990s. The number of Americans continued to increase without
significant alterations in the nation's "produce, consume, and throw away"
lifestyle. With each American producing almost thirty times as much carbon
dioxide per capita as a citizen of India, a gap that was widening, it had to be
admitted that after years of environmental effort U.S. citizens were not walking
more lightly upon the earth, for the conservation efforts of the decades since the
1960s had been erased by population growth. And the environmentalist movement itself was divided. One wing was convinced that science and technology
were the keys to success, while working within and through governments and
corporations. Others rejected the very idea of lobbying for incremental gains

within the existing political system, and urged a more radical politics backed by a profound religious conversion to nonmaterial values.

As the 1990s arrived, the environmental organizations were losing membership, the Sierra Club down from 630,000 to 500,000 in one year, the Wilderness Society shrinking by 31 percent, the Audubon Society laying off workers after recording a $1.7 million deficit in 1993. And their critics had increased in numbers and volume. Policy analysts attacked the basic "command and control" regulatory approach taken since the 1960s, urging greater use of market incentives and an abandonment of the environmentalists' stubborn adherence to a "zero-risk" goal which had led to such follies as spending $15 to $20 billion to remove asbestos from schools and public buildings at a cost of $250 million per life saved. Environmentalists were "dunderhead alarmists and prophets of doom," who had invented the global warming crisis where none existed, sneered popular talk-show host Rush Limbaugh to his multimillion listeners nationwide. EPA Administrator Browner conceded in 1995 that the nation was getting "too little environmental protection at too high a cost."

Thus the century approached its end with the conservation campaign of Teddy Roosevelt and Gifford Pinchot, now renamed environmentalism, reevaluating its methods, confronted by resistant social habits and articulate, well-financed critics.

On one matter American environmentalists agreed: Environmental problems once encountered locally were now global, requiring some planetary framework of law and cooperation. The United States and other Western governments had often urged global attention to the problems of overpopulation and environmental damage, but in a series of international meetings from the Bucharest Conference (1974) forward they had been sharply rebuked for impeding Third World economic development. By the 1990s, a new consensus seemed to be emerging. The 170-nation U.N. Conference on Environment and Development (or "earth summit") took place in Rio de Janeiro in June 1992, in a country with the largest levels of deforestation on the planet and in a city shrouded in pollution. Preconference bargaining revealed that developing nations now agreed that population growth and attendant environmental degradation was a problem for their own people's well-being, and that "sustainable development" ought to replace "development at all costs." First World nations concurred that their role as major industrial polluters and wealthy societies meant an obligation to reduce their own pollution and assist the developing world to do the same. It was hoped that the Rio meeting would extend the momentum established when fifty-nine nations agreed in the Montreal Protocol to phase out production of chemicals that destroy the earth's protective ozone layer.

The meeting in Rio was a disappointment, and the United States was the reason. The Bush administration would not sign, and worked to weaken, the conference's proposed agreements on sustainable development and curbs on the production and release of greenhouse gases. Without U.S. leadership, the Rio conference could only pass pious resolutions without enforcement mechanisms or financial support. The prospects for international environmental cooperation were cloudy at best.

LOOKING BACK, LOOKING FORWARD

In a book surveying the American nation as the end of the twentieth century approached, Alan Wolfe wrote: "Someone who visited the United States in the first decade after World War II and then came back in the last decade of the twentieth century would have seen two entirely different countries." A Rip Van Winkle who went to sleep around 1950 and awoke in 1995 would be astounded at the changes. In the 1940s women did not drive heavy trucks, attend West Point and Annapolis, or jog in the streets. No black American played in the white professional football, baseball, or basketball leagues. The overwhelming majority of the children in Los Angeles, Miami, and Houston public schools were Caucasian. Immigration was negligible, exerting no influence on the nation's demographic future. No American bought automobiles made in Germany or Japan, and very few made in Great Britain. The preferred drink at cocktail parties was bourbon or rye whiskey, not white wine. Sixty percent of the American people smoked cigarettes in restaurants, buses, theaters, or wherever they wished. Farmers fought weeds with hoes and mechanical disks more often than with herbicides. The government did not ration access to Grand Canyon boat trips, nor limit access to Yosemite National Park because of overcrowding. No one ate falafel in St. Louis, or MacDonald's hamburgers in Cairo. There was no Israel, but there was a Soviet Union. Almost no men were nurses, and none were airline flight attendants.

These few examples suggest the enormous changes experienced by Americans from World War II to our own time. Most of these changes reflect an enlargement of social opportunity. Also on the positive side, a Cold War of deadly potential had formed and then ended. The Jim Crow system had been eradicated, and remarkable though incomplete strides taken toward racial equality. Sexual mores had been liberalized, geographic mobility increased, regional differences narrowed. American tastes had been internationalized, and our national economy became linked to an industrializing global economy with consequences that are vast, and about which we cannot agree.

And what remained the same? America was still a capitalist economy, and a democratic republic. New social values, such as racial and sexual tolerance, existed side by side with older ones—respect for private property, individualism, wealth making, and physical size ("big is better"). People in 1995, just like their predecessors in 1950, felt proud when their high school or university put eleven males on a field wearing its colors and pushed an inflated pigskin across the goal line more often than the opponents. Domestic roles had changed a great deal, but household chores were still mostly done by females. Americans still avoided learning foreign languages, still feared baldness and shortness, and received the news that an entity was "growing" or "the largest" with pleasure and pride.

What was the biggest change? This book is built around the proposition that the biggest change was the movement of the issues of population, resources, and the environment from latent to manifest, from the margin of national discussion to the center. "The rescue of the environment," Al Gore wrote in 1990, should be "the central organizing principle for civilization." Whether one agreed with this view or not, there was no denying that post-Cold War America was much in need of a new vision of its central purposes.

BIBLIOGRAPHY FOR PART SIX

BERNSTEIN, RICHARD. *Dictatorship of Virtue: Multiculturalism and the Battle for America's Future.* New York: Knopf, 1994.

BLY, ROBERT. *Iron John: A Book about Men.* Reading, MA: Addison-Wesley, 1990.

BOLCH, BEN, AND HAROLD LYONS. *Apocalypse Not: Science, Economics, and Environmentalism.* Washington, DC: Cato Institute, 1993.

BORNELLI, PETER, ed. *Crossroads: Environmental Priorities for the Future.* Washington, DC: Island Press, 1988.

BRAMWELL, ANNA. *Ecology in the 20th Century: A History.* New Haven, CT: Yale University Press, 1989.

BROWN, LESTER. *State of the World.* New York: Norton, 1980–1994.

CHAN, SUCHENG. *Asian Americans: An Interpretive History.* Boston: Twayne, 1991.

CLINTON, BILL, AND AL GORE. *Putting People First: How We Can All Change America.* New York: Times Books, 1992.

COHEN, WARREN I. *America in the Age of Soviet Power, 1945–1991.* London: Cambridge University Press, 1993.

D'ANTONIO, MICHAEL. *Atomic Harvest: The Lethal Toll of America's Nuclear Arsenal.* New York: Crown, 1993.

DEGLER, CARL N. *At Odds: Women and the Family in America from the Revolution to the Present.* New York: Oxford University Press, 1980.

DREW, ELIZABETH. *On the Edge: The Clinton Presidency.* New York: Simon & Schuster, 1995.

EDSALL, THOMAS B., AND MARY D. EDSALL. *Chain Reaction: The Impact of Race, Rights, and Taxes on American Politics.* New York: Norton, 1991.

FELSENTHAL, CAROL. *The Sweetheart of the Silent Majority: The Biography of Phyllis Schlafly.* Garden City, NY: Doubleday, 1981.

FRANCK, IRENE M. *The Green Encyclopedia.* New York: Prentice-Hall, 1992.

FREDERICK, KENNETH D., AND ROGER A. SEDJO, eds. *America's Renewable Resources: Historical Trends and Current Challenges.* Washington, DC: Resources for the Future, 1991.

FRIEDMAN, NORMAN. *Desert Victory: The War for Kuwait.* Annapolis, MD: Naval Institute Press, 1991.

FRUM, DAVID. *Dead Right.* New Republic/Basic Books, 1994.

GILLIGAN, CAROL. *In a Different Voice: Psychological Theory and Women's Development.* Cambridge, MA: Harvard University Press, 1982.

GOLDIN, CLAUDIA DALE. *Understanding the Gender Gap: An Economic History of American Women.* New York: Oxford University Press, 1990.

GOMEZ-QUINONES, JUAN. *Mexican Students por La Raza: The Chicano Student Movement in Southern California, 1967–1977.* Santa Barbara, CA: Editorial La Causa, 1978.

———. *Chicano Politics: Reality and Promise, 1940–1990.* Albuquerque: University of New Mexico Press, 1990.

GORE, ALBERT. *Earth in the Balance: Ecology and the Human Spirit.* Boston: Houghton Mifflin, 1992.

GRMEK, MIRKO D. *History of AIDS: Emergency and Origins of a Modern Pandemic.* Princeton, NJ: Princeton University Press, 1993.

IRIYE, AKIRA, AND WARREN T. COHEN. *The U.S. and Japan in the Postwar World.* Lexington, KY: University Press of Kentucky, 1989.

JAYNES, GERALD DAVID, AND ROBIN M. WILLIAMS, JR. *A Common Destiny: Blacks and American Society.* Washington, DC: National Academy Press, 1989.

JENKS, CHRISTOPHER. *Re-thinking Social Policy.* Cambridge, MA: Harvard University Press, 1992.

———. *The Homeless.* Cambridge, MA: Harvard University Press, 1994.

KENNEDY, PAUL M. *Preparing for the Twenty-first Century.* New York: Random House, 1993.

MANES, CHRISTOPHER. *Green Rage: Radical Environmentalism and the Unmaking of Civilization.* Boston: Little, Brown, 1990.

MARANISS, DAVID. *First in His Class: A Biography of Bill Clinton.* New York: Simon & Schuster, 1995.

MARCUS, ERIC. *Making History: The Struggle for Gay and Lesbian Equal Rights, 1945–1990, An Oral History.* New York: Harper Collins, 1992.

MAYER, MARTIN. *The Greatest Ever Bank Robbery: The Collapse of the Savings and Loan Industry.* New York: Scribner's, 1990.

MCKIBBEN, BILL. *The End of Nature.* New York: Random House, 1989.

MILLER, JUDITH. *Saddam Hussein and the Crisis in the Gulf.* New York: Times Books, 1990.

OPPENHEIMER, MICHAEL. *Dead Heat: The Race against the Greenhouse Effect.* New York: Basic Books, 1990.

PEROT, H. ROSS. *United We Stand: How We Can Take Back Our Country.* New York: Hyperion, 1992.

SCHNEIDER, STEPHEN H. *Global Warming: Are We Entering the Greenhouse Century?* New York: Vintage Books, 1990.

SCHWARTZKOPF, H. NORMAN, WITH PETER PETRE. *It Doesn't Take a Hero: General H. Norman Schwarzkopf, the Autobiography.* New York: Bantam, 1992.

SHILTS, RANDY. *And the Band Played On.* New York: St. Martin's Press, 1987.

SHORRIS, EARL. *Latinos: A Biography of the People.* New York: Norton, 1992.

SHULMAN, SETH. *The Threat at Home: Confronting the Toxic Legacy of the U.S. Military.* Boston: Beacon Press, 1992.

SIFRY, MICAH L., AND CHRISTOPHER CERF. *The Gulf War Reader: History, Documents, Opinions.* New York: Times Books, 1991.

SMITH, JEAN E. *George Bush's War.* New York: Holt, Rinehart & Winston, 1992.

STAGGENBORG, SUZANNE. *The Pro-Choice Movement: Organization and Activism in the Abortion Conflict.* New York: Oxford University Press, 1991.

STEELE, SHELBY. *The Content of Our Character.* New York: St. Martin's Press, 1990.

TOBIAS, MICHAEL. *World War III: Population and the Biosphere at the End of the Millenium.* New York: Bear & Co., 1994.

U.S. NEWS AND WORLD REPORT. *Triumph without Victory: The History of the Persian Gulf War.* New York: Bear & Co., 1994.

WEYR, THOMAS. *Hispanic USA: Assimilation or Separatism?* New York: Harper & Row, 1992.

WILSON, WILLIAM J. *The Truly Disadvantaged: The Inner City, the Underclass, and Public Policy.* Chicago: University of Chicago Press, 1987.

WOLFE, ALAN. *America at Century's End.* Berkeley: University of California Press, 1991.

YERGIN, DANIEL. *The Prize: The Epic Quest for Oil, Money, and Power.* New York: Simon & Schuster, 1991.

Index

Aaron, Andy, 283
Abbey, Edward, 203
Abortion, 174–175
Acid rain, 249
Acquired immune deficiency syndrome
(AIDS), 296
AEC, 71–72
Affirmative action, 132, 199–200, 255, 282, 292
Agnew, Spiro, 177, 184, 186
AIDS, 296
Alaska Land Act, 217
Alliance for Progress, 110
Apollo 11, 109, 142
Aristide, Jean-Claude, 288
Armstrong, Neil A., 109, 142
Asia, 213
Atomic bomb, 36–38
    dropped on Hiroshima and Nagasaki, 3
    testing at Alamagordo, New Mexico, 3, 7
Atomic Energy Commission (AEC), 71–72
Audubon Society, 142, 202, 310, 312

Baby Boom. *See* Population
Baker, Howard, 184
Bakke v. Regents of the University of California,
200
Bay of Pigs Invasion, 110
Beat Generation, 82
Begin, Manachem, 217
Bennett, William, 297
Berlin, 30–31
Black Americans, 32
Black Nationalism, 129–130
Black Panther Party, 131
Bly, Robert *(Iron John)*, 296
Bohr, Niels, 5
Boland Amendment, 225–226

Bosnia, 288
Bouvier, Leon, 245
Bracero Program, 48
Bradley, Omar, 56
Bretton Woods Conference, 10
Brodie, Bernard, 37
Brown, Jerry, 218
Brown, Lester, 248
Brown v. Board of Education of Topeka, 66–68
Brownell, Herbert, 66
Browner, Carol, 312
Bucharest Conference, 312
Buckley, William F., Jr., 79
Burden of Brown, The (Wolters), 292
Burford, Ann, 223, 228–229
Burger, C.J. Warren, 206
Bush, George, 229, 255–256, 297
    in election of 1992, 275–278
    presidency, 261–266, 268–274, 284, 288, 304

Camp David Accords, 194, 217
Carson, Rachel *(Silent Spring)*, 54, 99–101, 141,
164
Carter, Jimmy, 189, 207, 243, 247, 304
    assessed, 220–221
    energy policy, 192–193
    presidency, 191–195, 213–218
Carter, Rosalyn, 190, 217
Casey, William, 226, 229
Castro, Fidel, 76, 110–111, 187
CCHW, 253
Central America
    and U.S. policy, 225–226. *See also* Nicaragua
        and El Salvador
Central Intelligence Agency (CIA), 77, 187,
265
    role in Central America, 225–226